RELIGION AND REALITY TV

Why is reality television flourishing in today's expanding media market? *Religion and Reality TV: Faith in Late Capitalism* argues that the reality genre offers answers to many of life's urgent questions: Why am I important? What gives my life meaning? How do I present my best self to the world? Case studies address these questions by examining religious representations through late capitalist lenses, including the maintenance of the self, the commodification of the sacred, and the performance of authenticity. The book's fourteen essays explore why religious themes proliferate in reality TV, audiences' fascination with "lived religion," and the economics that make religion and reality TV a successful pairing. Chapters also consider the role of race, gender, and religion in the production and reception of programming.

Religion and Reality TV provides a framework for understanding the intersection of celebrity, media attention, beliefs, and values. The book will be of interest to students and scholars of religion and media studies, communication, American studies, and popular culture.

Mara Einstein has worked as an executive at NBC, MTV Networks, and at major advertising agencies. She is Professor of Media Studies at Queens College, CUNY, USA and Director of the Masters program in Media and Social Justice.

Katherine Madden teaches media studies at Jesuit High School in Sacramento, California, USA.

Diane Winston holds the Knight Chair in Media and Religion at the USC Annenberg School for Communication and Journalism, USA.

RELIGION AND REALITY TV

Faith in Late Capitalism

Edited by Mara Einstein, Katherine Madden, and Diane Winston

Routledge
Taylor & Francis Group

LONDON AND NEW YORK

First published 2018
by Routledge
2 Park Square, Milton Park, Abingdon, Oxon OX14 4RN

and by Routledge
711 Third Avenue, New York, NY 10017

Routledge is an imprint of the Taylor & Francis Group, an informa business

British Library Cataloguing-in-Publication Data
A catalogue record for this book is available from the British Library

Library of Congress Cataloging-in-Publication Data
Names: Einstein, Mara, editor.Title: Religion and reality TV : faith in late
capitalism / edited by Mara Einstein, Katherine Madden, and Diane Winston.
Description: 1 [edition]. | London ; New York : Routledge, 2018. | Includes
bibliographical references and index.Identifiers: LCCN 2017052828| ISBN
9781138681279 (hardback) | ISBN 9781138681286 (pbk.) | ISBN
9781315545950 (ebook)Subjects: LCSH: Reality television programs--United
States. | Religion on television.Classification: LCC PN1992.8.R43 R48 2018 |
DDC 791.45/6--dc23LC record available at https://lccn.loc.gov/2017052828

ISBN: 978-1-138-68127-9 (hbk)
ISBN: 978-1-138-68128-6 (pbk)
ISBN: 978-1-315-54595-0 (ebk)

Typeset in Bembo
by Taylor & Francis Books

To David and Cayla, who bless my reality

—M.E.

To Sean, Mom, Dad, and my sweet Miles

—K.M.

To Izzy who introduced me to Chrisley and so much more

—D.W.

CONTENTS

CONTRIBUTORS

Erica Hurwitz Andrus, PhD (UC Santa Barbara, 2006) is a Senior Lecturer in the Religion Department at the University of Vermont, where she teaches courses on Religion and Pop Culture, Religion in America, and Comparing Religions. Her past work includes chapters on fan culture and *The Big Lebowski* and *Battlestar Galactica*, and the role religion plays in the creation of imagined worlds in television and literature.

Melinda Q. Brennan is an Assistant Professor in the Department of Women's and Gender Studies at SUNY Oneonta. She earned her PhD from the Department of Gender Studies at Indiana University. Her interdisciplinary work centers on the intersection of gender and race, focusing on the ways gendered racialization is activated across dissimilarly situated differences, such as ethno-religious Islamophobia and anti-brown xenophobia/anti-Latinx racisms.

Yoel Cohen is Associate Professor in the School of Communication, Ariel University, Israel (School Chairman 2009–2011). His research interests include religion news; religion and media in Judaism; foreign correspondents; and nuclear policy and media. His book publications include *God, Jews & the Media: Religion in Israel's media; Spiritual News: Reporting Religion Around the World; Whistleblowers and the Bomb: Vanunu, Israel and Nuclear Secrecy*; and *Media Diplomacy: the Foreign Office in the mass communications age*.

Mara Einstein is the author of a number of books, including *Black Ops Advertising: Native Ads, Content Marketing and the Covert World of the Digital Sell* (OR Books, 2016), *Advertising: What Everyone Needs to Know* (Oxford University Press, 2017), and *Brands of Faith: Marketing Religion in a Commercial Age* (Routledge, 2007). Dr. Einstein has worked as an executive at NBC, MTV Networks, and at major advertising agencies. She is Professor of Media Studies at Queens College, CUNY and Director of the Masters program in Media and Social Justice.

Amir Hetsroni is Associate Professor in the Department of Media and Visual Arts, Koç University in Istanbul Turkey. He has a Ph.D. in communication from the Hebrew University of Jerusalem. His research interests include applications of cultivation theory and content analysis of prime-time programming and advertising. He is a well-known media persona in his homeland of Israel where he also served as an expert in residence and a production consultant in the second season of the reality television series, *Big Brother* (2009–2010).

Annette Hill is a Professor of Media and Communication at Lund University, Sweden. Her research focuses on audiences and popular culture, with interests in media engagement, everyday life, genres, production studies and cultures of viewing. Her books include *Reality TV: Key Ideas* (Routledge, 2015); *Paranormal Media* (Routledge, 2011), *Restyling Factual TV* (2007), *Reality TV* (2005), *The Television Studies Reader* (with Robert C. Allen 2003), *TV Living* (with David Gauntlett, 1999), and *Shocking Entertainment* (1997). Her next book is *Media Experiences* (Routledge, 2018).

Stewart M. Hoover is Professor of Media Studies and Religious Studies at the University of Colorado at Boulder, where he directs the Center for Media, Religion, and Culture. He is an internationally-recognized expert on media and religion. He is author, co-author or editor of ten books, including *Media, Home, and Family, Religion in the Media Age*, and *Does God Make the Man: Media, Religion, and the Crisis of Masculinity*, co-authored with Curtis Coats, and the edited volume, *The Media and Religious Authority*.

Sharon Lauricella is a Communication scholar and Associate Professor in the Faculty of Social Science and Humanities at UOIT in Oshawa, Ontario, Canada. She holds a doctoral degree from the University of Cambridge (UK), and a BA from Wheaton College (Massachusetts). Dr. Lauricella's research focuses on spiritual/religious communication, digital feminist identities, and the use of mobile technologies in higher education. Dr. Lauricella has also been recognized for teaching excellence, having been awarded the UOIT Teaching Award twice (2007 and 2012) and the CJPS Faculty Teaching Award (2010).

Sean McCloud is Professor of Religious Studies and American Studies and Communication Studies Faculty Affiliate at the University of North Carolina at Charlotte. He teaches, publishes, and researches on American religions, religion and culture, and social theory. His publications include *Making the American Religious Fringe: Exotics, Subversives, and Journalists, 1955–1993* (2004), *Divine Hierarchies: Class in American Religion and Religious Studies* (2007), *American Possessions: Fighting*

Demons in the Contemporary United States (2015), and a co-edited volume, *Religion and Class in America: Culture, History, and Politics* (2009).

Katherine Madden holds a Ph.D. in Critical Studies from the School of Cinematic Arts at the University of Southern California. Her dissertation, *Father, Son, and the Holy Dollar: Rebuilding the American Dream in Post-Recessionary Reality Television and Mommy Blogging*, studies the ideological framework of Christianity and parenting in reality television and video blogs following the Great Recession of 2008. She also holds an M.A. in Critical Studies from the University of Southern California and a B.A. in Film and Media Studies from the University of California, Irvine. Dr. Madden teaches Media Studies at Jesuit High School in Sacramento, California.

Monique Moultrie is an Assistant Professor of Religious Studies at Georgia State University. She earned degrees from Vanderbilt University, Harvard Divinity School, and Duke University. Her scholarly pursuits include projects in sexual ethics, African American religions, and gender and sexuality studies. Duke University Press will publish her book *Passionate and Pious: Religious Media and Black Women's Sexuality* in December 2017. She is a co-editor of the recently published *A Guide for Women in Religion: Making Your Way from A to Z*, 2nd edition.

Myev Rees is a doctoral candidate in American Religions at Northwestern University. She studies the history and culture of religion in America, American Christianities, and the intersection of religion, gender, and media in the United States. She holds an MA in Comparative Religion from Miami University of Ohio and a BA in Philosophy from Barnard College, Columbia University.

Andrea Stanton is Associate Professor of Islamic Studies (PhD, MA Columbia University; BA Williams College) and an affiliate faculty member of the Center for Middle East Studies and Conflict Resolution Institute at the University of Denver. She has received grants from the American Academy of Religion, the National Endowment for the Humanities, and the US Institute of Peace. She has published on the intersection between national identity, religious self-formation, and various media forms, ranging from radio to emoticons. She blogs regularly for the academic website Political Theology Today (http://www.politicaltheology.com/blog/?s=Stanton).

Brenda R. Weber is professor and chair of the Department of Gender Studies at Indiana University, Bloomington. Her books include *Makeover TV: Selfhood, Citizenship, and Celebrity on Reality TV; Women and Literary Celebrity in the Nineteenth Century*; and *Reality Gendervision: Sexuality and Gender on Transatlantic Reality TV*. Her present book project is *Latter-day Screens: Gender, Sexuality, and Mediated Mormonism* (Duke).

Diane Winston holds the Knight Chair in Media and Religion at the USC Annenberg School for Communication and Journalism, USA. Her current research interests include religion, politics and the news media; American spirituality, and religion and the entertainment media. She has authored or co-edited *The Oxford Handbook on Religion and the American News Media* (Oxford University Press, 2012); *Small Screen, Big Picture: Television and Lived Religion* (Baylor University Press, 2009); *Faith in the Market: Religion and the Rise of Urban Commercial Culture* (Rutgers University Press, 2002); *Red-Hot and Righteous: The Urban Religion of the Salvation Army* (Harvard University Press, 1999).

ACKNOWLEDGEMENTS

We want to acknowledge the many colleagues, friends, and mentors who helped us develop and shape this collection. We are grateful to the International Society for Media, Religion and Culture which, during its 2014 Canterbury conference, hosted a religion and reality television panel that inspired us to further explore the topic. Thanks to Anthea Butler, Lynn Schofeld Clark, Nabil Echchaibi, Aniko Imre, Michele Rosenthal, and Ellen Seiter who provided initial support, encouragement and critiques. We are especially appreciative of Brenda R. Weber, whose invaluable advice was always helpful. We also want to extend thanks to our contributors, who embraced an area about which very little has been written – and good-naturedly submitted to feedback from multiple editors. Likewise, we are indebted to the team at Routledge for shepherding us through the publication process.

INTRODUCTION

Religion and American television have a long history. In the 1950s, during television's nascent age, "sustaining time" permitted mainstream religions to broadcast programming, usually sermons or inspirational messages, free of charge. When scripted dramas and comedies blossomed in the 1960s and 1970s, religiously-themed series such as *The Flying Nun, Bridget Loves Bernie* and *Highway to Heaven* were popular fare. By the 1980s, televangelists were a growing segment of the TV landscape, and evangelicals even had their own talk show, Pat Robertson's *The 700 Club*. When sexual and financial scandals toppled several televangelism empires, Robertson continued to thrive, using *The 700 Club* to launch his 1988 bid for the presidency.

Robertson did not make it past the Republican primaries, but almost 30 years later another businessman turned reality television star and champion of the Religious Right succeeded. Donald Trump, the embodiment of neoliberal spectacle and its apotheosis of nationalism, capitalism and the nuclear family, is living proof of television's entanglement with American beliefs and values. *Religion and Reality TV: Faith in Late Capitalism* explores how the reality genre has contributed to the current moment and religion's role in the process.

Two central arguments run through this collection. The first is that the proliferation of religious content in reality television, specifically, and post-network television genres more broadly, both produces and represents the ideological and policy reforms of late capitalism. While some scholars have begun to plumb the relationship between religion and neoliberalism, and others have explored the relationship between neoliberalism and reality television, this book is the first to triangulate these domains. Our second argument is that the "work" of reality television, the theme that links media discussed in this volume with so much more available content, is the lived religion of late capitalism. Precisely, then, what does the reality genre tell us about how men and women find meaning, identity and purpose in today's world?

In chapters that provide case studies of the ideological work performed by religion, the collection's authors examine themes common to reality television and late capitalism, including the exposition and maintenance of the self, the commodification of the sacred, the performance of authenticity, the targeting of niche markets, and the privileging of the individual over the community. Several chapters also argue that these themes are not only transforming the media landscape but also shaping and reflecting the "lived religion," that is the everyday practice, of viewers. At the very moment when polls show an increasingly smaller percentage of Americans identifying as religious and that church attendance is in free fall, millions are watching how beliefs and their corollary behaviors motivate their fellow citizens. What lessons are they learning from reality shows? And what does their popularity tell us about 21st century American culture and society? *Religion and Reality TV: Faith in Late Capitalism* is the first scholarly work to scrutinize the deeply entwined relationship among American religion, reality television and political culture. Moreover, with comparative chapters on Muslims and Jews, the volume places the American experience over/against reality genres in non-Christian contexts.

Religion and television: a brief history

In the mid-to-late 1990s, religious and spiritual motifs lit up scripted dramas. Cultural set pieces, spurred by the millennial fever, dove into supernatural themes. The success of *Touched by an Angel*, the second most popular show on television at that time, and 7th *Heaven*, the leading show on the then new WB network, opened the door to similar content. Other religion-related programs included *Nothing Sacred, Teen Angel, Promised Land* (a spinoff of *Touched*), *Twin Peaks, Buffy the Vampire Slayer*, and *Soul Man*. In addition to shows specifically presenting religious messages, religious content appeared regularly on dramas such as *Homicide: Life on the Streets* and *ER*, where police and doctors struggled with moral and ethical issues, and in sci-fi programming like *The X-Files*, where religion was presented in paranormal terms. This supernatural trend continued into the 2000s with shows like *Reaper*, about a 21-year-old whose parents had sold his soul to the devil, *Saving Grace*, featuring a detective visited by a tobacco-spitting angel, and sci-fi programming with spiritual themes, such as *Lost, Heroes*, and *Battlestar Galactica*.

More recently with the advent of digitization and non-traditional platforms, a growing number of scripted comedies and dramas have featured religious, spiritual and supernatural themes, content and characters. While many such shows are aimed at niche audiences, their compelling explorations of meaning, identity and purpose can attract millions of viewers as well as weighty critical attention. In the mid-2010s, examples ranged from the wildly topical *Transparent*, with its close-grain depiction of Los Angeles' Jews, to the epic fantasy *Game of Thrones'* inventive mix of religious, spiritual and supernatural elements, to the return of the supernaturally-saturated *Twin Peaks*.

A number of factors contributed to the success of religiously and spiritually-inflected scripted dramas (and comedies) on both traditional and non-traditional

TV platforms. First, generic faith is more widely acceptable for television presentation.[1] *Touched by an Angel*, for example, was successful in attracting large audiences because it presented an all-purpose belief system. This also was true of *7th Heaven*. On the other hand, *Nothing Sacred*, while praised by critics, was never able to attract a significant following. Commentators attributed this to its religious specificity. In this case, the central character's Roman Catholic identity was the basis for the drama; a handsome young priest continually testing his boundaries.[2] Audiences have preconceived notions about particular faiths and if a program does not deliver on that presupposition, they are likely to turn away. Second, combining religion with other genres also has been an effective means of presenting religious and moral themes. This is particularly true with sci-fi programs (*Quantum Leap* in the 1990s and more recently numerous shows ranging from *Ghost Whisperer* to the aforementioned *Game of Thrones*). Likewise it's not unusual for police procedurals, medical shows and legal series to have episodes based around religious conflict, scandal or sensationalism. The crime series, *Cold Case*, had several such episodes. One was about a virginity club in a high school. Another focused on an Amish girl who is killed during Rumspringa (a rite of passage when Amish teens can experience life outside their communities). A third featured a Scientology-like cult that was supposedly involved in killing a writer.

However, different factors came into play when religious content blossomed on cable television's reality genres as well as in digital media environments. Niche audiences, long tail economics and little to no regulation allowed for a broader array of programming content. In addition, the need for new genres to fill the pipeline as well as the advent of social media to drive the appeal of controversial content – something that is typically eschewed on legacy media – made religion an attractive topic. Combined with the market needs and drives of reality TV, religion offers the perfect mix of prurience, controversy and titillation that spurred a proliferation in the genre.

The rise of reality TV

Reality TV has been a staple of television for decades. Shows like *Candid Camera* and *Cops* had long and successful tenures; *Cops*, in fact, is still in production after almost 30 years. The television deregulation of the 1980s combined with corporate efficiencies enabled the reality format to proliferate.

By the 1990s broadcasters began looking for programming that was less expensive to produce and/or more easily sold into syndication to offset the increasing costs of popular television shows. Newsmagazines were one option. Shows like *Dateline* and *20/20* and *Primetime* often aired multiple times during the week. Variety shows, like *Whose Line is it Anyway*, also filled this bill as did *America's Funniest Home Videos*, a show made up of consumer generated content (CGC). Finally, game shows made a comeback at this time, starting with *Who Wants to Be a Millionaire?*, which at one point aired four times a week on ABC and moved the network from last place to first in the primetime ratings. Other networks hoped to replicate this success and produced familiar fare such as an updated version of the 1950s quiz show *21*, as well as new shows like *Fear Factor* and *The Amazing Race*, a program now categorized as a reality show which in 2017 had been on air for 16 years.

Regulation also played a significant factor in leading to the rise of reality TV. In the mid-1990s, the financial interest and syndication rules (fin-syn) were repealed. These rules were instituted in the early 1970s to insure independent television producers would not be strong-armed into giving away equity in their programs in order to get a coveted slot in the primetime lineup. Once eliminated, the broadcast networks could own the shows that they broadcast.

Unsurprisingly, deregulation led to a significant shake up in the industry. Shows that had been on the air for years and were up for license renewal suddenly had much higher price tags. The quintessential example is *ER*. The show, which premiered in 1994, was an anchor for NBC's "Must See TV" night. Five years later, the agreement with the network was up for renegotiation. At the time, NBC had lost football rights and *Seinfeld* was going off the air. Network executives were desperate to retain a hit for their Thursday night lineup, and Warner Brothers, the producers of *ER*, had them over a barrel. It was reported that NBC agreed to pay $13 million per episode to keep the show. This was a huge sum when a typical licensing fee at the time was approximately $3 million for a show of *ER*'s caliber. NBC agreed to pay, however, because the production company could take the show elsewhere including its own, newly-established WB network. Cost cutting to compensate for paying exorbitant license fees led to increased production of inexpensive programming. Initially, this meant televised newsmagazines, because at the time the only shows the networks produced internally were news. Shortly thereafter, reality programming became part of the networks' belt tightening measures, and shows such as *Survivor* and *Big Brother* on CBS were produced by the news divisions (Einstein, 2004).

The final piece of the puzzle was cable television. The growth of cable TV helped turn reality TV into a very popular programming genre. In the 1980s when cable was emerging, networks scheduled inexpensive options, often outdated syndicated fare like *Murder She Wrote*. But as cable became a viable outlet for advertisers and as carriage fees from cable operators increased, networks had more money to spend on original content. These shows were important because they enabled networks to differentiate themselves among an increasing lineup of channels. Because of its cheap production costs, reality became a cable TV staple; MTV's *Real World* is credited with launching the genre as we know it today. Since then, there have emerged three "generations" of reality programming: the camcorder era, surveillance and competition, and economies of celebrity (Kavka, 2012), with the last being the most operative today particularly in conjunction with religious-based content.

Religion and reality television

While reality TV grew, it would be another decade before faith was integrated into the genre with any regularity. Two early religion-related shows were *Amish in the*

City (2004), a series about five Amish teens on Rumspringa living with six city kids in a Hollywood Hills house à la *Real World*, and *God or the Girl* (2006), a series about four men deciding on whether to enter the priesthood. Both shows were produced as limited series and neither was picked up for renewal, which suggests they were not well received by audiences. More successfully, *Paranormal State*, a show about paranormal investigators, was a surprise hit on A&E, and came to spawn numerous copycat programs.

Today, religion and spirituality have become so successful that they claim their own subgenre within reality TV. The Amish continue to be a topic of particular interest, generating a slew of shows like *Amish Mafia, The Amish, Breaking Amish*, and *Amish in the City*, among others. Likewise, Mormons seeking to leave their church (*Breaking the Faith* and *Escaping the Prophet*) or participating in polygamous relationships (*Sister Wives* and *My Five Wives*) have had solid followings. Conservative Christians have attracted those outside their ranks through nominally secular programs like *19 Kids and Counting; Dog, the Bounty Hunter;* and *Duck Dynasty*. A significant number of shows examine African American religion, particularly through close-ups into the private lives of public figures, including *Divas for Jesus, Mary Mary, Thicker than Water*, and *Preachers of LA*. And the supernatural genre, with programs that focus on paranormal activity ranging from psychics to ghost hunting, continues to expand in popularity as a form of religious/spiritual entertainment.

Even in the most secular of reality shows – whether it is *Keeping Up With the Kardashians, Undercover Boss*, or *The Bachelor* and *Real Housewives* franchises – religion, ethics and spirituality are ever-present themes, albeit filtered through a late capitalist lens. Whether through their references to church, prayers to higher powers, or discussions of "proper citizenship" and the importance of family and self-fulfillment, characters on these and other programs reflect the same longings for identity, meaning and purpose – the building blocks of religion – as any other neoliberal citizen. Moreover, their "lived religion," daily rituals for meaning-making that point to ultimate values and concerns, raise up what is truly central in their lives.

And these conventional reality shows are not the only reality genre where such themes play out. The interface of religion, economics and politics is also found on game shows, talk shows, and magazine programs. Attentive viewers have seen and heard such allusions on *The Voice* and *Survivor, The Daily Show* and the *Late Show*, and *The Oprah Winfrey Show* and *60 Minutes*. We can attribute this to the ongoing appeal of religious themes, like martyrdom, messianism and the struggle between good and evil. The theme of redemption, in particular, is a popular late capitalist trope. Almost every game show from *Survivor* to *American Idol* to *It Takes a Church* is framed as a redemptive story: the underdog coming from behind to win.

Digitization has resulted in a range of new opportunities for representations of religion and mediated reality. We define mediated reality to include reality TV as well as "reality" in other video forms distributed via new media platforms. In user-generated media such as vlogs and YouTube, the impact that reality television has had on bottom-up media is evident, specifically in the commodification of emotion and the performance of the self. The ubiquity of video technology in everyday consumer life in conjunction with user-friendly video sharing platforms has resulted in a growing number of people able to widely distribute their lived experiences, in exchange for likes, shares, and views. Communities form around these video-sharing sites and social media where individuals both produce and consume the performance of beliefs, customs, emotions, or even the most mundane moments of their daily lives. Correspondingly, reality television producers and casting agents use vlogs and popular social media accounts to discover new talent and trends.

But why the current increase in content and in these formats? A confluence of factors contributed to the rise in religion, broadly construed, as mediated reality. First was the flux in the television's political economy. Starting in the 2000s, broadcast and cable networks faced competition from Internet outlets. The challenge came from both traditional websites that attracted viewers away from television as well as video sites, like Netflix and Hulu, that caused "cord-cutting," when consumers chose to watch content on computers rather than on television.

No longer guaranteed significant advertising income, television executives had to find new forms of revenue and, at the same time, decrease programming costs. Revenue was increased through product placement (or more broadly branded entertainment) and ancillary products like branded kitchen products from Food Network or text voting on *American Idol*. Program costs decreased through the increased use of reality content. The savings were significant: a typical 30-minute situation comedy costs approximately one million dollars per episode; established, long-running reality TV shows cost half as much. Newer reality shows can be done for as little as $100,000 per episode. In many instances, shows about religious people are among the least expensive to make.

Second, social media works synergistically with reality TV in two ways. First, social media has changed the way we think about privacy (Andrejevic, 2004, Poniewozik, 2010). Not so long ago audiences might have thought it untoward to watch the foibles of their neighbors and their ministers. Not so today. "Thus comes what you might call the realitization of reality: the evolution of once private, or at least obscure, acts into performance. The diary becomes the blog. The home-movie collection becomes the YouTube channel. The résumé becomes the public search-result page" (Poniewozik, 2010). In other words, prying into people's personal lives has become not only accepted, but also expected. In addition, programmers look for shows that compel viewers to interact online or through social media when the program is airing. (This drives the appeal of live programming, such as the Academy Awards, and contest shows like *The Voice*.) Seeking to replicate this with filmed content, networks create online content that requires interaction and/or inspires tweets while the show is in progress. Programs flash hashtags on the screen so that viewers can have a more interactive experience and engage with other audience members.

In conjunction with this interactivity, researchers have found that audiences are more likely to share content when it generates strong emotions (Berger, 2013;

Guadagno et al., 2013). Religious-based content is ripe for this type of media environment because it generates awe and anger – the two emotions that lead to online virality. For television programmers, this means more engaged viewers and, therefore, more advertising revenue. For many Americans, religion has been a private matter. Reality television turns intimate moments of prayer, confession, ecstasy and sin into spectacle.

Religion and Reality TV: Faith in Late Capitalism lays the foundation for understanding the complex interplay among faith, ideology, technology and television. We theorize the expansion of this genre as more content migrates into the digital space, where individualism, privatization, and commodification reign. Within this genre, the themes discussed in this collection, including the commodification of the sacred, the performance of authenticity, and the privileging of the individual over the community have an impact on how audiences think about themselves and society. Reality television has been dubbed "a guilty pleasure," but we argue it's much more. The reality genre helps to normalize late capitalist ideology, influencing who we think we are, what we want to be and how we hope to get there. Can we keep up with the Kardashians? The Chrisleys? And what would our lives look like if we try?

Case studies

This volume has four sections, each of which examines a particular theme illustrative of the relationship between religion and late capitalism. Some chapters focus on spectacle, others on lived religion, and still others on race and/or gender. In Part I, "Maintenance of the self," the authors explore how religion works to constitute gendered and racialized selves in late capitalist society. Diane Winston's "Flaunting Christian patriarchy in the 21st century: Todd Chrisley's straight guy with the queer eye" looks at how the eponymous Chrisley's metrosexual persona offers a new model for white, male Christian headship. In "Making over body and soul: gender, selfhood, and parables of spiritual neoliberalism on *Makeover TV*," Brenda R. Weber explains how the reality television makeover articulates the characteristics of spiritual neoliberalism. And Monique Moultrie's "Black female sexual agency and racialized holy sex in black Christian reality TV shows" is a close analysis of how the notion of racialized holy sex promotes patriarchy, heteronormativity, and sexual purity, while also responding to stereotypes of black hypersexuality.

The Part II, "The performance of authenticity," probes the ways in which reality genres use religious identities to contextualize advanced capitalism within a moral framework. Katherine Madden's "'This is just an incredible God thing': monetized domesticity in bottom-up media" shows how, following the Great Recession of 2008, the homes of conservative Christian vloggers became a stage to reaffirm patriarchy within the fractured American Dream. In "'The renovation starts now!': rite-of-passage reality television," Erica Andrus looks to *Extreme Makeover: Home Edition* as a form of American ritualization that reinforces the neoliberal tenets of privatization and materialism. Yoel Cohen and Amir Hestroni use Israeli adaptations of global reality television formats to highlight the discordance between Orthodox Jewish values and Western secularism. And in "All-American cancellation: spectacle and neoliberal performativity in *All-American Muslim*," Melinda Q. Brennan cites the cancellation of TLC's *All-American Muslim* as an example of the Religious Right's resistance to the neoliberal project of cultural assimilation.

Late capitalism drives profits by creating distinct sets of consumers, and reality genres reflect that process. In Part III, "Niche markets," the authors examine religious audience segments as both a window into lived religion and as an examination of "the other." In "*Sister Wives*: the Protestantization of Mormon polygamy," Myev Rees shows how reality TV works to make multiple wives appear "just like us" to attract female audiences. Paranormal reality has become a popular niche, so we include two chapters that address this segment. In Annette Hill's "Paranormal reality television: audience engagement with mediums and spirit communication," genre analysis is combined with audience research to understand viewers' connection to this content. Sean McCloud takes an analytical approach in "Conjuring spirits in a neoliberal era: ghost reality television, Third Wave spiritual warfare, and haunting pasts," connecting occultism to evangelism. Finally, Stewart M. Hoover examines viewers' fascination with the "otherness" of the Amish in "Amish reality and reality TV Amishness: agonism in the cultural marketplace," and why their outsider standing makes compelling television fare.

Exploring the "Commodification of the sacred," authors in the final part draw on examples such as praying, preaching and pastoring to demonstrate the marriage of marketing and religion. Sharon Lauricella's "Praying for reality: the invisible hand in Downey and Burnett's *Answered Prayers*" shows how religion adheres to the neoliberal ideal of individual responsibility by presenting the praying person as accountable for his or her personal salvation and spiritual agency. In "The search for a young Imam begins now: *Imam Muda* and civilizational Islam in Malaysia," Andrea Stanton discusses how a game show facilitates viewers' pious self-cultivation while also promoting a modern and youthful Islam. And Mara Einstein's "*Preachers of Oxygen*: franchising faith on reality TV" examines the packaging and promotion of Los Angeles' celebrity preachers as a convoluted mix of "everyman" and the unattainable.

Religion and Reality TV: Faith in Late Capitalism highlights the crucial role that religion plays in the creation and maintenance of political ideology. Even if viewers did not see *The Apprentice* as a try-out for a Trump presidency, they did perceive a leader whose core values of individualism, self-reliance and success mirrored theirs. These values, reflecting aspects of American religions from transcendentalism to New Thought to the Prosperity Gospel, are well-matched to the current moment. And that's why Donald Trump's presidency may have surprised many Americans but not the millions who tune in to undercover bosses, polygamous households and game shows predicated on the survival of the fittest.

Notes

1 Oprah's online school shows, however, that there is interest in very strong spiritual content through other media, specifically the Internet.
2 The show was also controversial in its subject matter which may have contributed to the show's demise.

Bibliography

Andrejevic, M. (2004). *Reality TV: The Work of Being Watched*. Lanham, MD: Rowman & Littlefield.
Berger, Jonah. (2013). *Contagious: Why Things Catch On*. New York: Simon & Schuster.
Einstein, M. (2004). *Media Diversity: Economics, Ownership and the FCC*. Mahwah, NJ: Lawrence Erlbaum.
Guadagno, R.E., Rempala, D.M., Murphy, S., and Okdie, B.M. (2013). What makes a video go viral? An analysis of emotional contagion and internet memes. *Computers in Human Behavior*, 29(6): 2312–2319. Doi: doi:10.1016/j.chb.2013.04.016.
Kavka, M. (2012). *Reality TV*. Edinburgh: Edinburgh University Press.
Poniewozik, J. (2010, February). Reality TV at 10: How its changed television and us. *Time magazine*. Retrieved from http://www.time.com/time/magazine/article/0,9171,1963739,00. html

PART I
Maintenance of the self

1

FLAUNTING CHRISTIAN PATRIARCHY IN THE 21ST CENTURY

Todd Chrisley's straight guy with the queer eye

Diane Winston

When *Chrisley Knows Best* (CKB) premiered in March 2014, reviewers called it an updated version of *Father Knows Best*. Similar to the classic sitcom that ran from 1954–1960, this new reality show featured an affluent family headed by a strong but loving dad. Both fathers were white, Christian suburbanites with patient wives, taxing teens and an adorably precocious youngster. But that's where the similarity ends.

In the quintessential 1950s series' first season, *Father Knows Best* opened with a natty businessman in a suburban foyer, starting his day with a smoke.[1] "This," says a rotund voice, "is the story of a man, his home and his family." The man glances at his watch, and an attractive female emerges from a side door, his hat and briefcase in hand. The two lean in for a kiss, but high-pitched laughter – pan to three smiling children on the staircase – stops them. Exchanging a knowing look, the parents chastely embrace. The black-and-white *mise-en-scène* is reassuringly middle class: four small windows on the front door's transom let in light, and a grandfather clock lends gravitas to the vestibule. The wife wears a white blouse with a Peter Pan collar, and the children are fresh-scrubbed portraits of wholesomeness. The message is clear: Father is off to work, and his family and home are in order.

Sixty years later, the opening for *Chrisley Knows Best* also spotlighted a man, his home and his family, but this patriarch's presentation was far removed from the fictional Jim Anderson. Anderson embodied the masculine myths of his time: a sincere, self-contained but distant presence. Dad worked outside the home, but his influence and expectations were pervasive. Todd Chrisley, however, is always there, always emoting and usually playing the angles.

The show's first 30 seconds – fast cuts of Chrisley wisecracking with his rambunctious brood – establish him as a no-nonsense authoritarian, albeit with a cutting wit.[2] Next comes an establishing shot of Todd and Julie Chrisley, dressed in complementary blacks and whites, perched on an oversized sofa. "We're the Chrisleys," says a thickly-accented Southern tenor, Todd himself, and the camera pulls out to reveal an imposing brick mansion. Official network publicity described Todd as a self-made, Atlanta-based millionaire who made his fortune in real estate, an assertion complicated by subsequent facts.[3] Now as he introduces his home and family, certain words seem to pop: "30,000 square feet," "gated community," "celebrities," "order," and "expectations." A visit to his room-size closet underlines the not-so-secret subtext: this is a home where personal consumption and self-control coexist. Rows of clothes are organized by season, says Todd, as he pulls an offending dark jacket from a wall of pressed pastel shirts. The family spends up to $300,000 a year on clothes, he notes, adding, "I approve every piece of clothing our children wear."

The message is clear here, too: Father's work *is* the home; he orders and controls the family. Home is traditionally the woman's sphere, but Chrisley's kingdom of excess, populated by unruly scamps, needs a firm male hand albeit attached to a slightly limp wrist. What could be viewed as gender confusion – and, in fact, looks gay to many viewers – is reality television's reconciliation of market needs, family values and self-surveillance. Todd Chrisley is neoliberalism's newest poster boy: a self-actualized metrosexual.

This chapter explores Todd Chrisley's performance of religion and gender. His metrosexual persona promotes neoliberal norms including a new model for white, male Christian headship. Evangelical Christian notions of freedom – religious, economic and political – are consistent with neoliberalism, and scholars have noted their symbiosis. Moreover, the Prosperity Gospel – a strain of evangelicalism that teaches God wants his followers to enjoy wealth and health – hews to neoliberal economic and political values. The synthesis of religion, economics and politics is potent. During the 2016 presidential race, journalists described Republican candidate Donald Trump's appeal to evangelicals as proof of the Prosperity Gospel's popularity.[4]

Neoliberalism advocates free markets, limited government, deregulation and privatization. A corollary to the concomitant economic freedom is personal responsibility, including accountability for one's family. That's why neoliberal administrations, beginning with Ronald Reagan's, have cut entitlement programs; "good" citizens take care of their own. Neoliberalism also "involves shifts from authoritarian government to individual responsibility; from injunction to expert advice; and from centralized government to quasi-governmental agencies and media, including television, as sources of information, evaluation and reproach."[5] According to media studies scholars, reality television correlates with neoliberalism because it is a media-based source of "expert advice" as well as "information, evaluation and reproach." Neoliberalism's supporters say it facilitates individual freedom, especially economic success, but critics counter that its emphasis on market values and personal success has damaged social cohesion.

Todd Chrisley fervently embraces key aspects of neoliberalism: the primacy of family and personal responsibility, and the right to pursue wealth and enjoy consumption. Yet, as a heterosexual male, he queers this embrace by enacting it through flamboyant performances of feminine behaviors, specifically displays of physical attractiveness, emotional volatility and luxury consumption. Misha Kavka calls this performance "flaunting," a useful term to "open up a critical interrogation of gendered performances within the specific conditions of contemporary reality television programs," because it "recognizes precisely the *gendered* pressures on the presentation of the self."[6] In Chrisley's case, flaunting may be a strategy to mask and mitigate his need for dominance and control which, at the same time, addresses the current "crisis of masculinity."

Kavka's analysis focuses on heterosexual performances, but other scholars have probed "the *gendered* pressures on the presentation of the self" of gays on reality television. Writing about the "Fab Five," the gay life coaches on *Queer Eye for the Straight Guy*, Katherine Sender does not use the term "flaunting," but her description of how gay stereotypes are deployed to remedy "the crisis of masculinity" accords with Kavka's thesis. According to Sender, the current "crisis" stems from the failure of heterosexual men to be good consumers and to value the importance of – and therefore buy products to improve – their appearance, their homes and their relationships. *Queer Eye for the Straight Guy*, which ran from 2003 to 2007 on Bravo, "puts gay style expertise to work to reform a heterosexual masculinity compatible with neoliberalism."[7]

Chrisley, whose television debut came seven years after *Queer Eye* ended, embodies the "reformed" heterosexual whom the Fab Five sought to fashion. Subverting traditional gender categories, Chrisley promotes consumption and personal responsibility even as he emphasizes his headship of the family by protecting and providing for its members. He accomplishes this by flaunting, displays of femininity that Todd treats as normal. When Grayson, the family's youngest child, notes that his father's eyebrows never move, Todd's retort is both immediate and unembarrassed: "They're not supposed to. It's called Botox."[8]

"We're the Chrisleys"

Chrisley Knows Best debuted in March 2014 on the USA Network. According to Todd, a producer-friend asked if the family would do a "sizzle reel," a short, fast-paced promotional video that could be shopped around. He later recalled: "Six weeks later, we got a call that said we have pitched your show to 10 networks and we have 9 offers."[9] USA Network, which was launching reality programming, had the winning bid, betting that Todd's flamboyance, the children's charm and Julie's level-headedness would attract audiences. As one network executive explained, "The family is not only over-the-top but they are fun, comedic characters."[10] A new spin on the successful formula of family-centered reality shows, the Chrisleys staked territory between the lavish, Los Angeles lifestyle of *Keeping Up With the Kardashians* and the Southern Gothic milieu of *Here Comes Honey-Boo*. Like the former clan, the Chrisleys were very wealthy people who always put family first. Similar to the latter, there was a constant stream of strange relatives, get-rich-quick schemes and beauty pageant preparations.

When the series debuted, Todd's wife Julie is a stay-at-home mom, and the mother of his three youngest children. Chase, their eldest, is a high-spirited teenager who frequently gets into trouble. Savannah, his slightly younger sister, is attractive and generally risk-averse. In the pilot, she is still in high school and preparing for a beauty pageant. Their younger brother Grayson is a preternaturally wisecracking mini-Todd. Todd's two children from his first marriage also are series regulars. Lindsie wed without her father's blessing, and Todd and her husband do not get along. She usually appears by herself or with her young son, Jackson. Todd has issues, too, with his oldest son Kyle, whom he describes as "our child that doesn't march to anyone's beat other than his own."[11] "Nanny Faye," Todd's septuagenarian mother, is the family's oldest "child." A fount of commonsensical advice, Nanny Faye has a surprising penchant for getting into trouble, including drinking, gambling, sexting and driving with a suspended license. Todd must manage his mother alongside his offspring. In Season Two, Todd and Julie also have custody of Chloe, Kyle's daughter from an out-of-wedlock relationship. Chloe, who was born in 2012, is of mixed race, the only character of color to appear regularly on the series. (In 2016, USA Network removed her from the show after Kyle requested payments for her appearance.)[12]

While these are the Chrisleys' onscreen personas, their "real" selves are difficult to track. Unlike the Kardashians, whose off-screen histories are well documented, the Chrisleys' paper trail is thin. There is little information on either Todd's or Julie's past, their relationship or their businesses. Official publicity depicts Todd as a loving, if idiosyncratic, family man whose worst faults are brashness, micromanagement and a "tough, and at times brutally honest, form of parenting."[13] But according to some online news outlets, the self-proclaimed "patriarch of perfection" is a rash and callous ex-husband and employer. His ex-wife Teresa Terry describes Todd's behavior during their marriage as controlling, abusive and violent.[14] Kyle, chafing under his father's dictates, left the show after the second season, and initiated a public feud.[15] In June 2017, Lindsie announced that she, too, would leave *Chrisley Knows Best*, citing Todd's callous comments about her marital problems.[16] In 2009 and 2010, Chrisley was sued for sexual harassment. (Both cases were settled out of court.[17]) In 2012, $49.4 million dollars in debt, he filed for bankruptcy protection.[18] (Three years later the case was resolved.[19]) Online sources report that Todd's current net worth is negative five million dollars, and that the family stays afloat because Julie is independently wealthy.[20] In 2017, the state of Georgia began investigating claims that the Chrisleys failed to pay state income tax, and subsequently filed liens against Todd.[21]

Consumption, control and Christian headship

Todd is an authoritarian. He believes in discipline, punishment and that father does know best. When his first marriage ended, his wife claimed he inflicted "mental and physical abuse," including his demand that "everything had to be picture perfect."[22] But Todd's control issues, wrapped in a sitcom, are played for laughs on the television series. On the show, Todd's power appears to come from money, which he uses to coax, cajole and bully the children into obedience. But his existential location – a white, Christian man – also imbues dominance. Although Todd does not call attention to these identities (as he does with his wealth), they surface in his references to his heterosexuality (frequent allusions to his virility) and his religiosity (invocations of the Bible, God, and morality). Todd lets it be known that Julie's father is a minister; the children attend Christian schools, and that the family attends church. He also boasts that he does not smoke, drink or take drugs, and he prides himself on his self-control. He does not use the term "headship" to describe his place in the household, but he represents it.

Headship, according to Stewart Hoover and Curtis Coats, "is a way of framing gender through a divine order and channeling it through a domestic ideal, where the man's role is particular, focused and ascendant."[23] In their research on men, media and Christianity, Coats' and Hoover's subjects, a mix of evangelicals and non-evangelical Christians, said that their churches did not adequately explain what headship is or how to enact it. As a result, many of the men looked for alternative ways to understand their roles, and discovered both positive and negative examples in popular culture, particularly movies and television programs. Pressed to articulate what they meant by "headship," interviewees mentioned a sense of purpose, which Hoover and Coats describe as "a quality of life, a state of mind, a moral claim" that "men should act in a way that shows that their commitments and actions matter."[24] Purpose, for many of these men, derived from protecting and providing for their families. Their jobs and careers supplied an income, but their domestic role provided meaning. Hoover and Coats call this "elemental masculinity," a wide consensus among their subjects that provision, protection and purpose surrounding family were fundamental to being a man and exercising headship.

Chrisley's headship is embodied by female behaviors, which, upon examination, demonstrate elemental masculinity. Todd's ostentatious displays of wealth – $300,000 on clothing and $140,000 on a car as well as vacations, parties and homes – reflect his ability to provide for his family.[25] They also indicate his sanctity. According to the Prosperity Gospel, a good Christian is faithful to God and family, and success signals divine favor. Todd may not act like a typical Christian (he curses, talks dirty and rarely engages in religious activities such as praying or attending church), but his values and behaviors – including enjoyment of health and wealth, personal responsibility and reliance on family –align with the Prosperity Gospel.

Likewise, Todd's zealous monitoring of Chase and Savannah (tracking their cars, controlling their social lives, and checking their social media) as well as his "cleaning up" after their escapades, indicates his attachment to family and his need to protect them. He tracks the teens online and through social media. If he finds something he does not like, he acts: throwing Chase's computer into the pool, docking Savannah's allowance and playing "dirty tricks" to teach them a lesson. These interventions are central to Todd's notion of parenting, "Ignorance I can fix, stupidity is forever,"[26] and surveillance, supervision and subterfuge are the means to his end. When Todd learns that Chase has two dates for Valentine's Day – "[he's] acting like a damned gigolo and going against every moral I've ever taught him,"[27] – he decides to step in. (Though he is less voluble about his son's sexuality than Savannah's, Todd does not want Chase to be a "ho."[28]) He catfishes Chase and sends Savannah, in sunglasses and a brunette wig, to rendezvous with him. When Chase realizes he has been set up and sending flirty texts to his father, the rest of the family laughs at his expense.

Todd's emotional involvement in the family reflects the sense of purpose he experiences from taking care of the Chrisley clan. Unlike Jim Anderson and "real" dads from earlier eras, Todd is more than the titular head of the household. He oversees almost all aspects of family members' lives, and his goal as "patriarch of perfection" is to hone each one into the best version of themselves; or, more precisely, his notion of who they should be. That person not only enjoys but also appreciates consumption: Chase does not want a car, he wants a Range Rover; Savannah does not ask for a dress, she expects a Valentino. But they also are responsible for themselves and, ultimately, their family. That's why many episodes revolve around Todd instructing Chase, Savannah and even Nanny Faye about accountability. In Season 4, the Chrisleys relocate to Nashville, and Todd decides that he will teach the teens to be entrepreneurs. He buys a juice bar that the family can run together and will "help the kids learn responsibility."[29] (The juice bar also offers opportunities for sight gags and family drama.)[30] Todd not only wants to provide for the children but also to instruct them in self-monitoring. This is an important lesson for Chase, whose onscreen persona, a mischievous Peter Pan, shirks work and serious commitment. Todd tries to explain that running a business requires conforming to social norms that govern adult behavior, but unsurprisingly – since this is a reality series-cum-sitcom – he is unable to change Chase's behavior.

The interrelationship among responsibility, self-monitoring and religion comes up in just one episode in the first four seasons. "The Wrath of Todd" also is the only episode that has the family in a church. At the start of the program, Chase is getting a tattoo. Wary of Todd's disapproval, he decides his best bet is to have John 3:16, a Bible verse, inked on his torso.[31] But before Chase can talk to his father, Todd sees the tattoo on Snapchat, thanks to Savannah, who is trying to deflect attention from her own failings. Home from college, Savannah has to tell her parents that she flunked her Bible class. Disgusted with both children, Todd tells Julie, "We've got one child failing Bible and another who has gone and branded himself with it. I don't know what the hell is going on in this house." Since the children are disrespecting their parents and the Scriptures, Todd vows to "teach them a lesson."[32]

Todd tells Chase that if he removes the tattoo, he will give him a $140,000 Range Rover. The teen accepts the deal not realizing that removing the tattoo is a very painful process, which takes several months. Watching Chase squirm and scream during the first session, Todd seems almost gleeful. Savannah's lesson in self-discipline is milder. Julie and Todd take her to their church, where the pastor suggests she follow Jesus' example and do something for others.[33] She agrees to teach a Sunday school class, which, despite some initial bumps, ends in success. Again, Todd seems satisfied when Savannah buckles down and assumes responsibility for her behavior. Todd's lessons convey his control over the teens' bodies. By inflicting pain on Chase and schooling Savannah in front of others, he aims to educate the two about responsibility, self-monitoring, and respect for religion. The episode is the closest Todd comes to explicitly enacting Christian headship.

Gender flaunting

Kavka notes "there is no singular political meaning" and "no particular ideological connotation"[34] attached to flaunting. But political and ideological readings are inevitable since gender displays illuminate the self's relationship to power. When women on reality television flaunt their bodies, their possessions and/or their feelings, the consequent show of "(hyper)femininity" instantiates their worth and power within the construct of their televised reality. What audiences make of that power – and whether they view it as authentic or artifice – is crucial. Anecdotal information from online forums and popular magazines is equivocal. *Kardashians* is a case in point; the double meaning of "keeping up" – to stay in touch and to compete with – reflects the strong if ambivalent hold the family has on viewers, including scholars. Their excesses intrigue, excite and disgust; their family bonds irk and inspire. Are they feminist icons or embarrassments to their gender?

The same might be asked of reality television's gay characters, whose flaunting is more akin to Kavka's description of (hyper)femininity than to straight men's displays of virility, villainy and sexuality.[35] The very aspects of gay male life that have been disparaged in the "real" world – including a preoccupation with appearances, objects and emotions – make gay men integral to reality television, especially for dating and makeover programs. As Joshua Gammon notes, "Reality television has exaggerated the gay-man-as-style-maven role and its class meaning: playing up queenly insight into the consumption and habits of the upper middle classes and the ability to transform a dowdy, 'taste challenged' man, woman or space into a fabulous, 'classy' one."[36] Pivoting between genders, gay men appeal not only to GLBTQI viewers but also to women who appreciate their guidance and men who need it. They promote consumption in the guise of providing expert advice. The real goal of *Queer Eye for the Straight Guy*, argues Sender, is to "reform a heterosexual masculinity compatible with neoliberalism,"[37] or, in other words, to turn men into metrosexuals.

The term "metrosexual" originated with Mark Simpson, a British journalist, in 1994.[38] According to Simpson, it connoted "a young man with money to spend, living in or within easy reach of a metropolis … He might be officially gay, straight or bisexual, but this is utterly immaterial because he has clearly taken himself as his own love object."[39] By the time *Queer Eye* debuted, the initially unflattering term had been "adopted by marketers and lost some of its bite." Metrosexuals had evolved from solipsistic narcissists into straight men who appreciated expensive haircuts and designer labels. Like the hapless heterosexuals whom the Fab Five groomed to be sensitive hunks, metrosexuals were a feminized evolution of the manly man, one whose commodity needs accommodated neoliberal norms.

Todd Chrisley did not need a queer eye, he had his own. His face is Botoxed, his nails manicured, and his trim frame fits snugly into a designer wardrobe. His 30,000 square foot house is well appointed,[40] and his family relationships are intense, extreme and commodity-based. Chrisley's displays of self, home and family echo Kavka's description of the gendered performances of female reality stars. He flaunts himself ("I want a life in fashion"[41]), his possessions ("He who has the gold rules"[42]), and his family ("I place nothing above my wife and children[43]). The series revolves around two poles fundamental to neoliberalism: Todd's desire to provide for his family and his need to teach them personal responsibility. The frisson between the two gives the show its humor. "Yes I spoiled the children. I created this monster," Todd says, when Savannah tells him about the Valentino and Chanel accoutrements she needs for college. "And now I am going to tame it."[44]

Onscreen and off, Julie and Todd Chrisley use the term "metrosexual" to explain Todd's seemingly gay behaviors. His arch mannerisms, fashion consciousness and conspicuous consumption have long fueled "is he or isn't he?" speculation. Even before the show debuted, he was denying rumors about his sexuality. In 2014, Chrisley told *People* magazine, "What you see is what you get. I am what I am. Other people's opinions of me are just not my business."[45] But even though he announced "there was no coming out," Todd's small screen persona, whether tossing a frosted blonde coif or dismissing Savannah's crotch-grazing couture with a deep-fried *bon mot,* e.g. "You ain't wearing a coochie cutter,"[46] seemed to belie the denial. In Season 4, Todd meets the innuendos head on. After catching the flu, he tells his family why he skipped a preventive shot, "Contrary to popular belief, I don't like anything penetrating my body."[47]

For Chrisley, the body is a nexus for religion, money and the enactment of gender. His headship gives him the authority to protect and provide for the children, especially their bodies. In the first season, Chrisley is as involved in Savannah's wardrobe as he is in safeguarding her virginity. In the fourth season, he is deeply disturbed when Chase defaces his body with a tattoo. Yet he controls their bodies not by physical force but by bribing and outsmarting them. The violence that Chrisley used to control his first wife has been replaced by enticement, subterfuge and manipulation. Flaunting (hyper)femininity rather than acting out hyper-masculinity enables Chrisley to have his cake (or TV series) and eat it, too. Chrisley's interest in the family's bodies extends to his mother Nanny Faye and the two children from his first marriage.[48] In the first season episode, "Jugs and Ammo," the family gathers in the kitchen to discuss Lindsie's upcoming "boob job." When Todd asks if she has decided on a bra size, Lindsie refuses to answer. "Why not?" Chase says. "He's paying for it."[49] Undeterred, Todd leaves the room and returns with "the newest members of the family," two enormous cakes shaped as breasts, which he calls, "the twins." Pointing to candles perched on the mounds, he tells Lindsie to "blow the nipple." The interchange is as telling about class as it is about gender. Despite Todd's wealth, his speech and behavior is more *Duck Dynasty* than *Kardashians.* The class commentary that began with "boob" jokes ends with Todd's efforts to bond with Will, Lindsie's husband, at a shooting range. Todd hopes that this masculine pastime will reassure his crew-cut, taciturn son-in-law, that he, too is a real man.

Conclusion

Onscreen and off, Todd is a flamboyant presence whose gay/metrosexual persona projects headship as a non-threatening, consumer-friendly, strong-parenting option. His effeminate affect and compone barbs mitigate the tactics of surveillance, subterfuge, and supervision that he uses to discipline his brood and inculcate his values. His religiosity is not overbearing, and like many Americans, he assumes wealth is a sign of God's blessing and that enjoying it is akin to a religious duty. Likewise, his neoliberalism is neither politicized nor polarizing. Rather, he enacts it in a manner recognizable to many American families, alternating between spoiling his children and teaching them a lesson.

Todd's flaunting is the metrosexual response to the crisis in masculinity. It plays well on reality television, though many "real" men may not want to emulate it. But the Chrisley alternative is especially intriguing in the Age of Trump. Some commentators have read Donald Trump's election as a sign that straight, white, Christian men feel threatened and endangered. In fact, Trump's posture as an aggressive, sexual, chauvinist male echoes Kavka's delineation of male flaunting on reality television. Todd Chrisley points to another alternative, one which demonstrates strength but also sensitivity, responsibility and self-monitoring. He juxtaposes a female style (queered figuratively if not literally) with the male message of Christian headship. He is the straight guy with the queer eye. Even though his headship is played for laughs – it's excessive with a hint of prissiness – Todd controls the home. He wants the rest of the Chrisleys to share his devotion to family as well as to the values of hard work and self-reliance. The substance of these lessons – personal responsibility within a cohesive and financially successful family unit, as well as the unthreatening style in which it is delivered – reflect the neoliberal dimensions of Chrisley's patriarchy as mediated by popular entertainment.

If Todd maintained his headship through aggression and violence, as his first wife claims, he would not star in a reality television show. But the very qualities that Teresa Terry says doomed her marriage – his demand for perfection and his need to control – are, in *Chrisley Knows Best*, played for laughs. It's headship enacted with a wink, a nod and a fully loaded luxury vehicle. Similar to many other reality shows, *Chrisley Knows Best* normalizes neoliberalism by embedding its tenets in attractive, if idiosyncratic, characters whose basic values include love of family, country and religion. It also reflects a cultural moment when many Christians envision God as a money machine, and the Religious Right's standard-bearer is a belligerent, sexist bully. To some viewers, *Chrisley Knows Best* may seem to be about a closeted gay man whose inner queen can't stay put. But it actually depicts a new style of white, Christian patriarchy, hiding an iron fist in a lavender racing glove.

Notes

1 *Father Knows Best*, "Season 1 Original Opening." https://www.youtube.com/watch?v=O64pR4IfYB0
2 *Chrisley Knows Best*, "Pilot," Season 1, episode 1. https://www.youtube.com/watch?v=sHc7DnzIs6I
3 "Todd Chrisley's Story: Net Worth, Bankruptcy & Quotes," *Investopia*, March 8, 2017, http://www.investopedia.com/insights/todd-chrisley/, accessed August 4, 2017.
4 Elizabeth Dias, "Donald Trump's Prosperity Preachers, *Time*, April 14, 2016; http://time.com/donald-trump-prosperity-preachers/, accessed August 6, 2017; Michael Schulson, "Why electing Donald Trump was a triumph for the prosperity gospel," *Washington Post*, November 30, 2016, https://www.washingtonpost.com/news/acts-of-faith/wp/2016/11/30/why-electing-a-billionaire-was-especially-a-triumph-for-the-prosperity-gospel/?utm_term=.21480c8f52c6, accessed August 7, 2017; Jeff Sharlet, "Donald Trump, American Preacher," *New York Times Magazine*, April 12, 2016, https://www.nytimes.com/2016/04/17/magazine/donald-trump-american-preacher.html?_r=0, accessed August 7, 2017.
5 Katherine Sender, "Queens for a Day: Queer Eye for the Straight Guy and the Neoliberal Project," *Critical Studies in Media Communication*, 23:2, August 16, 2006, 135.
6 Misha Kavka, "Reality TV and the Gendered Politics of Flaunting," (pp. 54–75) in Weber, Brenda R., ed. *Reality Gendervision: Sexuality and Gender on Transatlantic Reality Television* (Durham: Duke University Press, 2014), 57.
7 Sender (2006), 132.
8 *Chrisley Knows Best*, "A Very Chrisley Christmas 2," Season 3, episode 19.
9 Avery Thompson, "Todd Chrisley Reveals the Crazy Origin Story of 'Chrisley Knows Best'," *Hollywood Life*, October 31, 2016, http://hollywoodlife.com/2016/10/31/todd-chrisley-knows-best-origin-story-kim-kardashian-podcast-listen/, accessed June 22, 2017.
10 Rodney Ho, "USA's 'Chrisley Knows Best' stars Roswell's Todd Chrisley, a perfectionist with skeletons in his closet," *AJC.com*, November 4, 2014, http://radiotvtalk.blog.ajc.com/2014/03/07/usas-chrisley-knows-best-stars-atlantas-todd-chrisley-a-perfectionist-with-some-skeletons-in-his-closet/, accessed June 22, 2017.
11 "The Patriarch of Perfection," *Chrisley Knows Best*, Season 1, episode 1, 4:40.
12 Staff, "Todd Chrisley Explains Chloe's Absence on Show Exclusive," *The Real Mr. Housewife*, September 14, 2016, http://www.realmrhousewife.com/2016/09/14/todd-chrisley-granddaughter-no-longer-on-show-reason-exclusive/, accessed July 2, 2017.
13 Todd Chrisley, USA Network, http://www.usanetwork.com/chrisleyknowsbest/cast/todd-chrisley, accessed July 11, 2016.
14 Laura Collins, "'I thought I was fixing to get shot': Todd Chrisley's 'secret' ex-wife claims he 'stripped her naked and battered her', leaving her fearing for her life after vicious campaign of physical and mental abuse," *Daily Mail*, May 27, 2014, http://www.dailymail.co.uk/news/article-2635394/EXCLUSIVE-I-thought-I-fixing-shot-Todd-Chrisleys-secret-ex-wife-reveals-emotional-physical-abuse-suffered-seven-year-marriage-TV-reality-star.html, accessed July 11, 2016.
15 Laura Collins, "'My dad's a snake who shut me out of my child's life': Kyle Chrisley, now happily married and drug-free, reveals how reality star Todd has 'stolen' his daughter and ruthlessly kicked him off show," *Daily Mail*, October 24, 2014, http://www.dailymail.co.uk/news/article-2805604/EXCLUSIVE-s-snake-shut-child-s-life-Kyle-Chrisley-happily-married-drug-free-reveals-reality-star-dad-stolen-daughter-ruthlessly-kicked-show.html, accessed July 2, 2017.
16 James Vituscka, "I Quit! Todd Chrisley's Daughter Lindsie Leaves Reality Show Amid Feud With Father," *RadarOnline*, June 20, 2017, http://radaronline.com/celebrity-news/todd-chrisley-daughter-lindsie0quits-chrisley-knows-best-feud-father/, accessed June 22, 2017.
17 Melissa Cronin, "Does Chrisley Really Know Best? Millionaire Star of New USA Reality Show Sued by Employees for 'Vulgar' & 'Outrageous' Sexual Harassment, Filed

for Bankruptcy Last Year," *RadarOnline*, January 2, 2014, http://radaronline.com/exclu sives/2014/01/todd-chrisley-knows-best-usa-reality-tv-show-sexual-harassment/, accessed July 11, 2016; Melissa Cronin, "Proof Todd Chrisley Is 'Gay'? 'Chrisley Knows Best' Star Allegedly Asked Male Employee to Engage in Sexual Act, Court Docs Claims," *RadarOnline*, November 20, 2014, http://radaronline.com/exclusives/2014/11/todd-chrisley-gay-sex-claims-chrisley-knows-best/, accessed July 11, 2016.

18 Steve Helling, "Chrisley Knows Best: Inside Todd Chrisley's $45 Million Bankruptcy Case," *People*, March 7, 2014, http://www.people.com/people/article/0,,20794568,00. html, accessed July 11, 2016.

19 James Vituscka, "In The Clear? Todd Chrisley's $46 Million Bankruptcy Case Is Discharged! – 'We Have Moved On,' He Says," *RadarOnline*, April 1, 2015, ahttp://rada ronline.com/exclusives/2015/04/todd-chrisley-46-million-bankruptcy-case-discharged/, accessed July 11, 2016.

20 *Celebrity Net Worth*, https://www.celebritynetworth.com/richest-businessmen/busi ness-executives/todd-chrisley-net-worth/, accessed July 9, 2017.

21 Rodney Ho, "WSB-TV: Georgia files $700K in tax liens against Todd and Julie Chrisley ('Chrisley Knows Best')," *AJC.com*, March 23, 2017, http://radiotvtalk.blog. myajc.com/2017/03/23/wsb-tv-georgia-files-700k-in-tax-liens-against-todd-and-julie-chrisley-chrisley-knows-best/ accessed July 2, 2017.

22 Laura Collins, "'I thought I was fixing to get shot': Todd Chrisley's 'secret' ex-wife claims he 'stripped her naked and battered her', leaving her fearing for her life after vicious campaign of physical and mental abuse," *Daily Mail*, May 27, 2014, http://www. dailymail.co.uk/news/article-2635394/EXCLUSIVE-I-thought-I-fixing-shot-Todd-Chrisleys-secret-ex-wife-reveals-emotional-physical-abuse-suffered-seven-year-marriage-TV-reality-star.html, accessed July 11, 2016.

23 Hoover and Coats, 62.

24 Hoover and Coats, 147.

25 Even when the family is forced to scale down – selling their home mansion and moving to a smaller home in Atlanta and then relocating to Nashville – the family still lives comfortably. And while online sources say that Julie's money is keeping the family afloat, that is never mentioned on the program.

26 *Chrisley Knows Best*, "Pilot," Season 1, episode 1.

27 *Chrisley Knows Best*, "My Chrisley Valentine," Season 3, episode 4.

28 *Chrisley Knows Best*, "My Chrisley Valentine," Season 3, episode 4.

29 *Chrisley Knows Best*, "Smoothie Operator," Season 4, Episode 8.

30 The Chrisleys own the I Love Juice Bar in Nashville's Green Hills mall. But an online post reported they are rarely there. https://www.tripadvisor.com/Restaurant_ Review-g55229-d8836032-Reviews-Juice_Bar-Nashville_Davidson_County_Tennessee. html, accessed July 7, 2016.

31 @Chase Chrisley, "For God so loved the world that he gave his one and only Son, that whoever believes in him should not perish but have eternal life." *People*, March 22, 2016, http://www.people.com/article/chrisley-knows-best-todd-chrisley-talks-son-chase-scripture-tattoo, accessed July 13, 2016.

32 *Chrisley Knows Best*, "The Wrath of Todd," Season 4, episode 2.

33 The church identified in the episode is Clairmont Presbyterian in Atlanta, GA. In response to an email for information, I received this: "Hi Diane, The show featured our church as a backdrop, but that family nor the pastor in that show are a part of our church. They did not inform us that they would be using our name or pretending to be a part of our church in their filming. All of the people in that segment are actors. So unfortunately our pastors would skew your research because the group in the show and the church are two completely separate groups. Jenn Twitchell, Director of Communications, Clairmont Presbyterian Church" (July 1, 2016, author's email account).

34 Kavka in Weber (2014), 71.

35 Kavka in Weber (2014), 66.

36 Joshua Gamson, "Reality Queens," *Contexts*, Spring 2013, Vol. 12, No. 2, 52.

37   Sender (2006), 132.
38   "About Mark Simpson," MARKSIMPSON.COM, http://www.marksimpson.com/about/, accessed July 8, 2016.
39   Mark Simpson, "Meet the metrosexual," *Salon*, July 22, 2002, http://www.salon.com/2002/07/22/metrosexual/, accessed July 8, 2016.
40   The Chrisleys have since relocated to a smaller home in Nashville, Tennessee.
41   *Chrisley Knows Best*, season 1, episode 1.
42   *Chrisley Knows Best*, season 1, episode 1.
43   *Chrisley Knows Best*, season 1, episode 1.
44   *Chrisley Knows Best*, "Dollars and Sense," Season 3, episode 3.
45   Monica Rizzo, "Todd Chrisley on Gay Rumors: 'There's No Coming Out,'" *People*, March 10, 2014, http://www.people.com/people/article/0,,20794188,00.html, accessed July 8, 2016.
46   Liane Bonin Stark, "'Chrisley Knows Best' review: This family may be nuts, but that's okay," *HITFIX*, March 12, 2014, http://www.hitfix.com/starr-raving/chrisley-knows-best-review-this-family-may-be-nuts-but-thats-okay, accessed July 8, 2016.
47   *Chrisley Knows Best*, "Todd Goes Country," Season 4, episode 12.
48   Julie appears to be the only family member not under Todd's control. Unlike the others (with the exception of Nanny Faye), she is not toned and slender. She dresses well but does not seem consumed with designer labels. Todd never teaches her a lesson, and she remains at a distance when he plays his tricks on others.
49   *Chrisley Knows Best*, "Jugs and Ammo," Season 1, episode 3.

Bibliography

Bowler, Kate, *Blessed: A History of the American Prosperity Gospel* (New York: Oxford University Press, 2013).

Celebrity Net Worth, https://www.celebritynetworth.com/richest-businessmen/business-executives/todd-chrisley-net-worth/, accessed July 9, 2017.

Chrisley, Chase, "For God so loved the world that he gave his one and only Son, that whoever believes in him should not perish but have eternal life." *People*, March 22, 2016, http://www.people.com/article/chrisley-knows-best-todd-chrisley-talks-son-chase-scripture-tattoo, accessed July 13, 2016.

Chrisley, Todd, USA Network, http://www.usanetwork.com/chrisleyknowsbest/cast/todd-chrisley, accessed July 11, 2016.

Collins, Laura, "'My dad's a snake who shut me out of my child's life': Kyle Chrisley, now happily married and drug-free, reveals how reality star Todd has 'stolen' his daughter and ruthlessly kicked him off show," *Daily Mail*, October 24, 2014, http://www.dailymail.co.uk/news/article-2805604/EXCLUSIVE-s-snake-shut-child-s-life-Kyle-Chrisley-happily-married-drug-free-reveals-reality-star-dad-stolen-daughter-ruthlessly-kicked-show.html, accessed July 2, 2017.

Collins, Laura, "'I thought I was fixing to get shot': Todd Chrisley's 'secret' ex-wife claims he 'stripped her naked and battered her', leaving her fearing for her life after vicious campaign of physical and mental abuse," *Daily Mail*, May 27, 2014, http://www.dailymail.co.uk/news/article-2635394/EXCLUSIVE-I-thought-I-fixing-shot-Todd-Chrisleys-secret-ex-wife-reveals-emotional-physical-abuse-suffered-seven-year-marriage-TV-reality-star.html, accessed July 11, 2016.

Connolly, William E., *Capitalism and Christianity, American Style* (Durham, NC: Duke University Press, 2008).

Cronin, Melissa, "Does Chrisley Really Know Best? Millionaire Star Of New USA Reality Show Sued By Employees For 'Vulgar' & 'Outrageous' Sexual Harassment, Filed For

Bankruptcy Last Year," *RadarOnline*, January 2, 2014, http://radaronline.com/exclusives/
2014/01/todd-chrisley-knows-best-usa-reality-tv-show-sexual-harassment/, accessed July
11, 2016.

Cronin, Melissa, "Proof Todd Chrisley Is 'Gay'? 'Chrisley Knows Best' Star Allegedly Asked
Male Employee To Engage In Sexual Act, Court Docs Claims," *RadarOnline*, November
20, 2014, http://radaronline.com/exclusives/2014/11/todd-chrisley-gay-sex-claims-chri
sley-knows-best/, accessed July 11, 2016.

Dias, Elizabeth, "Donald Trump's Prosperity Preachers," *Time*, April 14, 2016, http://time.
com/donald-trump-prosperity-preachers/, accessed August 6, 2017.

Gamson, Joshua, "Reality Queens," *Contexts*, Spring 2013, Vol. 12, No. 2.

Helling, Steve, "Chrisley Knows Best: Inside Todd Chrisley's $45 Million Bankruptcy
Case," *People*, March 7,2014, http://www.people.com/people/article/0,,20794568,00.
html, accessed July 11, 2016.

Ho, Rodney, "USA's 'Chrisley Knows Best' stars Roswell's Todd Chrisley, a perfectionist
with skeletons in his closet," *AJC.com*, November 4, 2014http://radiotvtalk.blog.ajc.com/
2014/03/07/usas-chrisley-knows-best-stars-atlantas-todd-chrisley-a-perfectio
nist-with-some-skeletons-in-his-closet/, accessed June 22, 2017.

Ho, Rodney, "WSB-TV: Georgia files $700K in tax liens against Todd and Julie Chrisley
('Chrisley Knows Best')," *AJC.com*, March 23, 2017, http://radiotvtalk.blog.myajc.com/
2017/03/23/wsb-tv-georgia-files-700k-in-tax-liens-against-todd-and-julie-chrisley-
chrisley-knows-best/ accessed July 2, 2017.

Hoover, Stewart and Curtis Coats, *Does God make the Man?: Media, Religion and the Crisis of
Masculinity* (New York: New York University Press, 2015).

Kintz, Linda, *Between Jesus and the Market: The Emotions That Matter in Right-Wing America*
(Durham, NC: Duke University Press, 1997).

Kraidy, Marwan and Katherine Sender, eds. *The Politics of Reality Television: Global Perspectives* (New York: Routledge, 2010).

Ouellette, Laurie and James Hay, *Better Living Through Reality TV: Post-Welfare Citizenship*
(Hoboken, NJ: Wiley-Blackwell, 2008).

Rizzo, Monica, "Todd Chrisley on Gay Rumors: 'There's No Coming Out,'" *People*,
March 10, 2014, http://www.people.com/people/article/0,,20794188,00.html, accessed
July 8, 2016.

Robinson, Sally, *Marked Men: White Masculinity in Crisis* (New York: Columbia University
Press, 2005).

Schulson, Michael, "Why electing Donald Trump was a triumph for the prosperity gospel,"
Washington Post, November 30, 2016, https://www.washingtonpost.com/news/acts-of-fa
ith/wp/2016/11/30/why-electing-a-billionaire-was-especially-a-triumph-for-the-prosp
erity-gospel/?utm_term=.21480c8f52c6, accessed August 7, 2017.

Sender, Katherine, "Queens for a Day: Queer Eye for the Straight Guy and the Neoliberal
Project," *Critical Studies in Media Communication*, 23:2, 2006, 135.

Sharlet, Jeff, "Donald Trump, American Preacher," *New York Times Magazine*, April 12,
2016, https://www.nytimes.com/2016/04/17/magazine/donald-trump-american-prea
cher.html?_r=0, accessed August 7, 2017.

Simpson, Mark, "About Mark Simpson," marksimpson.com, http://www.marksimpson.
com/about/, accessed July 8, 2016.

Simpson, Mark, "Meet the metrosexual," *Salon*, July 22, 2002, http://www.salon.com/
2002/07/22/metrosexual/, accessed July 8, 2016.

Staff, "Todd Chrisley Explains Chloe's Absence On Show Exclusive," *The Real Mr. Housewife*,
September 14, 2016, http://www.realmrhousewife.com/2016/09/14/todd-chrisley-gra
nddaughter-no-longer-on-show-reason-exclusive/, accessed July 2, 2017.

Stark, Liane Bonin, "'Chrisley Knows Best' review: This family may be nuts, but that's okay," *HITFIX*, March 12, 2014, http://www.hitfix.com/starr-raving/chrisley-knows-best-review-this-family-may-be-nuts-but-thats-okay, accessed July 8, 2016.

Thompson, Avery, "Todd Chrisley Reveals The Crazy Origin Story Of 'Chrisley Knows Best'", *Hollywood Life*, October 31, 2016, http://hollywoodlife.com/2016/10/31/todd-chrisley-knows-best-origin-story-kim-kardashian-podcast-listen/, accessed June 22, 2017.

"Todd Chrisley's Story: Net Worth, Bankruptcy & Quotes," *Investopia*, March 8, 2017, http://www.investopedia.com/insights/todd-chrisley/, accessed August 4, 2017.

Vituscka, James, "In The Clear? Todd Chrisley's $46 Million Bankruptcy Case Is Discharged! – 'We Have Moved On,' He Says," *RadarOnline*, April 1, 2015, ahttp://radaronline.com/exclusives/2015/04/todd-chrisley-46-million-bankruptcy-case-discharged/, accessed July 11, 2016.

Vituscka, James, "I Quit! Todd Chrisley's Daughter Lindsie Leaves Reality Show Amid Feud With Father," *RadarOnline*, June 20, 2017, http://radaronline.com/celebrity-news/todd-chrisley-daughter-lindsie0quits-chrisley-knows-best-feud-father/, accessed June 22, 2017.

Weber, Brenda R., *Makeover TV: Selfhood, Citizenship, and Celebrity* (Durham: Duke University Press, 2009).

Weber, Brenda R., ed. *Reality Gendervision: Sexuality and Gender on Transatlantic Reality Television* (Durham: Duke University Press, 2014).

2

MAKING OVER BODY AND SOUL

Gender, selfhood, and parables of spiritual neoliberalism on *Makeover TV*

Brenda R. Weber

In 2009, I published *Makeover TV*, a book that examines the post-2000 surge in reality television programming centered on the concept of the makeover. At that time, the reality métier was booming, and each new week seemed to bring another show centered on transformation, from *Styled by Jury* to *Supernanny*. In viewing more than 2,000 hours of programming, it became clear to me that regardless of the body to be transformed (be it car, dog, child, house, business, finances, or the actual physical body from faces to teeth to fat removal) the reality TV makeover used and solidified many key tropes that emphasized self-awareness and self-regulation. These include the survey of the shameful pre-makeover body (what I call the Before-body), the subject's confession of failure to successfully manage that body, the actual work of the makeover and the conversion from before to after, and the big reveal, or moment when the results of the makeover process were put on full celebratory and exuberant display (what I call the After-body). Each respective makeover text also had its own pantheon of gods – style coaches, plastic surgeons, interior designers, life coaches, and personal trainers – all with the power to put the suffering soul on the path to better living. Indeed, in its emphasis on devotion, suffering, obedience, and salvation, the reality television makeover clearly speaks through a religious idiom. But, as I demonstrate in this essay, given the makeover's insistence on good choices, individualism, aspirationalism, and personal capacities for competition in a global marketplace, it is also steeped in the teas of neoliberalism.

Come unto the makeover

Before I discuss the neoliberal implications of these programs in greater detail, I'd like to solidify their working as a genre and the composite hailing of ideological and spiritual goals that are made evident through the makeover's common structure. The hallmark of the reality makeover requires that subjects be confronted with "secret footage" of how they appear to others, the visual evidence provided by hidden cameras offering an incontrovertible proof of fashion disasters or unmanaged homespaces that the unwitting subject cannot deny. Style shows often involve pedagogical moments where subjects must be taken outside of themselves through cameras, mirrors, or the judgments of others, so that they might finally begin to see the deplorable mess that others presumably see. It is only at this moment of shared recognition – we both see the same sad thing – that subjects on style shows recognize how bad they look and how much they need the extraordinary power of the makeover. With awareness comes shame, and subjects often make statements – such as Saira on the BBC version of *What Not to Wear* – that reinforce the power dynamics between all-powerful style hosts and debased makeover subjects. "Clearly I need to be taken in hand," Saira says in tears when confronted with her image in the 360-degree mirror. When prompted to elaborate on why she feels shame, Saira confesses to the presenters Trinny and Susannah that her dowdiness is due to "Not giving enough of a damn about what I look like. Not realizing how important it is and how it diminishes me. I am ashamed" (*What Not to Wear*, "Stylish Sisters," 2006). Awareness of her shame, as manifested through her poor fashion choices, her monochromatic clothing palate, and her premature gray hair, thus justifies the "saving" power of the makeover.

While both men and women participate in the reality television makeover, the ratio of men's representation to women's is 1:9, meaning that only ten percent of the suffering souls needing (or taking advantage of) the salvific powers of television makeover are men.[1] While men are also featured on such makeover shows as *The Biggest Loser* (2004–present) or *Pimp My Ride* (2004–2007), their need for help and assistance works against conventional codes of masculinity that require autonomy, agency, and authority. Men on the makeover have largely stalled in the hegemonic project expected of them, thus requiring that transformation is not solely of the body (or its symbolic referent like the car or the house) but also of gender itself. The Before-body is soft, pliant, needing to be shaped and coached. As such, the Before-body in need of redemption is resolutely coded as abject and gendered feminine. This is true even on a show such as *Queer Eye for the Straight Guy* (2003–2007), which often made over men who were "too masculine," if we understand scruffiness and messiness as reliable markers of masculinity. The makeover technology itself is a feminizing one that places the subject, regardless of sex, in a position of submission where improvement is imposed by a figure of authority. This gender dynamic does not, however, advantage women, since the threshold for what constitutes "desirable" femininity is extremely high. To be female but not to be conventionally feminine is a gender disorder of 911 proportions requiring the active intervention of RTV's various makeover SWAT teams.

In a Christian frame, if Adam and Eve were to be subjects of a reality television makeover, Adam would only figure as a body of shameful concern once for every ten times that Eve was targeted. In other words, the reality television version of this story would not begin with a male figure and then craft a secondary character out of his rib, but instead, the makeover would put Eve front and center. Further, it would continue to feature Eve, or Mary, or Madeline, or Joyce, or Yvette, in preference to lonely Adam. This favoritism for women is not, unfortunately, due to the makeover's woman-friendly politics. Although it is important that stories about women predominate on makeover television, thus situating women as the most important feature of narrative interest, these stories almost always accentuate female shame due to feminine ignorance. Not knowing how to dress is often raised as a gender crime committed by women, who allow their "natural" hourglass figures to be obscured. Or they simply inhabit the world in ways that code them as masculine. Such a body is referenced across makeover television by many derisive terms, including "sad," "insane," "mannish," and "delusional," but the primary means of verbally indicting the Before-body in need of a fashion/gender inter-vention is to say that the female subject is "not herself." In turn, this alienation from self is tacitly coded as deeply shameful, so that the makeover subject is made to feel both humiliation and regret for the degree to which she has failed in the project of properly governing gendered selfhood. The renovation of a woman's shabby style is thus positioned as bringing about her reinvention of a "true" self. Put in these terms that situate selfhood as at grave risk, the officious, imperious, demanding, and often masculinist politics of the makeover seem not only humanitarian but caring.

While in this essay I focus primarily on what might be considered a Christian reading of the makeover, its malleability and porousness make it adaptable to many faith systems, from New Age spirituality to pantheism. Indeed, there is more than a little hearkening to the Greek and Roman gods at work in the mythology of the makeover that calls upon style gurus and celebrity plastic surgeons, each – like Zeus or Athena or Poseidon – possessing a specific skill set necessary to master the combined elements of entropy, everydayness, and (perceived) evil. The makeover certainly employs Christian themes of suffering, redemption, and being born again, but Christianity is not the exclusive hermeneutic used by the makeover. Indeed, I would argue that the makeover's theology is far more polytheistic, adaptable, and idiosyncratic than a monotheistic Christian model might indicate. For this reason, I think of the makeover as being driven by a fluid theology of religiosity (rather than by a specific religion) that is quite willing to borrow elements from powerful religious systems, but it does so haphazardly and opportunistically.

The neoliberal element

As a term to describe a political economy, neoliberalism stresses the efficiency of privatization, the reliability of financial markets, and the decentralization of govern-ment, often announcing itself in cultural terms through practices and policies that use the language of markets, efficiency, consumer choice, and individual autonomy to shift risk from systems to persons and to extend this sort of market logic into the realm of social and affective relationships. Under neoliberalism, the individual is the primary unit of agency, and personal choice reigns supreme as the reason one succeeds or fails. Neoliberalism is fueled by governmentality, a concept made salient by Michel Foucault (1979) to indicate the degree to which systems, such as government, religion, and mainstream culture, produce citizens who are best suited to the policies of the state. Within the market-based logic of neoliberalism, governmentality colludes with other hegemonic factors to create the terms for a docile body, which is willing to write on itself the codes of success that will enable competition within a larger global marketplace. Critical to the idea of governmentality is the tacit regulation of micropractices – that is, self-control, guidance of the family, management of children, supervision of the household, and development of the "self." Neoliberalism and governmentality thrive on the pedagogies offered in and through Makeover TV, particularly as such instruction is often labeled a form of care, or, in the words of Oprah Winfrey, learning to "live your best life."[2]

The haphazard and opportunistic nature of the makeover is not to say, however, that the genre lacks the capacity to be compelling or coherent. Indeed, it offers supplicants a powerful and, by all accounts, desirable form of personal power that may seem transitory and superficial but actually speaks to compelling twenty-first-century fears and desires about loss, personal worth, and meaning. If we attend to the narrative reasons embedded in reality makeover shows that speak to why subjects elect to put their most embarrassing problems on international television (and indeed, many of these shows travel worldwide under the auspices of their parent networks), we see that the makeover crystalizes and mobilizes a very distinct neoliberal fear about economic competition, obsolescence, and feelings of being unloveable. In turn, the makeover promises a better place of hope and happiness post-makeover. *If I could only have whiter teeth,* the logic goes, *I would smile more, look happier, attract a partner, get a better job.* Personal transformation here stands as the gateway to the normative functions of a productive, happy, successful life. But the makeover is not so crass as to pin its transformational magic to material success – instead, the makeover works through a parable of sanctified selfhood. *We will help you find your true self, and in so doing, happiness and prosperity will follow.* This pledge is only a few steps removed from a prosperity gospel that promises material wealth as a reward for good living, good choices, and good stewardship of monies (largely through mandatory tithing; for more on the prosperity gospel, see Bowler, 2013). If you aren't healthy, wealthy, and wise, you aren't believing hard enough.

Such is the power of transformation that makeovers empower subjects to voice wondrous statements of jubilation and reward ("I can do anything now!" "I'm going straight to the top!"). These discourses tie the workings of the makeover to broader constitutions of democratic citizenship predicated on meritocratic mobility within free markets and societies. In so doing, they betoken an ideology of neoliberalism and free markets that posit looking good as the equivalent of being good, since an investment in one's self shows itself in one's appearance and manifests in an ability to compete (against less worthy others) and to live the good life. As Katherine Sender (2012, 48) has also noted about the reality television makeover, the format of the shows often assumes that "audiences aspire to be good citizens by adopting the shows' guidelines for living as a resource that they draw on to reform themselves in line with the values of the neoliberal state."

More to the point, however, reality television makeovers use a metric of worth as calibrated by one's ability to compete for a good job or to attract a spouse, positioning these mandatory achievements as prerequisites to more abstract outcomes: fulfillment, happiness, self-actualization. In this, makeovers participate in a broader cultural momentum that is increasingly upping the ante on the neoliberal mandate, a shift in abstractions from "making it" to "living one's best life." Doing so involves harnessing the aspirational powers of heaven through what I call spiritual neoliberalism.

Religion and commerce have long been bedfellows, yet advanced capitalism has shifted these dynamics to new ground so that churches now compete in a crowded field of brand culture. As Sarah Banet-Weiser writes, even in light of religion's long commodification,

> the contemporary political economy of advanced capitalism encourages a shift from commodification to the branding of religion, where brand strategies intersect with consumer activity and content to create a brand culture around religion, and where capitalist business practices merge with religious practices in an unproblematic, normative relationship.
>
> *(Banet-Weiser, 2012, 171; see also Einstein, 2007)*

In this symbiotic relationship between branding and religion, the makeover lends itself as a ready lens through which we might see a different organization of neoliberalism, or spiritual neoliberalism.

In using this term, I indicate a phenomenon at work even beyond the neoliberal exploitation of religion under advanced capitalism. Indeed, at stake in the term *spiritual neoliberalism* is less the co-opting of religion and more the establishment of spiritualized goals – such as salvation, peace, and fulfillment – as best (or only) achievable through neoliberal methods requiring "free" choice and "open" markets that are predicated on competition and advancement. This new domain in which spiritualism and neoliberalism fuse constitutes what might be viewed as a neoliberalism 2.0, where financial success in the market must be matched and bettered by benchmarks in both self-improvement and spiritual aspirationalism. I devote the remainder of this chapter to demonstrating these dynamics at work in the reality television makeover.

The ties that bind: suffering, shame, and the savior

Across the makeover canon, the gospel of reinvention requires that penitential subjects confess the sins of their bad choices to exalted demigod figures, the style guru or lifestyle coach. These confessions happen on camera for the combined pleasure and critique of the audiences, whose responses (thanks to social media) sometimes play on the screens in real time, like a Greek Chorus commenting on what it observes. Like the sacred trinity of Christian tradition (father, son, and holy ghost) and like many figures of Greco-Roman mythology, Eastern religions, or even comic book lore, the makeover expert is both human and divine. The style guru or makeover coach is both saint and intercessionary agent, with just a whiff of the celestial (a heady concoction typically marked by a degree of celebrity). Unlike these fused figures, however, the makeover expert's authority comes not from a familial or genetic relation to the most divine being but, in a more American parlance, to good old-fashioned meritocratic hard work. She or he represents what the sinful subject can become provided she works hard, makes good choices, and submits to authority – the American credo of individualism here taking a back seat to codes of leadership meant to install self-sovereignty. "Tell me what you don't like about the way you look," says Carson Kressley of *How to Look Good Naked*. "I'm not worthy," says the mournful woman, surveying herself in the full-length mirror. "Of course you are," says Kressley, "Just follow my advice, believe in me, and you will be saved from your bad choices and poor sense of self."[3]

Kressley is hardly alone in his role as censorious style agent and redemptive role model. Across the makeover canon, the guiding presence of the makeover authority functions as a kind of beatific blessing, guiding the makeover participant through a combination of compassion and tough love. Consider for instance *Revenge Body with Khloé Kardashian* (2017–present). *Revenge Body* is premised on helping slightly heavy people who have experienced emotional trauma due to their size trim down and shape up, thus asserting revenge on "haters" who made the chubby person feel bad about him or herself through overt criticism or romantic rejection. *Revenge Body* gathers together most of the requisite component parts of the makeover: the suffering subject, the promise for change, the demand for obedience to bodily discipline, the struggles for submission, the glamorous After-body. In this case, the show is made distinctive by the fact that each of the subjects is a fan of Kardashian's and thus is star-struck in her presence and emotionally overwhelmed by the fact of her interest, like a god come to earth. Let go and let Khloé.

Indeed, as the title indicates, *Revenge Body* is galvanized by the presence of Khloé, of the celebrated Kardashians, a family that has willed their celebrity into being through a series of reality shows, primarily *Keeping Up with the Kardashians* (2007–2017), and a conglomerate of high-profile social media platforms and tabloid scandals (particularly sister Kim's sex tape, her 40-day marriage to Chris Humphries, and her eventual marriage to rap provocateur Kanye West). Since 2015, the Kardashian family has also been in the public eye because of their relation to Caitlyn Jenner (formerly married to matriarch Kris Jenner), and Caitlyn's very public transition from male to female. Although Khloé had her own shows (*Khloé & Lamar* [2011–2012] and *Kocktails with Khloé* [2016]), she was long considered the second-tier sister, or as she says it, "I'm the ugly sister. I'm the fat one" (Fox News Network, 2011). In 2015 and after the breakup of her marriage, Khloé underwent a significant makeover. If tabloid reports can be believed, she spent nearly three million dollars on interventions ranging from high-end weight loss and workout coaches to plastic surgery so that she might achieve her resplendent new

After-body. As such, Khloé earns credibility as not only a do-it-yourself celebrity but as a suffering Before-body who transformed into a celebrated After-body. Like tales of lore, she transmogrified from ugly sister to glamorous goddess, in turn enhancing her currency as star and self.

As this fairy tale is told in an American parlance, it is not Khloé's ties to royalty or the attractions of a Prince Charming that allowed for her transformation, but her own grit, determination, and desire as conveniently augmented by a family treasure chest that can underwrite the cost of multi-million dollar renovations that turn her from drab to fab. As I will discuss later in this chapter, in keeping with the makeover's code of silence around social privilege, neither Kardashian's class nor race privilege is factored into the significance of her transformation. In a religious parlance, we might argue that Khloé's hard work, determination, and commitment to change allow her to transcend into a new-and-improved incarnation. Having done so in the public eye, she has also increased her currency as a celebrity, who possesses both compassion and empathy. Khloé gets it, the thinking goes. She has undergone the excruciating process of personal change and now deserves the spotlight. With her help (and professional style team), perhaps I can do what she has done. But the logic of the makeover extends beyond living well on the mortal plane. Khloé's personal transformation, no matter how temporal, is positioned as timeless – an investment in personhood and appearance that will bear fruit in the spiritual neoliberal frame of idealized living – the After-body afterlife.

Divine intervention in the name of normativity

As I argue in *Makeover TV* (Weber, 2009), most reality television makeover programs are not at all sure what to do with forms of social difference as expressed through race, class, sexual orientation, gender identity, religion, or disability. While the makeover needs (and indeed, seeks out) non-normativity, it cannot handle systemic oppression. Before-bodies must therefore be malleable, capable of change and transformation and able (post-intervention) to emit the signs of normativity. The self-conscious and chubby white housewife might apply to be changed; the paraplegic cannot. What about poor people? Can a working class woman be made over but not a homeless one? Can a woman in hijab be transformed into someone with glowing and flowing hair? The complexities of style-as-identity explode the makeover's narrative of saving the self if that person does not or cannot or will not conform to normative iterations of selfhood.

Similarly, gay and lesbian subjects might seek renewal through the makeover, but the makeover does not tackle transformations that overtly link to oppression. Actual sexual orientation is very rarely overtly mentioned. So far (thank goodness), there have been no makeovers designed around reparative therapy to make LGBT people straight. And while reality television might document post-transition lives, it has not imagined a makeover show that would involve and reward transitioning. As I discuss in the final section of this chapter, brown and black people featured on makeover shows often experience a process of symbolic deracination that lightens and whitens them.

So, though the makeover traffics in big themes of shame, selfhood, and salvation, it resolutely avoids a direct address of social discrimination. As a consequence of these foundational positions, most people who participate in television makeovers are otherwise normative – white, straight (or not outwardly gay), cis-gendered. Their flaw is whatever has brought them to the casting couch. The tacit promise is to restore them to a place of ethnic anonymity, where what has marked them as different is suddenly erased (for more on the concept of ethnic anonymity, see Haiken, 1999). The makeover invites no sinners whose bodily defects cannot be washed away through a good dose of compassion, tough love, or eight weeks of extensive plastic surgery.

Stigmata

While the makeover's bread and butter is the contrast between before and after, it is really the "during" that functions as the narrative reason for being. The "during" is where the work of the makeover takes place – it is the heart of the show itself and often requires that the makeover subject become a passive and docile body that might invite the skill, craft, cunning, and inspiration of the makeover team, be it stylists or surgeons. Consider, for instance, the reality show *Bridalplasty* (2010). The show positioned twelve brides-to-be in a secluded mansion, each vying against the other so that she might win her "fairy-tale wedding." The requisite items for such a wedding ranged from the obvious to the surprising. Included in the prizes that each woman might win were not only designer dresses and high-carat diamond rings but individualized plastic surgery procedures that accorded with each woman's "wish list" for the perfect body. The participants elected to try out for the show for various reasons. The winner of season one, Allyson Donovan, told *Life & Style Magazine*, "We wouldn't have had a wedding without the show," primarily because both she and her now-husband John, had both lost their jobs within two months of one another (*Life and Style*, 2011, 29). As is fairly common in makeover television, reality TV here serves as the palliative for economic precariousness. Allyson could still have her dream wedding, which in this case ran a tab of about $300,000; she just had to earn it by competing on reality TV against other women, equally desiring their own fairy tales.

What struck me most when watching the show was not really the premise itself (which became the occasion for a whole new set of sighs and screams about reality TV as the lowest common denominator). More, I was amazed that the surgical procedures happened within the diegetic unfolding of the show, so in any given week, a bride might win one procedure from her wish list, only to appear in ensuing episodes bandaged and swollen. Such representation directly cuts against the dominant frame of Makeover TV that might show the bloody, swollen, and oozing aftermath of cosmetic surgery, but never dwells overly long on it. Indeed, in most plastic surgery makeover programs, the gruesome aspects of cutting into a woman (and seeing steam rise from her body's warm and moist inside spaces) was always a mandatory feature of the shows, but the effort of doing so belonged to the doctors, not the patients. Recovery was typically limited temporally so that in any given hour of transformation television, only a few minutes would be given to the body's healing. By contrast, toward the end of each season of *Bridalplasty*, when remaining contestants would gather together for group challenges, their bandages and swelling made them seem more like wounded soldiers on the battlefield than brides hoping for happiness through glamour and spectacle. (This is perhaps fitting given that modern plastic surgery as we know it now began soon after World War I, as a way to re-integrate wounded and disfigured soldiers back into mainstream society.)

This display of wound-as-spectacle in itself serves as a visual link to the religiosity of the makeover project. The gospel of the twenty-first-century makeover fuses work, spectacle, and media, so that being telegenic or able to capture the gaze are not only critical to an age-old notion of the marriage market but also to the global marketplace, where a neoliberal mandate requires that one be an entrepreneur of the self, marshaling resources and making investments in one's person and appearance that will result in an increase in one's overall personal worth.

As I've already suggested, shame stands at the heart of the makeover, the evidence of poor choices, bad living, and poor self-governance written on the body in drab clothing, garish makeup, bulging waistlines, and cellulited thighs. Whether critiques are offered by intimates, strangers, or style gurus, shame-inducing assessments tend to be detailed and harsh ("You have yellow teeth!" "Your cellulite looks like cottage cheese stuffed in a polyester sack!"). Makeover subjects are often left with the unsettling realization that any negative self-talk they might feel is minimal compared to the invective of others. These shows announce: the world is watching, and it is not pleased with what it sees. Across the makeover canon, the motivating necessity that initiates transformation reinforces that at all times the body and its behavior are seen and judged. The gaze is always present, and shame falls on those who do not work hard enough to be pleasing to the gazer. The makeover intervention, as so imagined, serves not to avert the gaze but to convert judgments from negative to positive, so that subjects might somehow achieve the impossible: pleasing the critical gaze, a task that not only locks the makeover subject into a cycle of unending labor but inevitably invites increased self-scrutiny and shameful reflection.

The apotheosis

Every makeover requires a reveal, a moment where we might not only see but revel in the power of transformation. I see these moments as quasi-religious ceremonies of transformation, transubstantiation, and resurrection that promise some relief from shame. Most makeovers – whether of style, body, car, dog, kids, or house – require a scene of staged celebration that allows subjects to stand before friends, family, and style gurus (and, of course, the camera and us as viewers), bathed in the adoring affection and the ritualized language best summarized in "You look amazing!" or "You're like a super star!" The reveals are frozen moments in time that highlight the change from Before-body to After-body, and they are invariably accompanied by gasps, amazement, and enthusiastic approval – sometimes even by sobbing, fainting, and hyper-ventilating. Much like the religious convert, makeover contestants believe their journeys of humiliation and affirmation will empower others to experience surrender, redemption, and rebirth. Makeover subjects have been granted the confidence to be visible, to have faith in their body, to be seen by public and private eyes without fear of shaming censure. Being-seen-ness in this regard functions as the locus and limit of salvation, there being no place where one can be out of the gaze since a new-found inner peace requires full focus on one's dress and appearance in order to access internal strength manifest through notions of the self and the soul. Indeed, if both selfhood and the state of the soul are at stake, as most makeover texts so powerfully argue, a therapeutic salvation gospel of shame, surrender, and salvation through fashion might, to many women, be quite literally irresistible. In this case the mandate is clear: surrender to trans-formation or face something worse than shame, resign yourself to perpetual invisibility.

The alpha and the omega: *The Swan*

Most any one of the makeover's many shows might allow us to see all of these elements at work, but by far, one of the most vivid assemblages of religiosity, normativity, and spiritual neoliberalism is the plastic surgery, psychotherapy, life coaching, and pageant reality show called *The Swan* that aired on Fox in 2004 (for a more detailed analysis of this program see Weber and Tice, 2009). *The Swan* is based on the Hans Christian Anderson fairytale *The Ugly Duckling*, which tells the story of a sad homely bird, misplaced and ungainly amidst a family of cute ducklings. The ugly duckling experiences abuse and privation, suffering in alienation, only to discover that he was all along a beautiful swan, the power of personal transformation made palpable and enduring through mythology. In the context of reality televi-sion, each season of *The Swan* identified twelve woeful women, whom they termed ugly ducklings. In season one, all of these women were white. In season two, several of the twelve women were Latina or African American, yet this hardly assured them legitimacy as raced subjects. For example, when Sylvia Cruz is selected to be a contestant on *The Swan* in season two, viewers are told that she has faced a lifetime of romantic rejection because of her appearance. In documentary-style footage, Sylvia stands before a mirror and critiques her bikini-clad body, speaking of her desires for smaller thighs and less pronounced ears. Sylvia's boyfriend pro-vides additional testimony, acknowledging they have a limited sex life because of Sylvia's body issues. "It's always been a challenge for Sylvia to stay in shape," her boyfriend explains, "and it is simply because the Latino community, when it comes to food… " He need not finish his sentence because the camera does it for him, immediately cutting to Sylvia in sweat pants, approaching a food truck parked on a city street from which she purchases elote, a (delicious sounding) dish made of corn, butter, cheese, and mayonnaise.

The panel of Swan experts who are watching this footage on a television monitor in a mansion-like setting turn to each other laughing. "Something tells me those desserts and Latin foods won't be on the menu at the Swan program," says the host. In addition to losing thirty pounds, Sylvia's conversion from ugly duckling to swan requires that she undergo multiple cosmetic procedures that address what her surgeon terms "bland bone structure." She needs a chin implant and cheekbone lifts, as well as extensive liposuction in seven areas of her body to give her a "more feminine look." Veneers on all of Sylvia's teeth will "make her mouth look a little smaller." All of this and extensive psychotherapy addressing Sylvia's reluctance to trust authority figures, in general, and men, in particular, will bring about Sylvia's full transformation, making her "pageant worthy" in three months' time.

Those three months are filled with what *The Swan* terms a "grueling curriculum" of pain, isolation, sacrifice, and temptation. Though Sylvia struggles, she – like all of *The Swan*'s contestants – sheds her "ugly duckling" appearance and ego, emerging for her reveal ceremony as a beautiful Swan. When Sylvia enters the Swan mansion for her big reveal dressed in a long formal gown, full make-up, hair extensions, false eye lashes, and four-inch heels, her metamorphosis as an After-body draws gasps from the Swan experts of surgeons, workout coaches, psychotherapists, and life coaches, called the Dream Team. Throughout the narrative told by the show, Sylvia has engaged in a televised version of shame, surrender, and salvation: she has confessed her failings, undergone trials, learned to submit to a higher authority, exposed her wounds, and now possesses a face and body that mark her as not only beautiful but, in the words of *The Swan*'s creator, producer, and life coach Nely Galan, "resurrected," "transcendent," and "powerful." She is no longer a woman whose body makes her ethnic and class excesses visible; indeed, before she can be a transcendent Swan, the Latin food she has consumed must quite literally be sucked from her body. Posing in her sequined gown amidst the opulence of chandeliers and marble staircases, we get the sense that in order to be saved Sylvia had to lose her fondness for eating fattening "ethnic" food from a truck as much as she needed to "feminize" her body, refine her nose, and pin back her ears. Sylvia's body now fully emits the signs of ethnic anonymity, a condition of being unmarked that typically accords with idealized whiteness.

Sylvia's story fully expresses the race- and class-centered story of shame, surrender, and salvation told by *The Swan*. Her transformation illustrates a logic whereby makeover renewals require a conversion that produces a conventionally gendered woman for whom other signifiers of identity – such as race, class, and ethnicity – are still present but have been subordinated to an image representing what the show calls "gorgeous womanhood." If we consider that those targeted for Swanly renovations are, like Sylvia, coded as "ugly ducklings," whose poor choices, ethnic excess, and downward mobility stem from their appearance, then we begin to see how *The Swan* illustrates the complex relationships between gender, race, ethnicity, and class at work in the making of the beautiful image, all sutured together through a religious framework that draws heavily from both Christian and self-help spiritual rhetorics.

Since such miraculous conversions often require the diminishment of bodily markers indicating "non-normative" iterations of race and class, it seems clear that transcendent empowerment offered to women on *The Swan* is presumed to exist in an unmarked category, where race and class factors tacitly contribute to social identity location. Such reasoning that claims the unmarked as the natural and normative is frequently dedicated to the production of a middle-class whiteness, here transmitted through the transformation rhetoric that fuels Galan's mediated makeovers. In the case of Sylvia, to remove the markers of ethnicity from her body is to make her both normal and normative, a category of absence that is also one of whiteness. The invisibility of the normative is also a critical element of the function and performance of class, so that Sylvia's transformation from someone who eats food from trucks (before it was trendy) to someone who lives a sequined life in a Hollywood mansion here seems a natural consequence of her weight loss, plastic surgery, and new emotional discipline. On *The Swan*, such classed and raced values are coded through image, so that passing as a glamorous woman requires not cultural or knowledge capital but semiotic signification. In other words, Sylvia doesn't need to acquire new knowledge; she must only appear different in order to be perceived as improved. Such reliance on the image in turn transforms conventional ways of inscribing and interpreting race, ethnicity, and class, since what is valued in the made-over woman are signifiers that connote middle-class discipline (restrained forms of emotional and embodied excess), while surrounded by and clad in upper-class accouterment (gowns, chauffeurs, tuxedo-clad doormen, Romantic paintings, mansions). So, we see that class- and race-based messages about the image are communicated through the makeover's discourses of religiosity, all of which naturalize the feminized subject's transformation from ugly duckling to swan. Much like *The Swan*, the larger makeover mandate speaks in redemptive discourses that blend free choice, consumerism, individualism, personal empowerment, and spiritualism.

Conclusion

So again, it's necessary to think of the makeover as a system that relies on religiosity to make its goals seems more desirable to participants and viewers, but the make-over is not committed to the same outcomes as a single religious tradition. For instance, let us return to the place of perfection, the After-body. While Christianity posits the resurrected body and everlasting life as the divine endpoint of earthly suffering and reward for faithful living, the makeover's desired state of being, the After-body, is just as mortal and worldly as the Before-body. Frankly, it is also just as capable of feeling pain, humiliation, and shame as the Before-body, but these truths go unnamed in the makeover's teleology of transformation. Instead, the After-body is positioned as an idealized form of celebrity and celebration in which the critical gaze undergoes its own makeover into an adoring spotlight. And because of the change in both gazer and gazed at, to be the object of the gaze post-makeover is not to be objectified and shamed but to be granted worthy subject status – the After-body is, according to the gospel of the makeover, loveable, capable, empowered, fabulous. Resplendent in the spotlight. The reality television makeover thus offers an important and religion-infused parable not about life eternal but about life in the here and now. It's a potent salve that promises it might heal the wounds of the living, and it does so by harnessing its redemptive messages to religious systems of shame, suffering, submission, and salvation.

Notes

1 Reality television itself is becoming more transgender aware and inclusive, but the makeover tends to be uncertain of how to address transgender experiences. For this reason, when I use the terms "men" and "women," I refer to the makeover's understanding of sex and gender and identity as those who were assigned male or female at birth.

2 For more on reality television's ties to neoliberalism, see Laurie Ouellette and James Hay, *Better Living through Reality TV: Television and Post-Welfare Citizenship* (Walden, MA: Blackwell, 2008); June Deery, *Consuming Reality: The Commercialization of Factual Entertainment* (New York: Palgrave Macmillan, 2012). For more on the makeover's tie to neoliberalism, see Heidi Steinhoff, *Transforming Bodies: Makeovers and Monstrosities in American Culture* (New York: Palgrave Macmillan, 2015). It is not by accident that "live your best life" is one of the primary credos of Oprah Winfrey, who touts self-actualization as a religion unto itself. Kathryn Lofton argues, for instance, that Winfrey endorses the concept of an "ideal self" that "feeds into a neoliberal politics of beauty," celebrating "choice as the attitudinal gauge of quality." Kathryn Lofton, *Oprah: The Gospel of an Icon* (Berkeley: University of California Press, 2011): 124–125. For more on Oprah Winfrey and neoliberalism, see Cecilia Konchar Farr, *Reading Oprah: How Oprah's Book Club Changed the Way America Reads* (New York: State University of New York Press, 2005); Eva Illouz, *Oprah Winfrey and the Glamour of Misery* (New York: Columbia University Press, 2003); Janet Peck, *The Age of Oprah: Cultural Icon for the Neoliberal Era* (Boulder, CO: Paradigm Publishers, 2008); Sharon Heijin Lee, "Lessons from 'Around the World with Oprah': Neoliberalism, Race, and the (Geo)politics of Beauty," *Women & Performance: a journal of feminist theory* 18:1 (March 2008): 25–41.

3 Carson Kressley has made a career for himself as one of the many gods in the style guru heavens. First appearing on the hit *Queer Eye for the Straight Guy* as the expert on fashion, Kressley also branched into hosting the American version of *How to Look Good Naked* and an eponymous makeover show on Oprah Winfrey's network called *Carson Nation* (OWN, 2011). He is presently a fixture on transatlantic reality television, often appearing in the character of "self" as host, participant, and special guest on a range of programs including *Hollywood Game Night* (NBC, 2013–) and *RuPaul's Drag Race* (Logo, 2009–2017). As such, Kressley offers a powerful example of self-as-celebrity that fuels the makeover mandate.

Bibliography

Banet-Weiser, Sarah. 2012. *Authentic^{TM}: the Politics of Ambivalence in a Brand Culture*. New York: New York University Press.

The Biggest Loser. 2004–present. National Broadcasting Company.

Bowler, Kate. 2013. *Blessed: a History of the American Prosperity Gospel*. New York: Oxford University Press.

Bridalplasty. 2010. E!

Deery, June. 2012. *Consuming Reality: The Commercialization of Factual Entertainment*. New York: Palgrave Macmillan.

30   Brenda R. Weber

Einstein, Mara. 2007. *Brands of Faith: Marketing Religion in a Commercial Age*. New York: Routledge.

Farr, Cecilia Konchar. 2005. *Reading Oprah: How Oprah's Book Club Changed the Way America Reads*. New York: State University of New York Press.

Foucault, Michel. 1979. *Discipline and Punish: the Birth of the Prison*. Translated by Alan Sheridan. New York: Vintage Books.

Fox News Network. 2011. "Khloe Kardashian: I'm the Ugly Sister." *Fox News Entertainment*. March 31. http://www.foxnews.com/entertainment/2011/03/31/khloe-kardashian-im-ugly-sister.html.

Haiken, Elizabeth. 1999. *Venus Envy: a History of Cosmetic Surgery*. Baltimore: Johns Hopkins University Press.

How to Look Good Naked. 2008. "Natasha and Juanita." January 19, 2008. Lifetime Real Women.

Keeping Up with the Kardashians. 2007–2017. E!

Khloé & Lamar. 2011–2012. E!

Kocktails with Khloé. 2016. E!

Illouz, Eva. 2003. *Oprah Winfrey and the Glamour of Misery*. New York: Columbia University Press.

Lee, Sharon Heijin. 2008. "Lessons from 'Around the World with Oprah': Neoliberalism, Race, and the (Geo)politics of Beauty," *Women & Performance: a journal of feminist theory* 18(1): 25–41.

Life and Style. 2011. "Surgery Changed My Life." *Life and Style Magazine*, February 15.

Lofton, Kathryn. 2011. *Oprah: The Gospel of an Icon*. Berkeley: University of California Press.

Ouellette, Laurie and James Hay. 2008. *Better Living through Reality TV: Television and Post-Welfare Citizenship*. Walden, MA: Blackwell.

Peck, Janet. 2008. *The Age of Oprah: Cultural Icon for the Neoliberal Era*. Boulder, CO: Paradigm Publishers.

Pimp My Ride. 2004–2007. MTV.

Queer Eye for the Straight Guy. 2003–2007. Bravo TV.

Revenge Body with Khloé Kardashian. 2017–present. E!

Sender, Katherine. 2012. *The Makeover: Reality Television and Reflexive Audiences*. New York: New York University Press.

Steinhoff, Heidi. 2015. *Transforming Bodies: Makeovers and Monstrosities in American Culture*. New York: Palgrave Macmillan.

The Swan. 2004. Fox Broadcasting Company.

Weber, Brenda R. 2009. *Makeover TV: Selfhood, Citizenship, and Celebrity*. Durham: Duke University Press.

Weber, Brenda R., and Karen W. Tice. 2009. "'Are You Finally Comfortable in Your Own Skin?' The Raced and Classed Imperatives for Spiritual/Somatic Salvation in The Swan." *Genders* 49. https://www.colorado.edu/gendersarchive1998-2013/2009/06/01/are-you-finally-comfortable-your-own-skin-raced-and-classed-imperatives-somaticspiritual.

What Not to Wear. 2001–2006. "Stylish Sisters." December 12, 2006. British Broadcasting Company.

3

BLACK FEMALE SEXUAL AGENCY AND RACIALIZED HOLY SEX IN BLACK CHRISTIAN REALITY TV SHOWS

Monique Moultrie

Using womanist cultural analysis, this chapter examines how three black Christian reality TV shows – *Sisterhood, Preachers of LA*, and *Match Made in Heaven* – present black religion's and black religious leaders' depictions of sexuality and specifically of black female sexuality.[1] More particularly, the shows depict and reinforce the notion of racialized holy sex in that each promotes the concepts of patriarchy, heteronormativity, and demands for sexual purity, while also dealing with the stereotypical images of black hypersexuality. Enlisting this concept of racialized holy sex not only pulls in black female audience members, it also provides space in the shows for critiquing this foundation. Yet while black women are influenced both by church and by television, these three shows to some extent depict women using their sexuality to counter this tension and oppression and find their agency in a patriarchal system.

By and large, these TV depictions of black Christian sexuality rehearse the position that heterosexual, Christian marriage is God's intended plan for humanity and within this plan is the promise of "good sex." Good sex requires work, and the shows highlight black female sexual agency as the women work to fulfill God's alleged plan. Since Christianity is so central to the culture of the black women who are the target audiences of these television programs, understanding their sexual agency and empowerment requires taking seriously their general spiritual concerns.

The focus on black female sexual agency shows the myriad ways that black women negotiate a system that is otherwise patriarchal and heteronormative as they craft a "sexual ethic with which they can peacefully live."[2] Even then, that the women are doing the work testifies not only to their agency but also to the assumption that women do the work of pleasing men. Such programs and their assumptions about normative roles for women show how the "diverse cultural productions of everyday life" influence the decision-making of black women, as Linda Thomas reminds us.[3]

I harness poststructuralist cultural studies and womanist sexual ethics to propose womanist cultural analysis as an alternative theoretical lens for examining these shows. The shows' religious rhetoric I examine with Layli Phillips's understanding of womanism as a "social change perspective rooted in black women's and other women of color's everyday experiences and everyday method of problem solving in everyday spaces." Phillips characterizes womanism as being: (1) intentionally anti-oppression; (2) concerned with everyday experiences; (3) non-ideological; (4) communal; and (5) spiritual.[4] My deliberate use of womanist sexual ethics is, on the one hand, a response to traditionally white feminist theological ethics, which often excludes black women's experiences, and, on the other, a response to black feminist cultural theory, which often seems to undervalue black women's specifically religious lives.

Just as womanism foregrounds black women's experience, I use womanist cultural analysis to investigate Christian reality TV *foregrounding the interests and experiences of black women*. For black women are both cultural readers and cultural producers and their agency is what interests me. Locating that agency is made harder by the sense that the three shows are arguably filmed from male-centered perspectives.[5] How each of the female cast members comports herself on the shows is a deliberate tactic that in general seems to be meant to present them as model Christians and as participants in the dominant notion of "racialized holy sex." By "racialized holy sex" I mean an interpretation of evangelical Christians' valuing sexual purity within a larger cultural discourse where black female sexuality is hypersexualized. In the case of black women viewing and participating in these shows, they are wrestling with the diverging messages provided as they accept an evangelical emphasis on marriage because it resonates with their desires while simultaneously resisting other expectations such as abstinence, submission in marriage, etc. They are savvy negotiators that are navigating Christian boundaries regarding sexuality on the small screen.

Black churchwomen and religious television: a case study

Numerous studies have documented that black women constitute the majority of the membership of historically black churches and that US black women are the most religious (in observation and belief).[6] Their religiosity influences their TV viewing habits. Small wonder that religious programming has responded to this audience and its preferences. Eli Lehrer, former Lifetime senior VP of unscripted programming and current executive vice president of MTV2, noted the need to reach out to faith-based audiences and in particular African American audiences, whom he deemed to be respectively underserved and underrepresented on TV.[7] The market pushed past initial apprehensions to focus on promoting black Christian reality TV programming. While there have been numerous entrances into television programming by white Christian cultural producers, attention to black Christianity in the reality TV format is a recent phenomenon.

The move to television is more recent but black Christians are certainly not strangers to religious media more broadly. Research and Nielsen ratings show that

blacks view more religious television than any other group (which is also a result of
the fact that blacks consume more television than any other group), and these
shows are produced with them quite specifically in mind.[8] Black consumers of
varying ages tune in to secular shows and there is a handful of religious cable networks that cater to black audiences. Despite this familiarity, the venture into black
Christian reality television did not really begin until 2012 with the debut of WE
TV's *Mary Mary*, a show that followed Erica and Tina Campbell, the gospel-singing
sisters also known as *Mary Mary*. Based on that show's success, 2013 was a banner
year for religious reality TV with predominantly black casts as there were five
reality shows debuting across five different networks. Three of these shows were
connected with gospel recording artists, namely, *The Sheards* on BET, *Preachers of
LA* on Oxygen, and *Thicker than Water: The Tankards* on Bravo. This is not surprising,
as the Gospel Music Association noted their appreciation that major networks were
peering into the Christian world demonstrated by each of these shows averaging
one million viewers per episode.[9] This early success led to the production of five
additional shows: *Preachers' Daughters* on Lifetime, a dating reality show called *Match
Made in Heaven* on WE TV, *Preachers of Detroit* and *Preachers of Atlanta* on Oxygen,
and Lifetime's show *Preach*, chronicling the lives of four prophetesses. Each of these
entries into reality TV presented distinctive images of black women worthy of
further exploration.

There is stellar scholarship documenting the stereotyping of black female reality
TV participants as the shows arguably edit women's realities to match consumer
demand for perpetuating particular depictions of black women. Communications
scholar Adria Goldman notes the substantial increase in reality television programming and how unscripted shows are constructing and perpetuating certain images
of black women as Angry Black Bitch, Hoochie Mama, Ghetto Girl, and Chicken
Head.[10] In their research that gauges the correlations between religiosity and black
and Latino marriage rates, sociologists W. Bradford Wilcox and Nicholas Wolfinger
note that these stereotypes now amplify in popular culture what they term the
"street subculture," and that this acts as a deterrent for black and Latino marriage.
They suggest that acceptance of such stereotypes leads persons to reject the norms
of "decent society," in this case of marriage.[11] I wonder whether depictions of
"racialized holy sex" in the reality TV shows I investigate here, even with their
embedded stereotypes, might mitigate the impact of such pervasive "street culture"
values and depictions on black viewers' conceptions of black Christian marriage. I
suggest that the sexual agency that women demonstrate in these three distinct black
Christian reality TV shows is key to such mitigation.

Each of the shows I analyze was produced on a network whose target audience
is women. *Sisterhood* premiered on The Learning Channel (TLC) on January 1,
2013 and was promoted to document the lives of five Atlanta pastors' wives
(known as First Ladies). During the time of its expansion into black Christian reality
TV production, TLC had an "audience skew of 79% female" and ranked sixth
among the "most-watched networks by women 18–34."[12] *Preachers of LA* aired on
Oxygen, a network that shifted its marketing strategy (which began by targeting all

women) to a more concentrated emphasis on attracting "young, multicultural women," specifically black, Hispanic, Asian, and white women.[13] The final show to be examined is *Match Made in Heaven*, which premiered on WE TV, which was launched as the Romance Classics channel, renamed Women's Entertainment in 2001, and is now WE TV (2006). WE TV was one of the first networks to promote shows targeting African American women and then-president of the network Kim Martin explained that WE TV wanted to provide stories that allowed women to see themselves or someone they know or would want to know. This push to have media represent the interests of black women audiences reflects a symbiotic relationship: viewers tune in because they see themselves or an amusing caricature of themselves. Because it is beyond the scope of this argument to provide substantive audience response analysis of specific episodes, it is necessary to situate these three shows within the larger marketplace to indicate the significance of the shows for viewers.[14]

Cultural studies' concept of interpellation reflects exactly what the president of WE TV had in mind for viewers because interpellation refers to the moment that a subject realizes a message is meant for her. For example, in poststructuralist Louis Althusser's discussion of interpellation he imagines someone hailing a cab and when the cab stops he believes it is for him (despite others who may be on the street doing the same thing).[15] Part of the genius of interpellation is that the subject thinks that this is real regardless of what is actual. Althusser proffers that interpellation is a means for reproduction of social relationships because we interpret the messages of the media not as abstract but as made "by us for us." In the example of these shows, one sees a cooperative relationship where black women accept the message (or much of the message and ideology) because they find a connection to other black women, a connection fostered by the greater intimacy of a TV show than is possible with a movie. These women's stories are not just pure imagination pitched by advertisers. These stories become believable to them because often they replicate parts of their own narratives or those of someone they know.

Racialized holy sex

The stories shared in black Christian reality TV shows depict what early on I identified as a "racialized holy sex" and are themes addressed in the broader evangelical culture. Black evangelicals participate in a larger white evangelical sphere where they share belief in the inerrancy of scripture, spiritual rebirth as a criterion for entering heaven, and an expectation of certain types of behavior, but there are different denominational histories, theological perspectives, and class and political differences that shape their sexual realities.[16] Racialized holy sex re-envisions the larger evangelical concept of sexual purity from being centered on holy sex performed in Christian marriages because it must match a black community with a much lower marriage rate.

The notion of racialized holy sex also re-conceptualizes the concept of holy bodies given the historic negative attributes associated with black humanity to show the possibility of redeeming black bodies from the white moral imagination and black moral indoctrination that finds whiteness more pure.[17]

Black evangelicals in the US enter the sexual purity conversation aware that the white evangelical community has already laid claim to linking their sexual purity with the purity of the nation, which is the result of the racialization of sexual purity in both the secular and religious realms. For example, historians Sarah Moslener and Victoria Wolcott present secular narratives of white sexual purity as a way to connect sexual immorality with national insecurity, a declining white middle class, and even the impending apocalypse; whereas, black sexual purity was viewed as a response to stereotypes of black hypersexuality and a private strategy to protect black women from sexual violence.[18] Black evangelicals are working within larger white religious conversations on chastity/sexual purity that mark the mature Christian as heterosexual and married and which disadvantages anyone who falls short of this benchmark. Black evangelical responses to the category of holy sex must construct this category in line with the black female experience. Thus, they must adjust the white-dominant purity culture message to "reflect a history where a woman's purity is not automatically considered the property of her father, a woman's purity can be denied because of stereotypes of her being sexually available, and finally, a woman's path to a God given marriage is not guaranteed."[19]

White evangelical purity culture operates in a schema where God ordains fathers as the heads of their households who then "release" their daughters to the headship of their husbands. In black households this framework is not always replicated, as the overall number of black marriages is below the national average and as unmarried black couples are less likely to marry after a child is born.[20] Social ethicist Robert M. Franklin summarizes the vast literature on black families to state that although African Americans initially embraced marriage after Emancipation, there has been a downward spiral of black marriage since the 1950s, which can be attributed to declining job prospects, female independence, increased education leading to delays in marriage, and changing social, cultural, and moral standards.[21] Despite the decline in black marriages, within the black evangelical sphere, high value is placed on marriage as the solution to many social and spiritual woes. Yet, the realities of black female experience, e.g. increased periods of singleness due to partner shortages and the hypersexualization of black women often complicate these expectations.

Womanist cultural analysis – analyzing primary texts

John Fiske's three ways of analyzing texts by interpreting the relationship between them facilitate our task of ferreting out depictions of racialized holy sex in black Christian reality TV. The first way of analysis is interpreting the primary text as produced by/for a dominant ideology; the second analysis is of texts produced by the same culture industry, but perhaps a different part of it, like network publicity, cast biographies on the show's website, the choices and forms of sharing deleted scenes, etc. Third and finally, such interpretation discusses the ways that viewers produce themselves in these messages.[22] As I said at the outset of the chapter, all three shows depict racialized holy sex in that each promotes the concepts of patriarchy, heteronormativity, and demands for sexual purity, while concurrently dealing with the stereotypical images of black hypersexuality. Depictions of racialized holy sex both enlist black female audience members' interest and provide them with a space to critique its assumptions.

Analyzing the first show, *The Sisterhood*, from Fiske's first level of textual analysis reveals both what the TLC network wanted audiences to perceive and demonstrates participation in the larger black evangelical realm. In the stories of five women married to senior pastors, TLC producers introduce the wives and direct the audience in very deliberate ways. They depict these women as dutiful spouses (and in some cases co-pastors) who also have something distinctive going on in their lives outside their husbands' ministries.[23] The Atlanta-based cast is diverse in terms of education, career, and income levels. The cast includes: Dominique, a former drug addict turned educator who is married to Brad, an evangelical pastor who lost their church due to hard financial times;[24] Tara, a fitness instructor married to Brian, a Jew for Jesus, who also lost his church; Ivy, a former member of the R&B group Escape, who is married to Pastor Mark; Christina, a Dominican co-pastoring a successful megachurch with her black husband Anthony, and DeLana, a white Christian rock musician co-pastoring with her husband Myles.

Each of the episodes begins with a riff on one of the Ten Commandments. In episode 6, "Thou Shalt Not Brawl at a Bar Mitzvah," (referring to the constant battling that cast members engaged in during the Christian Bar Mitzvah of one member's son), a Christian sex therapist gives the cast sex tips and recommendations for sex toys. They are told that sex is a ministry and should be treated like a worship service. The Christian sex therapist also demonstrates sexually suggestive role-play with bananas to simulate more adventurous ways to engage in oral sex. While Tara (the mother of the son featured in this episode) is against sex toys, two of the other women acknowledge the need to be sexually adventurous in their marriages. Perhaps these scenes were filmed because the shock value of hearing pastors' wives discuss sexuality was expected to boost ratings and generate interest and controversy through social media; but it is also in keeping with the logic of racialized holy sex that encourages the proper performance of sexuality (meaning something quite particular, as we have seen).

This proper ordering is duplicated in the first episode "Thou Shall Not Cross a First Lady" as Christina and her husband discuss sex with their teenage daughters and their expectations that their daughters abstain from sex until marriage. Later in the same episode First Lady Ivy and her husband openly joke about sexual role-play as he gifts her with handcuffs to use in the bedroom. Ivy coyly tells the viewing audience "people don't expect a preacher and his wife to have a good sex life." Christina admits that if church folk see the episodes there will be problems with seeing their first ladies having a sex toy party, but the episodes reiterated a need to remain open to pleasurable godly sex. These first ladies couch their need for sexual expression in spiritual language by considering sex as ministry or worship; and, they do not act as if sex is a taboo topic.

In *Preachers of LA*, a show centered on the personal lives of six Los Angeles, CA, mega-church pastors and their families, sexuality is a dominant theme. The show documents five black and one white senior male pastor, but the inclusion of the two unmarried pastors magnifies the trope of racialized holy sex. While this show is also predominantly about male pastors, womanist cultural analysis uplifts the experiences of the black women on the show. In keeping with Fiske's view of analyzing the primary text provided, my analysis focuses on the experiences of the two unmarried women on the show to demonstrate how their presence adds to the "drama" of the show and reiterates the parameters of racialized holy sex.

During the first season, Dominique is engaged to former Detroit pastor Deitrick Haddon, whose career focus is now gospel music. During Deitrick's first marriage, he fathered a daughter with Dominique. During the first season, they plan a wedding while Dominique is pregnant with their second child.[25] Bishop Ron Gibson and his wife LaVette, who have been married for thirty-six years, invite Dietrick and Dominique to dinner to discuss their "shaky engagement" or, more aptly, whether they are still engaging in premarital sex. Dominique wants to take time planning an official wedding and she resents hearing that she should not live out-of-wedlock with her child's father.[26] When Lady LaVette tells Dominique that the Bible says she should not live in sin, Dominique retorts that her biblical definition of marriage is "once a man enters a woman." Responding "No, that's called fornication," Lady LaVette dismisses Dominique's interpretation as her opinion versus the word of God. Dominique is faced with the consequences of having unholy sex and she is chastised back into the framework of sexual purity.

In addition to exposing the negative parameters of racialized holy sex, Season 1 of *Preachers of LA* also demonstrates the benefits of engaging in God-sanctioned sexuality. Pastor Chaney and his wife describe themselves as "saved, sanctified, and sexual," and their public displays of affection and sexual bantering underlie the show. Prior to the wedding, Dominique asks the First Ladies for marital advice and she is given explicit advice like having sex in different places and saying yes to sex as often as possible. Again, the program's producers have reasons for crafting such a narrative but it also strengthens the doctrine of those that take the position that sexual relations within marriage are godly unions that are sexually freeing as evangelicals often quote Hebrews 13:4 which states that marriage should be honored above all and the marriage bed be undefiled, as evidence that God blesses the sexual intimacy of a husband and a wife. Communications scholar Elizabeth Whittington Cooper contends that this particular scene of marital advice conveys the Christian theme that women's bodies no longer belong to them, but to their husbands, and that it is their Christian responsibility to please their spouse.[27] Ironically, seeking advice for a godly marriage can also be a marker of success as a key component to the black evangelical message being disseminated.

The concept of being "found" by a godly man likewise fits this framework of godly sex as focused on pleasing one's husband. In *Match Made in Heaven*'s first season, the audience follows Shawn Bullard, a black real estate mogul attempting to find love among a bevy of eligible women. There were 24 women vying for Bullard's affections with the help of Pastor Ken Johnson, the spiritual advisor for the Indianapolis Colts. Deemed a remake of the hit-show *The Bachelor, Match Made in Heaven*'s hour-long episodes show how a love connection can be made with Christian morals as a centerpiece. While ultimately Shawn is the one voting women off the show, the 24 women exert great agency through their participation.

For example, of the 24 women originally cast for the show, 16 identified as women of color, the majority of these as African American. These women ranged in age from their early twenties to mid-thirties and had a vast range of educational and career backgrounds. In the interest of time and space, I chose to focus just on these three women because of their interactions with Pastor J and how they represented the concept of racialized holy sex. These cast members' sexual agency is also noteworthy because on a show focused on singleness there was no overt discussion of the media's attention to the plight of single black women.

In Season 1's ten episodes, the women displayed sexual agency in a variety of ways. Two of the women were virgins, Mercedes, a born-again virgin[28] and Nes, a former lesbian who had never had sexual contact with a man. In episode 2 "Virgin Territory," Pastor J keeps Mercedes in the competition because he respects her decision to remain pure. Mercedes and Nes have private dates with the bachelor, but he decides to let Mercedes go because, despite her commitment to celibacy, she is not a good match for him. Her elimination is noteworthy for several reasons. First, the non-virgins in the house speak out against what they declare to be Pastor J's biased opinion towards them. (One contestant named Dani said she felt like she was wearing a scarlet "A" because Pastor J had said if they had premarital sex they were not worthy of marriage.) Second, while it was clear that the bachelor appreciated Mercedes' choice of celibacy, ultimately he did not choose a virgin as his potential wife. This counters prevailing notions of philandering men primarily seeking virginal spouses. Nes, the other virgin, spent most of the show/series battling her feelings for one of the female participants and the bachelor. In episode 5 when Nes finally confesses her girl crush on Alex, the two women enjoy a passionate pool make out session. Then the two retreat to the pastor's office, which is the only place off limits to cameras. This complicated sexual agency of denying herself heterosexual sexual contact while simultaneously engaging in same-sex desire was significant as Shawn chooses to eliminate her female crush and keep Nes in the competition until two episodes from the end.

The dominant theme of evangelical sexual purity is challenged in this show but ultimately not undone. There are penalties for not performing and participating in a godly manner and each week contestants were eliminated from the show for having questionable morals. For example, women were given options: to go with the bachelor to a club or to church; to spend the night with the bachelor or not; or to eat the forbidden apple, the show's mechanism for ending the bachelor's date with one of the other contestants. Pastor J meted out consequences for women's less than holy choices and, in a perpetuation of blaming women for both their own and men's consensual actions, expressed his vocal disdain for some of their sexually suggestive actions even if Shawn was a willing participant. In *Match Made in Heaven*, the boundaries of racialized holy sex remain intact with rewards for those seeking godly unions and penalties for those expressing their sexuality outside of these realms.

Womanist cultural analysis – sublevel of texts

In each of these shows, the primary text produced (the show itself) is mediated and strengthened through various external texts (like feature articles, network publicity, and gossip columns on the show). Publicists for *The Sisterhood* not only produced publicity typical for any show, they ramped up their efforts in a desperate attempt to increase audience share by magnifying the publicity around the more sensational and sexy discussions of their cast. As one of the first black Christian reality TV shows, the producers cast a wide net to market themselves not only to Christians but also to secular fans of shows like *Real Housewives*. The cast did many interviews, often justifying their show's existence. In many of these interviews, cast members were asked to discuss scenes that dealt with sexuality. First Lady Ivy remarked that she was open about the subject because she didn't think sex is talked about in a healthy way, which she believes leads to "broken marriages and children being born out of wedlock from the pulpit." She noted that she felt particularly free to share explicit remarks with audiences because as a married person she doesn't "have any shame" talking about sexual matters.[29] Drawing attention to her sexual freedom in marriage reinforces the values of evangelical women who share her perspective.

First Lady Christina, however, was vocal about her dissatisfaction with some of the show's editing choices. The episode in which she and her husband discuss sex with their teenage daughters had, she told interviewers, been filmed in church and with an emphasis on scriptures that supported God's desire for purity, but these important elements were cut in editing. Whereas in some *Sisterhood* episodes, such "Bible thumping" produces catty division between the women, in Lady Christina's interviews regarding her message of sexual purity for her daughters she vocalized her regret that the televised message was made to appear so neutral.[30] In an interview before the show aired, cast members were asked about reality TV because their show was being publicized as the *Real Churchwives of Atlanta*. First Lady Dominique noted that she saw reality TV shows as ministry because they were able to show limits on behavior. First Lady Ivy said she was a fan of reality TV because it offered a release from her hectic life.[31] In other words, as much as the First Ladies participated in evangelical culture, they were also aware of being participants in the subculture of reality television.

The various subcultures of reality television are also present in *Match Made in Heaven*. In the first season, Nes' same-sex desire is mentioned in nearly every episode as she battles her growing attraction to Alex. Nes and the pastor discuss her desire to marry a man, but the bachelor does not find out about her desires until the pastor threatens to out her if she doesn't out herself. In evaluating the show at the second level of meaning, one can see that the cast biographies already outed her as a lesbian at the beginning of the season, so there was clearly a remapping of her desire from the publicity team. Similarly, one of the later finalists is described on the WE TV cast page as learning a key lesson from her mom, "be a good cook and give good head to get a man!" This is not displayed in the show directly but highlighted in the deleted scenes and on the cast webpage, which provide additional meanings to the portrayals on the show itself.

Preachers of LA likewise had massive media blitzes to promote the show and its cast members. It debuted after *The Sisterhood* was canceled and tried to avoid the plight of its predecessor. The longest running of the three shows, the cast members received diverse coverage. Numerous media outlets picked up on Dietrick's seeming support of shacking up or living with his fiancée without marriage and on the ensuing scandal from his impending marriage to the mother of his child. He even had a contentious interview with BET talk show host Wendy Williams and was forced to admit his sexual impurity. In the midst of Haddon's press junkets, the network encouraged his fiancée Dominique to give interviews as well. In one of them, she testified that she had hesitated morally about getting into a relationship with Dietrick, but caved to her desires. When she subsequently became pregnant, they kept the birth of their child a secret. That only fueled gossip magazines' reporting, and inquiries for more interviews.[32]

As ratings climbed for *Preachers of LA* and as Dominique earned greater notoriety, she used this opportunity to grow her brand. She promoted herself on her website and blog as a "nationally known reality TV personality" who also is a college graduate and was one class and an internship shy of a master's degree.[33] In interviews, she discusses being a first lady (Dietrick starts a church) but primarily speaks of her role as a mother. In this sense, she is referencing and enlisting another community, stay-at-home mothers, who she deems will relate to her experiences as a mother of three children under the age of five. Transforming the negative publicity or perhaps thriving in spite of it, she remains vocal on social media (especially Facebook), and this medium in turn brings us to the third area of textual analysis.

Womanist cultural analysis – viewer production

All of the shows examined reiterated messages of racialized sexuality in their blogs, Instagrams, and social media representations of their relationships. This in turn cued the various audiences to participate in the cultural production of black Christian reality television. The third level of textual analysis involves tracing how viewers reproduce, negotiate or oppose those same ideologies in their lives. Rather than delve into specific audience analysis, viewer commentary, etc. to discuss this third level of textual analysis, the chapter concludes by exploring what these examples of sexual agency mean for black women viewing these shows. Black feminist cultural critic Jacqueline Bobo points out that when a person reads and interprets a text, "she/he does not leave his/her histories, whether social, cultural, economic, racial, or sexual, at the door."[34] In fact, this is part of the promise of poststructuralist cultural theory: one's identity matters. How one sees oneself as existing in the world is a cultural construction that influences how one views a text. Black women who wrestle with the stereotypes of insatiable Jezebel and asexual Mammy are active audience members. As they watch these shows they must decide whether to accept what they see as representative of their life experiences, negotiate within that displayed image, or reject it outright.[35] When examining the commentary and chat rooms after the airing of each of these shows, it seems that black Christian reality television involves multiple types of what Parkin calls negotiated readings. After it was canceled, *Sisterhood* was denounced for not making a more overt Christian witness. Women in the show were often fighting, name-calling, gossiping, etc. Viewers who read the show oppositionally protested to have this show removed. That eventually their networks did not renew any of the three shows could suggest that oppositional readings were particularly significant.

And yet: that these shows live on in how viewers have been able to replicate these themes in their personal lives and in the support of other shows that share their themes surely suggests that the shows were influential and resonated with some of their audiences. For instance, *Match Made in Heaven* survived a second season and modified its format to include a black female co-host whose womanly counsel balanced the moral messaging of Pastor J. Moreover, the show's format has since been imitated by the Game Show Network's *It Takes a Church* reality TV show, which allows congregations to choose daters and make matches. This show was sponsored by the Christian dating site *Christian Mingle*, demonstrating the continued cross-appeal of the genre to various markets.

Preachers of LA had three successful seasons and broke records for the number of viewers and the most social cable reality program.[36] The show consistently had over one million viewers per episode and spawned two spinoffs, *Preachers of Detroit* and *Preachers of Atlanta*. Yet just as these shows were hitting their strides, the Oxygen network rebranded itself to focus on crime programming and canceled many other popular shows.

One could read the decrease of black Christian reality TV shows as evidence that audiences have moved on, but the larger concept of racialized holy sex is resilient and continues in spaces beyond reality TV. These shows are examples of a larger evangelical theme that is still being consumed by masses of black Christian women who may be fully aware that the empire that they are creating and sustaining is the empire of patriarchy and heteropatriarchy. Viewing these shows critically demands simultaneously being concerned with what black women find appealing and with the implications of these depictions on black female sexual agency.

Black Christian women cultural readers often navigate life while trying to live up to the constraints of holy sex as narrowly prescribed by religious communities. Of course, this does not undo the psychic, social, and cultural damage involved with women who are never able to participate in this model of Christianity. They may struggle to carve out their own new meanings and ways to be caretakers of the Holy Spirit. Yet, for many seeing the flawed nature of black Christians on television provides needed alternatives and perhaps even value centers that are concerned with their sexual and social lives.

Notes

1 I will only be examining the first seasons of each of these shows to fairly assess discussions of sexuality since *The Sisterhood* only aired for one season.
2 Susan D. Newman, *Oh God!*, 162.
3 Linda Thomas, "Womanist Theology, Epistemology," 497.
4 Layli Phillips [later Maparyan], *The Womanist Reader*, xx, xxvi. Phillips is expanding upon the original theorizing of Alice Walker's whose definition from her text *In Search of Our Mother's Gardens: Womanist Prose,* describes a womanist as a responsible, grown, black woman who is sometimes a lover of individual men, sexually and/or nonsexually, is sometimes a separatist, but is always a lover of the Spirit. This definition created the burgeoning genre of womanist theology and ethics. See Alice Walker, *In Search of Our Mothers' Gardens,*, ix.
5 Even though *Sisterhood* is a show about the lives of pastors' wives, the series often depicted them as merely appendages of the male pastor.
6 Gina Wingood, et al., "Comparative Effectiveness," 2226. Theola Labbe-Debose, "Black Women are among country's most religious groups." *The Washington Post*, July 6, 2012.
7 Andrea Seikaly, "Religion Makes an Appearance on Reality TV Landscape."
8 Chetachi Egwu, "The God in Me," 23.
9 "Gospel Artists Cashing in on Reality TV." Perhaps there is a symbiotic relationship between consuming gospel music and interest in religious reality TV.
10 Adria Goldman, "Meet the Braxtons and the Marys," 39, 43. She notes how production teams create "reality TV" by editing footage, making strategic casting calls, and staging different situations to foster more dramatic storylines. Several authors have written about these stereotypes in reality TV shows most notably Jennifer Pozner, Tia Tyree, and Adria Goldman. The angry bitch stereotype is an update of the Sapphire caricature that characterized black women as rude, loud, and overbearing. According to Tia Tyree, Hoochie Mama is considered a gold digger, typified by being uneducated and using her sexuality as her primary commodity; Ghetto Girl is cast as violent, low class, deemed lazy and lacking discipline; and the chicken head is a sexual freak known by her dangerous, high-risk sexual behaviors. See Tia Tyree, "African American Stereotypes," 398, 405.
11 They posit that such a street subculture emerged in the late 1960s and is representative of "criminal activity, violence, sexual conquest, alcohol and drug abuse, and other deleterious behaviors." W. Bradford Wilcox and Nicholas Wolfinger, *Soul Mates*, 48–49.
12 John Consoli, "WE TV, TLC, and Investigative Discovery Targeting Women's Upfront Advertisers."
13 Stuart Elliott, "Oxygen Shifts Focus to Millennial Viewers." It has now shifted strategy again and 2017 announced that the network is rebranding itself as a crime-focused network that will still seek to reach female audiences.
14 Oprah Winfrey's OWN network is the number one network in primetime among black female audiences. See Corporate Discovery, https://corporate.discovery.com/dis covery-newsroom/own-set-to-deliver-its-highest-rated-and-most-watched-year-in-net work-history/.
15 Louis Althusser, "Ideology and Ideological State Apparatuses" in *Cultural Theory and Popular Culture: A Reader*, 2nd edition. Edited by John Storey. New York: Prentice Hall, 1998, 162.
16 According to the historian Randall Balmer, *evangelical* refers broadly to conservative Protestants, including fundamentalists, Pentecostals, and charismatics (*Mine Eyes Have Seen the* Glory, xv–xvi).

17 Kelsy Burke notes that the logic of godly sex is framed against firmly prohibiting "sexual unions between anyone other than heterosexual, monogamous, married people." In regulating God sanctioned sexuality, white evangelicals are reconstructing an "us vs. them" framework that celebrates the supreme capacity for whites to be model exemplars of sexual purity. See Kelsy Burke, *Christians Under Covers*, 43.

18 See Sara Moslener, *Virgin Nation*, 3, and Victoria Wolcott, *Remaking Respectability*, 24–25.

19 See Monique Moultrie, *Passionate and Pious*.

20 Centers for Disease Control and Prevention data report that 72% of black children are born out of wedlock; yet, this does not equate to absentee black fathers as the number of unmarried black women living with their children's father has increased. See https://www.cdc.gov/nchs/data/nvsr/nvsr61/nvsr61_01.pdf; and Pew Research Center, http://www.pewsocialtrends.org/2014/09/24/record-share-of-americans-have-never-married/

21 Robert M. Franklin, "Generative Approaches," 112–113.

22 John Fiske, "British Cultural Studies and Television," 143.

23 In TLC's advertisements for the show, the president of the show's production company (who incidentally is also the producer of the *Real Housewives of Atlanta*) remarked that they were excited to "profile the lives of these strong-willed women" and thus turn the attention and praise more typically reserved for male preachers to give these "ladies the spotlight they crave and deserve." See Witherspoon, "Offensive or entertaining."

24 Brad and Dominique Scott claim their church failed because the church had low-income members who lost their jobs in the recent recession and members did not have funds to support the ministry. Ironically, in 2015, Dominique was sentenced to fifteen years of jail time (with 14 years waived) for forgery related to money mismanagement so one can wonder how the church failed.

25 They did not disclose details of their prior relationship during Season 1, and Season 2 began with questions of whether the second child was also conceived before they were married. Haddon later admitted that he fathered their first child while divorcing his second wife and that they both submitted to spiritual leadership for forgiveness of their sins. See PraiseWorld Radio, https://praiseworldradio.com/deitrick-haddon-new-ba by-dominique/.

26 Dominique tells her mother in episode 3 that she is being forced to be a single mother to please Christians because the episode shows her having to schedule time for Dietrick to see his daughter since they are not living together anymore.

27 Elizabeth Whittington Cooper, "High Tea, Church Hats," 12.

28 A born-again virgin or secondary virgin is someone who after engaging in sexual intercourse decides that he/she is going to abstain from any further sexual activity until after marriage.

29 Derrick Bryson Taylor, "Sisterhood Stars on Religion, Sex, and Being Preacher Wives."

30 For most evangelicals, the Bible is the most authoritative text on sexuality, as they believe scripture contains all they need to know about sex. Thus, following the Bible's instructions on sexual purity (scriptures from 1 Corinthians 6:18–20; 1 Thessalonians 4:3–8; 1 Thessalonians 4: 4; Romans 6:19–22; and Romans 12:1–2) is the evidence of living a sanctified life. See this example of Christina's interviews: https://ressurrection.wordpress.com/2013/02/14/exclusive-interview-christina-murray-of-tlcs-reality-show-the-sisterhood-on-love-marriage-and-the-business-of-ministry/

31 Rodney Ho, "Interviews with The Sisterhood cast."

32 Jessica Martinez, "Preachers of LA Deitrick Haddon Says He Has Second Chance at Life," *The Christian Post*, September 3, 2014, http://www.christianpost.com/news/prea chers-of-la-deitrick-haddon-says-he-has-second-chance-at-life-125814/.

33 Dominique Haddon, www.dominiquehaddon.com/blog.

34 Jacqueline Bobo, "The Color Purple: Black Women as Cultural Readers," 312.

35 Political social theorist Frank Parkin developed the concept of dominant, negotiated, and oppositional readings, but Stuart Hall used these readings within a poststructuralist framework to interpret texts. Frank Parkin, *Class Inequality;* Stuart Hall, "Encoding and Decoding."

36 Elizabeth Whittington Cooper, "High Tea, Church Hats," 3.

Bibliography

Balmer, Randall. *Mine Eyes Have Seen the Glory: A Journey into the Evangelical Subculture in America*. New York: Oxford University Press, 2014.

Bobo, Jacqueline. "The Color Purple: Black Women as Cultural Readers," in *Cultural Theory and Popular Culture: A Reader*, ed. John Storey, 237–245. New York: Prentice Hall, 1998.

Burke, Kelsy. *Christians Under Covers: Evangelicals and Sexual Pleasure on the Internet*. Oakland: University of California Press, 2016.

Centers for Disease Control and Prevention. "Births: Final Data for 2010." https://www.cdc.gov/nchs/data/nvsr/nvsr61/nvsr61_01.pdf.

"Christina Murray of TLC's Reality Show The Sisterhood on Love, Marriage, and the Business of Ministry." https://ressurrection.wordpress.com/2013/02/14/exclusive-interview-christina-murray-of-tlcs-reality-show-the-sisterhood-on-love-marriage-and-the-business-of-ministry/.

Consoli, John. "WE TV, TLC, and Investigative Discovery Targeting Women's Upfront Advertisers," *Broadcasting & Cable*, February 26, 2013. http://www.broadcastingcable.com/news/news-articles/we-tv-tlc-and-investigation-discovery-targeting-womens-upfront-advertisers/114183

Corporate Discovery. "OWN Set to Deliver Its Highest-Rated and Most-Watched Year in Network History." https://corporate.discovery.com/discovery-newsroom/own-set-to-deliver-its-highest-rated-and-most-watched-year-in-network-history/.

Egwu, Chetachi. "The God in Me: Faith, Reality TV, and Black Women." In *Black Women's Portrayals in Reality Television: The New Sapphire*, edited by Donnetrice Allison, 17–37. Lanham: Lexington Books, 2016.

Elliott, Stuart. "Oxygen Shifts Focus to Millennial Viewers." *New York Times*, April 8, 2014.

Fiske, John. "British Cultural Studies and Television," in *What is Cultural Studies? A Reader*, ed. John Storey, 115–146. New York: Arnold, 1997.

Franklin, Robert M. "Generative Approaches to Modernity, Discrimination, and Black Families," in *American Religions and the Family: How Faith Traditions Cope with Modernization and Democracy*, edited by Don S. Browning and David A. Clairmont, 104–123. New York: Columbia University Press, 2007.

Goldman, Adria. "Meet the Braxtons and the Marys: A Closer Look at Representations of Black Female Celebrities in WE TV's Braxton Family Values and Mary Mary." In *Black Women and Popular Culture: The Conversation Continues*, edited by Adria Goldman, et al, 33–54. Lanham: Lexington Books, 2014.

"Gospel Artists Cashing in On Reality TV." http://linwoodsinspiredmedia.com/gospel-artists-cashing-in-on-reality-tv/.

Haddon, Dominique. Conversations with Domerella. www.dominiquehaddon.com/blog.

Hall, Stuart. "Encoding and Decoding" in *Culture, Media, Language: Working Papers in Cultural Studies, 1972–79*, ed. Stuart Hall, et al. New York: Routledge, 1980.

Ho, Rodney. "Interviews with The Sisterhood cast," *Atlanta-Journal Constitution*, January 1, 2013. http://radiotvtalk.blog.ajc.com/2013/01/01/2013-flashback-interviews-with-tlcs-the-sisterhood-cast/.

Labbe-Debose, Theola. "Black Women are among country's most religious groups." *The Washington Post*, July 6, 2012.

Martinez, Jessica. "Preachers of LA Deitrick Haddon Says He Has Second Chance at Life," *The Christian Post*, September 3, 2014.

Moslener, Sara. *Virgin Nation: Sexual Purity and American Adolescence*. New York: Oxford University Press, 2015.

Moultrie, Monique. *Passionate and Pious: Religious Media and Black Women's Sexuality*. Durham: Duke University Press, 2017.

Newman, Susan. *Oh God! A Black Woman's Guide to Sex and Spirituality*. New York: One World/Ballantine Books, 2002.

Parkin, Frank. *Class Inequality and Political Order: Social Stratification in Capitalist and Communist Societies*. London: MacGibbon & Kee, 1971. Pew Research Center, "Record Share of Americans Have Never Married." http://www.pewsocialtrends.org/2014/09/24/record-share-of-americans-have-never-married/.

Phillips [Maparyan], Layli. *The Womanist Reader*. New York: Routledge, 2006.

PraiseWorld Radio. "Deitrick Haddon Welcomes New Baby with Wife Dominique." https://praiseworldradio.com/deitrick-haddon-new-baby-dominique/.

Seikaly, Andrea. "Religion Makes an Appearance on Reality TV Landscape." *Variety*. July 11, 2014. http://variety.com/2014/tv/news/religion-makes-an-appearance-on-reality-tv-landscape-1201217493/.

Taylor, Derrick. "Sisterhood Stars on Religion, Sex, and Being Preacher Wives." *Essence*. January 1, 2013. http://www.essence.com/2012/12/31/exclusive-sisterhood-stars-being-first-ladies-religion-sex-and-more.

Thomas, Linda. "Womanist Theology, Epistemology, and a New Anthropological Paradigm," *Cross Currents* 48.4(1998): 488–499.

Tyree, Tia. "African American Stereotypes in Reality Television," *Howard Journal of Communications* 22.4(2011): 394–413.

Walker, Alice. *In Search of Our Mothers' Gardens: Womanist Prose*. New York: Harcourt Brace Jovanovich, 1983.

Whittington Cooper, Elizabeth. "High Tea, Church Hats, Pastor Wives, and Friendships: A Critical Race Feminism Analysis of Black Women in Preachers of LA." In *Black Women's Portrayals on Reality Television: The New Sapphire*, edited by Donnetrice Allison, 3–16. Lanham: Lexington Books, 2016.

Wilcox, Bradford and Nicholas Wolfinger, *Soul Mates: Religion, Sex, Love, and Marriage among African Americans and Latinos*. New York: Oxford University Press, 2016.

Wingood, Gina, Lashun Robinson, Nikia Braxton, et al., "Comparative Effectiveness of a Faith-Based HIV Intervention for African American Women: Importance of Enhancing Religious Social Capital," *American Journal of Public Health* 103.12(2013): 2226–2233.

Witherspoon, Chris. "Offensive or Entertaining? 'The Sisterhood' reality show about preacher's wives in Atlanta." The Grio.com. http://thegrio.com/2012/11/30/offensive-or-entertaining-the-sisterhood-reality-show-about-preachers-wives-in-atlanta/.

Wolcott, Victoria. *Remaking Respectability: African American Women in Interwar Detroit*. Chapel Hill: University of North Carolina Press, 2001.

PART II

The performance of authenticity

4

"THIS IS JUST AN INCREDIBLE GOD THING"

Monetized domesticity in bottom-up media

Katherine Madden

In the crowdsource-funded documentary *Vlogumentary*, Mormon vlogger Shay Carl declares, "If a life's worth living it's worth recording," and for Carl, the life worth living is a life serving God. His statement is emblematic of a media industry in flux. In the reality era the intimacy of everyday life is commodified and exchanged through a digital currency of ratings, views, likes, and shares. Vloggers like Carl coexist with reality television in a media landscape where the mundanity of daily life is the spectacle. The two forms of media are irrefutably interwoven; reality television producers and casting directors scour through vlogs for new personalities, and vloggers borrow from reality genre conventions; many hope to be discovered someday and make the leap to mainstream media.

For Christian vloggers like Carl, the larger the platform they land on, the greater the opportunity to share their faith. Carl's introductory video to his vlog channel on YouTube has over 12 million views and counting. To put this into context, *The Real Housewives* franchise averages around 2.5 million viewers between all of its shows. While religion is featured prominently on many reality television shows, including the *Housewives* franchise, the under-produced rawness of these vlogs creates a uniquely intimate dynamic between the viewer and producer. These Christian vlogs work within the conventions of reality television, but also actively distinguish themselves as outside of mainstream media. These vloggers not only star in their vlogs, but also edit them, promote them, and distribute them directly to their fans on their own YouTube channels. Unlike reality television programs, vlogs are produced from beginning to end inside the home. The very means of their production distinguish them from corporately produced mainstream media and humanize the vloggers' Christianity in a way reality television and even churches fail to do. These videos do what churches and mainstream media cannot: they provide the emotion and intimacy of the home to contextualize Conservative Christian ideology. While the labor conditions of producing these vlogs characterize the neoliberal media space from which they are born, these often challenging conditions are justified by their decidedly Conservative Christian lifestyle. When their lifestyle or the content of their vlogs are confronted, as this chapter will demonstrate, the vloggers are able to position themselves as helpless victims against a Godless mainstream media.

This essay will explore two of the most popular family vlogs, Shay Carl's YouTube channel *The Shaytards*, with a total of 4,938,222 subscribers and 2,657,857,324 views, and Sam and Nia Rader's channel *Sam and Nia*, with a total of 2,100,903 subscribers and 647,578,286 views. Vlogs could not be more personal, yet one cannot watch these videos without reflecting on Conservative Christian beliefs regarding marriage, pregnancy, and gender norms. Christian media is overwhelmingly more personal than political, but it is impossible to ignore the political undertones in even the most personal moments. These vlogs reproduce neoliberal rationalities by conflating labor and pleasure and emphasizing self-reliance and self-fulfillment.[1]

Heather Hendershot argues that "today's conservative evangelicals want to engage with the wider culture because they think their belief system is the truth – indeed the only hope for mankind – and they want to share their reality with others."[2] Enter Christian vloggers Sam and Nia Rader, who summarize the purpose of their YouTube channel in an August 2015 video titled, "THE IMPORTANCE OF FAMILY VLOGS!":

> We call our fans on the Sam and Nia Channel "fanBASIC". It's a play on words with fan base. BASIC is an acronym for Brothers and Sisters in Christ. We understand that not all of you are believers in Christ, but we do this because this is what we want for you. Here on our channel, this is a part of our mission for God. In order to have the most fulfilling life possible, you need to have Christ in your life.[3]

The duo began posting daily vlogs in 2014, after a video of them eagerly lip-synching to Disney's *Frozen* soundtrack for their daughter's amusement made its rounds on parenting and lifestyle blogs. Most of the family's videos feature them participating in the mundane activities of domestic life. Vlog titles in all capital letters like "I LOST MY PURSE IN CALIFORNIA" or titles that insinuate a major catastrophe create drama and suspense. For example, in one video titled "Tragic Beach Accident," the thumbnail of the video is of their toddler face-down in the ocean as he appears helpless. In the vlog, the child is knocked over by a wave but is helped up quickly by his parents, all while the camera is trained on him. In another video titled "Scary brake failure," the thumbnail is of their oldest daughter on her bike. In the vlog, the child just has minor difficulties using the brakes on her bike.

After the *Frozen* video went viral, Sam said, "I've always had a dream to be famous."[4] Then in August 2015, fame came: their video, "HUSBAND SHOCKS WIFE WITH PREGNANCY ANNOUNCEMENT!", which featured Sam revealing to Nia that she was pregnant after he had collected and tested urine she had left in the toilet, went viral. Their next vlog celebrates their going viral, with Sam raving over the number of views they had racked up: "Oh my gosh, you guys, I pulled up the views again. We're like twenty-two minutes in this hour, and it's already beat the last hour. So we're at twenty, over twenty-two thousand views in twenty-two minutes. Can you believe that? Oh my gosh, it's really happening! This is nuts!"[5] Overwhelmingly, the majority of their views come from any of their many videos surrounding pregnancy. As is the case with the Raders, the viewers watch as the couple learns what any television producer could have told them: babies and pregnancies are good for ratings.

Three days later, in an unexpected turn of events, the couple tearfully reveal in a follow-up video that they miscarried; they admit to never actually confirming with a doctor either the pregnancy or (suspiciously enough) the miscarriage. Sam begins the vlog by solemnly addressing the camera: "I told Nia, I said God is ready to use us in a huge way." Nia then explains how overjoyed she is to have been pregnant, and cites their previous two videos as evidence of her joy. She states that she now understands what a profound loss a miscarriage can be and that she will forever shoulder her loss with all grieving mothers. Sam adds, "I just hope this video continues to be a way for God to shine His light to the world through us. This is a time when especially the U.S. needs that light and God knew that. And this video is just getting so big. We never imagined this could happen to us, but this baby came along, made us happier than we remember."[6]

Following the miscarriage, Sam tweeted that their unborn baby's purpose must have been to bring views and new followers to their account. "Our tiny baby brought 10M views to her video & 100k new people into our lives. She turned our life around & brought us closer together."[7] The comment unleashed a wave of criticism in mainstream media, which Sam and Nia have deflected by claiming that their account's primary purpose is to spread the word of God.[8]

Sam and Nia are part of a growing number of Christian vloggers who use their pregnancies and children to attract viewers to their sites. Sam and Nia exemplify a much wider trend in post-recessionary culture of Christian entrepreneurs who have monetized pregnancy and domestic labor through creative venues like YouTube, Etsy, Instagram, or their own personal blogs, in an effort to promote, but also make possible, the conservative Christian family lifestyle they desire. Sam and Nia have not left a single box unchecked, as they are active on YouTube, Instagram, Twitter, and Facebook; Nia even sells her homemade wreaths on Etsy. There are countless Christian families who are using children, family homes, spouses, and their family lifestyle to give credibility to their brand, but also to a Christian doctrine that advocates for stay-at-home parenting. A theme running throughout this media is the gratitude the vloggers express for being able to spend extra time with their children because of the flexible schedule that their entrepreneurial lifestyle affords. The perpetual gratitude moralizes the "individualization of our working lives."[9] A post-Fordist economy, "which is characterized by destabilized employment, the concomitant rise of casualized and contract-based work, and the logic of flexible specialization,"[10] is framed in these sites as a blessing for mothers who want to fulfill their calling as Christian women and care for their children while also having a career that helps support their families. Young Christian creatives repackage the conservative Christian lifestyle for their devoted audiences. In the process, they provide a moral context of Christian family values to a DIY economy by establishing it as family-friendly, despite the reality that jobs in this arena require around-the-clock labor. Moreover, very few succeed, and there are limited safety nets in place for those who fail.

Pregnancy functions in these vlogs as a prolonged narrative with big reveals, such as the baby's sex, the baby's name, and the baby's nursery.[11] In her essay "Pregnant Beauty: Maternal Femininities under Neoliberalism," Imogen Tyler states, "the emergence of pregnant beauty signals the deeper commodification of maternity under neoliberalism, a process which is shaping maternal experience and contributing to lived gender inequalities."[12] Expectant Christian families who use the experience of pregnancy to legitimize and expand their businesses provide a Christian moral context to the inherent gender inequality of commodifying the pregnant body. Furthermore, the Christian male headship ideology inherent to these projects excuses the inequalities of a DIY economy.[13] The labor is usually performed by women, and, building upon the work of Brooke Erin Duffy and Emily Hund, the mothers often suggest that the DIY labor they are performing allows them to be at home raising their babies, as God intends for them. Coincidentally, two of the most successful family vlogs, *Sam and Nia* and *The Shaytards*, are mostly shot from the perspective of men, unlike the majority of family vlogs, which are shot and maintained by women. The male presence and leadership in these vlogs perhaps partially explains how these vlogs were able to stand out from the thousands of domestic vlogs produced by women. The expository nature of this content borrows from the larger trends of blogging, reality television, and undoubtedly the chronicling of celebrity pregnancies in tabloid media.

In his book, *The Digital Sublime: Myth, Power, and Cyberspace*, Vincent Mosco explains that many Internet experts envisioned the end of the Cold War and the acceleration of cyber technology as the end to politics, science, and economics as we knew it. Mosco argues that "constraints once imposed by scarcities of resources, labor, and capital would end, or at least loosen significantly, and a new economics of cyberspace (a 'network economics') would make it easier for societies to grow, and especially, to grow rich."[14] Yet, despite the imagined potential for utopia, the social and economic change that was envisioned has not materialized. Instead, the field has replicated the advanced capitalist policies in which it was born. "The difference between the audience commodity on traditional mass media and on the Internet is that in the latter case the users are also content producers; there is user-generated content, and the users engage in permanent creative activity, communication, community building, and content production."[15] The often underpaid or unpaid labor that generates content for sites like YouTube or Instagram yields a profit for the owners of these platforms, which rarely trickles down to the media creators. Andrew Ross argues that this economy echoes the era prior to industrialization "when the careful and laborious nurturing of relationships with wealthy and powerful names were sources of considerable worth."[16] Ross argues that the affective currency of shares and likes "has replaced the wages of industrialization" and "by far the most substantial rewards are allocated, on an industrial basis, to those who build and maintain the technologies of extraction, who hold the system's intellectual property, and who can trade the aggregate output of personal expression as if it were a bulk commodity."[17] Jodi Dean makes a similar argument that bloggers are paid in little more than publicity for exposing themselves and, in the case of these vlogging parents, the lives of their children.[18] The affective labor of those who participate in the production of user-generated content is sacrificing their time and privacy, while the owners of these media-sharing platforms accumulate wealth. The producers of these vlogs are dealing in a currency that goes beyond mere publicity and wages; they are performing the work of God.

A 2012 episode of Anderson Cooper's now-defunct daytime talk show, *Anderson*, which focused on the making of "easy money," featured the Shaytards and their endorsement deals with Foot Locker, AT&T, Kia, Kodak, Google, Sanyo, A1, and GE.[19] The family's nickname refers to a leotard that the family's patriarch, Shay Carl, wore in an early video. Cooper opened the segment by saying, "Have you ever wondered how some people make money off of a viral video? You see all of those videos on YouTube, there are some people actually making money on YouTube. Here's what happens, this year YouTube invested over one-hundred million dollars into its contributors, which created a new kind of mogul, the YouTube millionaire." Cooper's subsequent introduction of the Shaytards as "the first family of YouTube" mythologizes YouTube success stories. Despite the reality that the majority of content producers are performing affective and underpaid labor, YouTube goes to great lengths to publicize the success stories of families like the Carls who are "co-founders of Maker Studios, a conglomerate of YouTube channels that was sold to Disney for $500 million in 2014."[20]

The aesthetics, content, and format of Mormon stay-at-home mothers' mommyblogs have greatly influenced blogging and vlogging communities. Mormons, in general, have been so prolific in their blogging that the portmanteau, "Bloggernacle," has been created in recognition of their abundant presence.[21] In a September 2013 vlog titled "ARE THE SHAYTARDS CHRISTIAN?", Shay Carl addresses the camera as he shaves in preparation for visiting their local temple in Idaho to see their son leave for his mission. "Like I have said before, [Mormonism] is the answer to the question, 'Why are you guys so happy? Something seems different about you guys.' [Mormonism] is the basis for me and Collette's relationship, for my relationship with my kids, for all of that."[22] Carl reminds the viewer that they will die one day and perhaps they should look into the Mormon faith before that day comes. Carl then bounces around the house saying goodbye to his children before he and his wife leave for the temple.

In the Mormon faith, there is a strong push for genealogy and record keeping.[23] In *Doctrine and Covenants*, Joseph Smith commands: "And again, let all the records be had in order, that they may be put in the archives of my holy temple."[24]

Former president of the Church of Latter-day Saints, Spencer W. Kimball stressed the importance of journal keeping by arguing that even the most mundane of details will help generations get to know one another so that in eternity everybody will be familiar. "Begin today," Kimball states,

> … and write in it your goings and your comings, your deeper thoughts, your achievements, and your failures, your associations and your triumphs, your impressions and your testimonies. We hope you will do this, our brothers and sisters, for this is what the Lord has commanded, and those who keep a personal journal are more likely to keep the Lord in remembrance in their daily lives.[25]

Kimball encourages his flock to journal with an optimistic and positive tone, stating that journals should be triumphant. Kimball's recommendations for journaling help to explain the omnipresent rosy outlook in Mormon mommyblogs and family vlogs. Kimball adds that:

> the truth should be told, but we should not emphasize the negative. Even a long life full of inspiring experiences can be brought to the dust by one ugly story. Why dwell on that one ugly truth about someone whose life has been largely circumspect?[26]

In an address to the graduating class of Brigham Young University in Hawaii, church elder Russell M. Ballard advised the graduates that blogging is an excellent way to chronicle their day and spread the Mormon message to people outside of the church.[27]

> May I ask that you join the conversation by participating on the Internet, particularly the New Media, to share the gospel and to explain in simple, clear terms the message of the Restoration. Most of you already know that if you have access to the Internet you can start a blog in minutes and begin sharing what you know to be true.[28]

In the case of the Mormon Church, blogging is a directive from the elders and leaders of the church.

Indeed, these vlogs do not dwell on "ugly truths," but instead promote themselves and their homes as wholesome. Justin G. Wilford argues that "the home is an ideal setting for evangelical performances because it is a foundational environment for postsuburban identity and thus one for authentic, intentional action."[29] The staging of the home serves as evidence for a Christian life well-lived: "In the postsuburban home, prayer becomes more intimate, singing becomes more authentic, fellowship becomes more emotional, and scripture becomes more relevant."[30] Vlogs featuring Christians at home with their children doing the work of God personalize the domestic experience in a way that pastors and media executives cannot. Wilford argues that home, in the evangelical performance, is an "endlessly adaptable tool for working on the self."[31] In these videos, the families often comment and reflect upon mundane chores like picking up after the kids, leaving luggage unpacked for weeks after a family vacation, or introducing new foods to a baby.

After Sam posted the video in which he states that he would be quitting his job to vlog full-time, the social news and entertainment site, *Buzzfeed*, posted an article that questioned the veracity of Sam and Nia's original pregnancy claim and suggested that the entire event, including the miscarriage, was possibly staged in order to grow their fan base. The *Buzzfeed* article cites "their cheerfulness in their video the day after they said they miscarried, combined with Sam's glee at finally having enough success to quit his job," as reason for questioning their motives. Two days after the *Buzzfeed* article was published, Sam and Nia posted a vlog in response. Sam addresses the camera as he sits on his front porch; his two children splash in a kiddie pool behind him.

> It seems as though the media out there, all the articles being written about us, are trying to put us in a bad light for the most part. And I feel like those are the ones that represent the world. And it makes me think of the verse John 15:19. "If you are of the world the world will love you as its own. But because you are not of the world but I have chosen you from the world, the world hates you." I just think that's so amazing. "Because I chose you, the world hates you." So we're hated. I mean God told us we were going to be hated. So what we are seeing is God's will being played out for our lives as Christians. We are being persecuted somewhat. And, um, this is what God told us is going to happen so I can't help but let it excite me every time I read these articles.[32]

Sam perpetuates the familiar narrative, popularized during the culture wars, of a secular media elite shutting Christianity out of the public sphere.[33] As Rhys H. Williams argues, "many of the conservative political activists have been particularly successful at attacking the 'cultural elite' that supposedly governs the fine arts and universities worlds – worlds from which many Americans do in fact feel estranged."[34] Sam is appealing to a class of people whose conception of morality is not replicated in the political and cultural spheres.

The media production of cultural and political conservatives has flourished in user-generated spaces like YouTube; and as Henry Jenkins argues, paradoxically, those who feel the most alienated by mainstream media have been the most successful at seeing their content cycled back into the mainstream.

> Ironically, perhaps the biggest success story in niche media production has been the emergence of alternative spheres of popular culture reflecting the tastes and ideologies of cultural conservatives, the very groups who are also working to impose those ideological norms onto mainstream media through governmental regulation of media content.[35]

Chip Berlet argues, "since Christians have a mandate to spread the gospel of Christ throughout the world, there is a powerful motive to be on the cutting edge of new information technologies."[36] Berlet cites the 1980s and '90s as a particularly prolific period of bottom-up conservative media production, as technology became increasingly user-friendly. Undoubtedly, the ubiquity of cameras and video sharing sites since the mid-2000s contributes to the vast quantity of Conservative Christian families, like the Raders, who broadcast their day-to-day lives and promote themselves as an alternative to mainstream media.

These families draw heavily from secular reality television and vlogs in the production of their media. Hendershot's book, *Shaking the World for Jesus*, looks to the ways evangelicals appropriate secular media for their own message. In a passage that echoes Sam's earlier sentiment, Hendershot argues that "to be 'in' but not 'of'" the world is to engage with people outside of the evangelical belief system, and hopefully lead them into that system, without becoming more like the outsider yourself. Hendershot contends that:

> examination of evangelical media reveals the complex ways that today's evangelicals are *both* in and out of the world. This is not a value judgment; evangelicals have not simply "sold out" or been "secularized." Rather, evangelicals have used media to simultaneously struggle against, engage with, and acquiesce to the secular world.[37]

Robert Wuthnow makes a similar yet broader argument in *After Heaven: Spirituality in America since the 1950s*:

> Compared with societies that have a longer history with secularity, the United States is in the throes of major transition. They are not marching steadfastly into a secular age, but are reshaping deep religious traditions in ways that help make sense of the realities of their lives.[38]

Additionally, Conservative Christians are engaging with secular media not only to evangelize but also to support their families. Domestic Christian laborers, therefore, must employ their faith to give moral purpose to their post-recessionary labor.

The balancing act of walking the line between secular and evangelical cultures was tested in the month following the Raders' viral pregnancy video, when Sam's name appeared among those listed as customers of Ashley Madison, the online dating site for married or committed individuals.[39] In a now private video, the duo swiftly responded, stating that both God and Nia had already forgiven Sam's sin.[40] Sam states that:

> the account was open out of fleshly desires and just sinful curiosity. Some of you are questioning my faith and me being a Christian and doing this and I guess what some people don't understand is we're all broken, even Christians. We come to God as broken people and He has sent Jesus on the cross to save us from those sins.

In her book, *Between Jesus and the Market*, Linda Kintz speaks to the rhetorical advantage of invoking the Christian belief that God sacrificed his only son: "He gave up his own *child* for us, and in the postmodern context, in which people are struggling to keep families intact, this is the most moving, powerful sacrifice one could imagine."[41] According to *People* magazine, the Raders were asked to leave a blogging conference, following the Ashley Madison scandal, after Sam got into a physical altercation with a fellow conference attendee who questioned the veracity of their miscarried pregnancy.[42] The altercation resulted in a media blackout until they announced, once again, that Nia was pregnant. A new pregnancy afforded the Raders a new opportunity to reclaim their domestic authority because, as Kintz argues, "the child proves to be the key to reconstruction and legitimation of sacred gender and the kind of politics that collapses family, religion, and patriotism into the same highly sensual configuration."[43]

Similarly, in February 2017, amidst a six-month "break from the internet" that had begun in September 2016, a leaked chat transcript between Shay Carl and an "adult cam" Instagram star revealed that he had been cheating on his wife. Carl responded with a tweet explaining his struggle with alcoholism and announcing that he would continue to halt production of their exceedingly popular vlog. The fact that the family blamed their fame and expanding social media presence for their woes, suggests that the more mainstream their media became, the more challenging it became for them to maintain the conservative and wholesome lifestyle they promoted.

The labor produced by Christian vloggers is undoubtedly creative and a product of a post-recessionary economy, which makes necessary domestic and creative labor. In his revision of *The Rise of the Creative Class*, Richard Florida speaks optimistically to the potential of an evolving labor market:

> A great stumbling block in the United States has been the huge rise in inequality, the bifurcation of the labor market between higher-skilled, higher-wage Creative Class jobs and lower-skilled, lower-pay Service Class jobs in fields like food preparation, home health care, and retail sales, where more than 60 million Americans work, 45 percent of the labor force.

Florida adds that:

> this stark divide in economic prospects has been exacerbated by the dreams of so many once high-paying Working Class jobs. The only way forward is to make all jobs creative jobs, infusing service work, manufacturing work, farming, and every other form of human endeavor with creativity and human potential.[44]

The burden to learn new creative skills, however, is often placed on underpaid and undereducated labor in order to adapt to a changing economy. Florida does not take into account the role of unpaid domestic labor in the economy, and the particular demands that a post-recessionary economy places on domestic labor to become monetized; already taxed domestic laborers must acquire creative skills to supplement their household incomes.

The economic value of domestic laborers has been associated historically with their ability to support the economy through their consumptive practices.[45] Elizabeth Nathanson argues that a conflation between consumption and production is a hallmark of user-generated convergence culture. The statistics reported by organizations like Etsy and the Hobby Association indicating that the DIY movement is both lucrative and growing obscure the fact that the profit does not go to the laborers, but rather to the crafting supply chains.[46] Similarly, vloggers like the Raders and the Shaytards are ultimately supporting the consumer technology and video sharing industries. The "DIY movement advocates for a different engagement with work that circumvents global mass-production, mass-marketing and passive mass-consumption."[47] Yet, the consumption and production practices the movement attempts to circumvent are ultimately insurmountable, and domestic labor is again tied to traditional consumptive practices. Imogen Tyler asserts that "within a neoliberal society the ability (and desire) to work and to spend are key measures of value and ideal neoliberal subjects cooperate with their subjectification within these markets (and compulsive consumption and workaholism are symptomatic pathologies.)"[48] The DIY movement requires the laborer to be both a workaholic and to compulsively consume in order to produce a product. In this sense, the movement is a complete recapitulation of neoliberalism. In her study of recessionary fashion blogs, Nathanson argues that these sort of blogs "celebrate the potential for the individual to become a successful entrepreneur through online work in consumer culture, offering a means to reconcile postfeminist identities with recessionary anxieties by transforming shopping into a kind of pleasurable work."[49] In the case of these vlogs it is not just shopping that is transformed, but domestic labor as well.

While these creative ventures may not be monetarily successful, many of these families have an ideological investment in monetizing a Conservative Christian lifestyle that prefers that wives are at home to care for their children and spouses, and that husbands are providing financially for their families. These families are not simply in it for the income, but are simultaneously trying to fulfill their Christian obligations as men and women.

A post on the liberal blog *Salon* noted that there is an abundance of self-described feminist women who fanatically read Mormon mommy blogs.[50] In a comment, reader BrookeD admits: "I read about 5 different blogs by Mormon women every day. (I am not Mormon) The life that they portray on these blogs are just lovely, they have lovely homes, picture perfect kids, loving super attentive husbands, and things seem very normal and calm. (I love the blogs, btw)."[51] BrookeD adds that she did not realize that the framing of the families in this way was so closely related to Mormon beliefs about family life. BrookeD's revelation illustrates the subtle ways in which these Christian creatives are repackaging and effectively selling Conservative Christian ideology to a willing audience. As Henry Jenkins, Sam Ford, and Joshua Green argue, "there is an implicit and often explicit proposition that the spread of ideas and messages can occur without users' consent and perhaps actively against their conscious resistance; people are duped into passing a hidden agenda while circulating compelling content."[52] Perhaps it is not that audiences are duped, but that the content speaks to them in ways not necessarily intended by the producer. In the case of Christian DIY laborers, they produce content that speaks to the economic and domestic realities of a post-recessionary economy. There is limited support for parents and families in traditional careers, and these parents bring to life the realities of choosing an alternative, albeit not much simpler, path. In the case of these vlogs, the specificity of the medium is entirely relevant to their reception. The very economics of the production of these vlogs exemplifies domestic realities in post-recessionary culture in a way that traditional forms of media cannot.

Notes

1 Nicole Dawkins, "Do-It-Yourself: The Precarious Work and Postfeminist Politics of Handmaking (in) Detroit," *Utopian Studies* 22, no. 2 (2011): 262, doi:10.5325/utopianstudies.22.2.0261.
2 Heather Hendershot, *Shaking the World for Jesus: Media and Conservative Evangelical Culture* (Chicago: University of Chicago Press, 2004), p. 11.
3 Sam Rader and Nia Rader, "THE IMPORTANCE OF FAMILY VLOGS!," You-Tube, August 15, 2015, accessed August 12, 2016, https://www.youtube.com/watch?v=hqpPeBRmwjo.
4 Kelsey Miller, "Even If Sam & Nia Did Fake It, What Does Our Reaction Say About Us?" Refinery 29, August 16, 2015, accessed August 11, 2016, http://www.refinery29.com/2015/08/92311/sam-nia-pregnancy-miscarriage-hoax-bias.
5 Sam Rader and Nia Rader, "We're Going Viral!," Sam and Nia (video blog), August 6, 2015, https://www.youtube.com/watch?v=LiknIo5N2IU.
6 Sam Rader and Nia Rader, "Our Baby Had a Heartbeat!," Sam and Nia (video blog), December 31, 2015, accessed August 11, 2016, https://www.youtube.com/watch?v=vTVui7Ff-68.
7 Sam Rader, Twitter, August 9, 2015, accessed May 1, 2016, www.twitter.com.
8 Aditi Roy et al., "Christian Vloggers Sam and Nia Rader Have No Regrets Posting Family Videos," ABC News, August 25, 2015, accessed August 12, 2016, http://abcnews.go.com/Lifestyle/christian-vloggers-sam-nia-rader-regrets-posting-family/story?id=33291322.
9 Melissa Gregg, "The Normalisation of Flexible Female Labour in the Information Economy," *Feminist Media Studies* 8, no. 3 (2008), accessed August 11, 2016, doi:10.1080/14680770802217311.
10 Duffy, Brooke Erin and Emily Hund, "Having it all." See also, Andre Wigfield's *Post-Fordism, Gender, and Work* and Linda McDowell's "Life without father and Ford" for a study of how the economic restructuring in post-Fordist economies reconfirms gendered labor.
11 Allie Jones, "A Guide to the Christian Vlog Community Where the Biggest Blessing Is a Baby," Gawker, August 14, 2015, accessed August 12, 2016, http://gawker.com/a-guide-to-the-christian-vlog-community-where-the-bigge-1723334784.
12 Imogen Tyler, "Pregnant Beauty: Maternal Femininities under Neoliberalism," in *New Femininities: Postfeminism, Neoliberalism, and Subjectivity*, ed. Rosalind Gill and Christina Scharff (Houndmills, Basingstoke, Hampshire: Palgrave Macmillan, 2011), 23.
13 Priscilla Pope-Levison's essay "Separate Spheres and Complementarianism in American Christianity" and Sally K. Gallagher's "The Marginalization of Evangelical Feminism"

both offer thoughtful reflections of how women navigate complementarianist beliefs in the modern evangelical practice.

14 Vincent Mosco, *The Digital Sublime: Myth, Power, and Cyberspace* (Cambridge, MA: MIT Press, 2004), 4.

15 Christian Fuchs, "Labor in Informational Capitalism and on the Internet," *The Information Society* 26, no. 3 (2010): 192, doi:10.1080/01972241003712215.

16 Andrew Ross, "In Search of the Lost Paycheck," in *Digital Labor: The Internet as Playground and Factory*, ed. Trebor Scholz (New York: Routledge, 2013), 13.

17 Ibid., 18–19.

18 Jodi Dean, "Whatever Blogging," in *Digital Labor: The Internet as Playground and Factory*, ed. Trebor Scholz (New York: Routledge, 2013), 127.

19 Irena Slutsky, "Meet YouTube's Most In-Demand Brand Stars," Advertising Age Digital RSS, September 13, 2010, accessed August 12, 2016, http://adage.com/article/digital/meet-youtube-s-demand-brand-stars/145844/.

20 Belinda Luscomb, "The YouTube Parents Who are Turning Family Moments into Big Bucks." *Time*, May 17, 2017, accessed August 11, 2017, http://time.com/4783215/growing-up-in-public/.

21 Krista Kapralos, "Mormon Bloggernacle Is No Choir," Religion Dispatches, June 19, 2009, accessed August 11, 2016, http://religiondispatches.org/mormon-bloggernacle-is-no-choir/.

22 Shay Butler, "ARE THE SHAYTARDS CHRISTIAN?," YouTube, September 4, 2013, accessed August 12, 2016, http://www.youtube.com/watch?v=fgwodehtWEI.

23 See Leonard J. Arrington and David Bitton's *The Mormon Experience: A History of the Latter-Day Saints* and Terryl L. Givens, *By The Hand of Mormon.*

24 D&C 127:9.

25 Spencer W. Kimball, "President Kimball Speaks Out on Personal Journals," New Era, Dec. 1980, accessed August 12, 2016, https://www.lds.org/new-era/1980/12/president-kimball-speaks-out-on-personal-journals?lang=eng.

26 Ibid.

27 Kapralos, op. cit.

28 Russell M. Ballard, "Using New Media to Support the Work of the Church," www.mormonnewsroom.org, December 15, 2007, accessed August 12, 2016, http://www.mormonnewsroom.org/article/using-new-media-to-support-the-work-of-the-church.

29 Justin G. Wilford, *Sacred Subdivisions: The Postsuburban Transformation of American Evangelicalism* (New York: New York University Press, 2012), 166.

30 Ibid.

31 Ibid.

32 Sam Rader and Nia Rader, "RESPONDING TO HATE COMMENTS!," YouTube, August 14, 2015, accessed August 12, 2016, http://www.youtube.com/watch?v=IF_DBFt5ax8.

33 See Todd Gitlin's *The Twilight of American Dreams*, Ronald William Dworkin's *The Rise of the Imperial Self*, and James Davison Hunter's *Culture Wars* for examples that look to media as a site for a moral divide. Rhys H. Williams argues in his edited collection *Cultural Wars in American Politics* that academics and media producers have perhaps overly invested in the idea that cultural wars are a crisis because of their own role in the production and dissemination of ideas.

34 Rhys H. Williams, *Culture Wars in American Politics: Critical Reviews of a Popular Myth* (New York: Aldine De Gruyter, 1997), 5.

35 Henry Jenkins, "The Cultural Logic of Media Convergence," *International Journal of Cultural Studies* 7, no. 1 (2004): 5, doi:10.1177/1367877904040603.

36 Chip Berlet, "Who Is Mediating the Storm," in *Media, Culture, and the Religious Right*, ed. Linda Kintz and Julia Lesage (Minneapolis: University of Minnesota Press, 1998), 261.

37 Hendershot, op. cit., p. 11.

38 Robert Wuthnow, *After Heaven: Spirituality in America since the 1950s* (Berkeley: University of California Press, 1998), ii.

39 Anna Chan, "Sam Rader Admits He Had Ashley Madison Subscription: Christian Vlogger Says Wife Nia Has Forgiven Him," Us Weekly, August 22, 2015, accessed August 12, 2016, http://www.usmagazine.com/celebrity-news/news/sam-rader-adm its-he-had-ashley-madison-subscription-2015228.
40 See "Viral Pregnancy YouTuber Admits to Having Ashley Madison Account," You-Tube, https://www.youtube.com/watch?v=OVFmxDHsE_g.
41 Linda Kintz, *Between Jesus and the Market: The Emotions That Matter in Right-wing America* (Durham, NC: Duke University Press, 1997), 30.
42 Maria Coder, "Sam Rader Admits He Got Physical with Another Vlogger Before Being Thrown out of Convention – but Denies Making Threats," People.com, August 24, 2015, accessed August 12, 2016, http://www.people.com/article/sam-rader-christia n-vlogger-kicked-out-vlogger-fair-conference-violent-threats.
43 Kintz, op. cit., p. 30.
44 Richard L. Florida, *The Rise of the Creative Class, Revisited* (New York: Basic Books, 2012), xiv.
45 See Shannon Hayes' *Radical Homemakers*, Lynn Spigel's *Make Room for TV*, Elaine Tyler May's *Homeward Bound*, Leila J. Rupp and Verta Taylor's *Survival in the Doldrums*, and Eugenia Kaledin's *Mothers and More*.
46 Elizabeth Nathanson, "Dressed for Economic Distress: Blogging and the 'New' Pleasures of Fashion." *Gendering the Recession: Media and Culture in an Age of Austerity*, edited by Diane Negra and Yvonne Tasker (Durham: Duke University Press), 2014, pp. 136–160.
47 Ibid.
48 Tyler, op. cit., 22.
49 Nathanson, 137.
50 Emily Matchar, "Why I Can't Stop Reading Mormon Housewife Blogs," Salon, January 15, 2011, accessed August 12, 2016, http://www.salon.com/2011/01/15/feminist_ obsessed_with_mormon_blogs/.
51 Emily Matchar, "Why I Can't Stop Reading Mormon Housewife Blogs," Salon, January 15, 2011, Comments, accessed August 12, 2016, http://www.salon.com/2011/01/ 15/feminist_obsessed_with_mormon_blogs/.
52 Henry Jenkins, Sam Ford, and Joshua Green, *Spreadable Media: Creating Value and Meaning in a Networked Culture* (New York: New York University Press, 2013), 18.

Bibliography

Arrington, Leonard J., and Davis Bitton. *The Mormon Experience: a History of the Latter-Day Saints*. Champaign: University of Illinois Press, 1992.

Ballard, Russell M. "Using New Media to Support the Work of the Church." www.mormonnewsroom.org. December 15, 2007. Accessed August 12, 2016. http://www.morm onnewsroom.org/article/using-new-media-to-support-the-work-of-the-church.

Berlet, Chip. "Who Is Mediating the Storm." In *Media, Culture, and the Religious Right*, edited by Linda Kintz and Julia Lesage. Minneapolis: University of Minnesota Press, 1998.

Butler, Shay. "ARE THE SHAYTARDS CHRISTIAN?" YouTube. September 4, 2013. Accessed August 12, 2016. http://www.youtube.com/watch?v=fgwodehtWEI.

Chan, Anna. "Sam Rader Admits He Had Ashley Madison Subscription: Christian Vlogger Says Wife Nia Has Forgiven Him." *Us Weekly*. August 22, 2015. Accessed August 12, 2016. http://www.usmagazine.com/celebrity-news/news/sam-rader-admits-he-had-ashley-madison-subscription-2015228.

Coder, Maria. "Sam Rader Admits He Got Physical with Another Vlogger Before Being Thrown out of Convention – but Denies Making Threats." People.com. August 24,

2015. Accessed August 12, 2016. http://www.people.com/article/sam-rader-christian-vlogger-kicked-out-vlogger-fair-conference-violent-threats.

Dawkins, Nicole. "Do-It-Yourself: The Precarious Work and Postfeminist Politics of Handmaking (in) Detroit." *Utopian Studies* 22, no. 2(2011): 261–284. doi:10.5325/utopianstudies.22.2.0261.

Dean, Jodi. "Whatever Blogging." In *Digital Labor: The Internet as Playground and Factory*, edited by Trebor Scholz, 127–146. New York: Routledge, 2013.

Duffy, B. E., and E. Hund. "'Having It All' on Social Media: Entrepreneurial Femininity and Self-Branding Among Fashion Bloggers." *Social Media Society* 1, no. 2(2015). doi:10.1177/2056305115604337.

Dworkin, Ronald William. *The Rise of the Imperial Self: America's Culture Wars in Augustinian Perspective*. Lanham: Rowman & Littlefield Publishers, 1996.

Florida, Richard L. *The Rise of the Creative Class, Revisited*. New York: Basic Books, 2012.

Fuchs, Christian. "Labor in Informational Capitalism and on the Internet." *The Information Society* 26, no. 3(2010): 179–196. doi:10.1080/01972241003712215.

Gallagher, Sally K. "The Marginalization of Evangelical Feminism." *Sociology of Religion* 65, no. 3(2004): 215. doi:10.2307/3712250.

Gitlin, Todd. *The Twilight of Common Dreams: Why America Is Wracked by Culture Wars*. New York: Metropolitan Books, 1995.

Givens, Terryl. *By the Hand of Mormon: The American Scripture That Launched a New World Religion*. Oxford: Oxford University Press, 2002.

Gregg, Melissa. "The Normalisation of Flexible Female Labour in the Information Economy." *Feminist Media Studies* 8, no. 3(2008): 285–299. Accessed August 11, 2016. doi:10.1080/14680770802217311.

Hayes, Shannon. *Radical Homemakers: Reclaiming Domesticity from a Consumer Culture*. Richmondville, NY: Left to Write Press, 2010.

Hendershot, Heather. *Shaking the World for Jesus: Media and Conservative Evangelical Culture*. Chicago: University of Chicago Press, 2004.

Hunter, James Davison. *Culture Wars: the Struggle to Define America*. New York: BasicBooks, 2001.

Jakob, D. "Crafting Your Way out of the Recession? New Craft Entrepreneurs and the Global Economic Downturn." *Cambridge Journal of Regions, Economy and Society* 6, no. 1 (2012): 127–140. doi:10.1093/cjres/rss022.

Jenkins, Henry. "The Cultural Logic of Media Convergence." *International Journal of Cultural Studies* 7, no. 1(2004): 33–43. doi:10.1177/1367877904040603.

Jenkins, Henry, Sam Ford, and Joshua Green. *Spreadable Media: Creating Value and Meaning in a Networked Culture*. New York: New York University Press, 2013.

Jones, Allie. "A Guide to the Christian Vlog Community Where the Biggest Blessing Is a Baby." Gawker. August 14, 2015. Accessed August 12, 2016. http://gawker.com/a-guide-to-the-christian-vlog-community-where-the-bigge-1723334784.

Kaledin, Eugenia. *Mothers and More: American Women in the 1950s*. Boston: Twayne Publishers, 1984.

Kapralos, Krista. "Mormon Bloggernacle Is No Choir." Religion Dispatches. June 19, 2009. Accessed August 11, 2016. http://religiondispatches.org/mormon-bloggernacle-is-no-choir/.

Kimball, Spencer W. "President Kimball Speaks Out on Personal Journals." New Era, Dec.1980. Accessed August 12, 2016. https://www.lds.org/new-era/1980/12/president-kimball-speaks-out-on-personal-journals?lang=eng.

Kintz, Linda. *Between Jesus and the Market: The Emotions That Matter in Right-wing America*. Durham, NC: Duke University Press, 1997.

Luscomb, Belinda. "The YouTube Parents Who are Turning Family Moments into Big Bucks." *Time*, May 17, 2017, accessed August 11, 2017, http://time.com/4783215/gro wing-up-in-public/.

Matchar, Emily. "Why I Can't Stop Reading Mormon Housewife Blogs." Salon.com RSS. January 15, 2011. Accessed August 12, 2016. http://www.salon.com/2011/01/15/fem inist_obsessed_with_mormon_blogs/.

May, Elaine Tyler. *Homeward Bound: American Families in the Cold War Era*. New York: Basic Books, 1988.

Miller, Kelsey. "Even If Sam & Nia Did Fake It, What Does Our Reaction Say About Us?" *Refinery 29*, August 16, 2015. Accessed August 11, 2016. http://www.refinery29.com/ 2015/08/92311/sam-nia-pregnancy-miscarriage-hoax-bias.

Mosco, Vincent. *The Digital Sublime: Myth, Power, and Cyberspace*. Cambridge, MA: MIT Press, 2004.

Nathanson, Elizabeth. "Dressed for Economic Distress: Blogging and the 'New' Pleasures of Fashion." In *Gendering the Recession: Media and Culture in an Age of Austerity*, edited by Diane Negra and Yvonne Tasker, Durham, NC: Duke University Press, 2014, pp. 136–160.

Pope-Levison, Priscilla. "Separate Spheres and Complementarianism in American Christianity." In *Sex, Gender, and Christianity*, edited by John R. Levison. Eugene, OR: Cascade Books, 2012.

Rader, Sam, and Nia Rader. "Our Baby Had a Heartbeat!" Sam and Nia (video blog), December 31, 2015. Accessed August 11, 2016. https://www.youtube.com/watch?v= vTVui7Ff-68.

Rader, Sam, and Nia Rader. "RESPONDING TO HATE COMMENTS!" YouTube. August 14, 2015. Accessed August 12, 2016. http://www.youtube.com/watch?v=IF_DBFt5ax8.

Rader, Sam, and Nia Rader. "THE IMPORTANCE OF FAMILY VLOGS!" YouTube. August 15, 2015. Accessed August 12, 2016. https://www.youtube.com/watch?v=hqp PeBRmwjo.

Rader, Sam, and Nia Rader. "We're Going Viral!" Sam and Nia (video blog), August 6, 2015. https://www.youtube.com/watch?v=LiknIo5N2IU.

Rader, Sam. Twitter, August 9, 2015. Accessed May 1, 2016. www.twitter.com.

Ross, Andrew. "In Search of the Lost Paycheck," in *Digital Labor: The Internet as Playground and Factory*, ed. Trebor Scholz. New York: Routledge, 2013.

Roy, Adit, Hana Karar, Jasmine Brown and Lauren Effron. "Christian Vloggers Sam and Nia Rader Have No Regrets Posting Family Videos," ABC News, August 25, 2015, accessed August 12, 2016, http://abcnews.go.com/Lifestyle/christian-vloggers-sam-nia-ra der-regrets-posting-family/story?id=33291322.

Rupp, Leila J., and Verta Taylor. *Survival in the Doldrums*. Oxford: Oxford University Press, 1987.

Slutsky, Irena. "Meet YouTube's Most In-Demand Brand Stars." Advertising Age Digital RSS. September 13, 2010. Accessed August 12, 2016. http://adage.com/article/digital/m eet-youtube-s-demand-brand-stars/145844/.

Spigel, Lynn. *Make Room for TV: Television and the Family Ideal in Postwar America*. Chicago: University of Chicago Press, 1992.

Tyler, Imogen. "Pregnant Beauty: Maternal Femininities under Neoliberalism." In *New Femininities: Postfeminism, Neoliberalism, and Subjectivity*, edited by Rosalind Gill and Christina Scharff. Houndmills, Basingstoke, Hampshire: Palgrave Macmillan, 2011.

"Viral Pregnancy YouTuber Admits to Having Ashley Madison Account," YouTube, August 22, 2015, accessed August 12, 2016, https://www.youtube.com/watch?v=OVFm xDHsE_g.

Wilford, Justin G. *Sacred Subdivisions: The Postsuburban Transformation of American Evangelicalism.* New York: New York University Press, 2012.

Williams, Rhys H. *Culture Wars in American Politics: Critical Reviews of a Popular Myth.* New York: Aldine De Gruyter, 1997.

Wuthnow, Robert. *After Heaven: Spirituality in America since the 1950s.* Berkeley: University of California Press, 1998.

5

"THE RENOVATION STARTS NOW!"

Rite-of-passage reality television

Erica Hurwitz Andrus

"Move that bus!" The cathartic cry rises up from the crowd gathered at the peak moment of this hour of television, the moment that brings to a climax a week of work and a lifetime of struggle: the "reveal" – a new home unveiled, bringing the promise of hope and redemption to a deserving family. A journalist for the *Brattleboro Reformer* wrote that the volunteers and fans on the local episode chanted this cry "with cult-like force" (Orne, 2007). This moment marks the end of "before" and the beginning of "after," a moment that creates the pivot point essential to all "makeover" reality television shows and creates a starting point for understanding how one show, *Extreme Makeover: Home Edition* (EMHE), enacted week after week a powerful ritual of integration into American culture for participating families, host and crew, and audiences – a particularly neoliberal version of American culture, where salvation comes from corporations, and continues through the consumption of goods and services, including the consumption of ritual catharsis itself by millions of viewers in the comfort of their own homes.

Using the ideas and theories of scholars like Wendy Doniger and Bruce Lincoln on myth and Victor Turner and Catherine Bell on ritual, I explore the way that this long-running reality show (2003–2012) used the techniques of ritual to create a powerful myth through the medium of television. The repeated segments of the show in their strongly formulaic style demonstrate how rituals are structured to both reflect and create certain emotional moods and social roles by enacting narratives of suffering and redemption and by placing participants' bodies in particular relationship with each other and with spaces that are physically and symbolically constructed to reflect desired identities. The family and audience, shepherded by host Ty Pennington and his team, move through a process of telling their story, going on vacation, and returning to be re-introduced to the new living space, demonstrating an example of Victor Turner's theory of three-stage initiation. Each stage provides examples of how the show uses emotions, role inversions, and the performance of ordinary actions as extraordinary, to reinforce the idea that a successful family is the goal of a good American life, and that that success can be achieved through ownership of a perfectly tailored home, designed by experts. The Victorian era model of the home as the domain of an "angel of the hearth" has all but disappeared from this twenty-first century, neoliberal context, but EMHE retains the sense of home as refuge, or even sacred space, capable of shaping the family members' characters and fates. The inherited narrative that drove twentieth-century families from urban centers to suburban havens continues to provide the underlying assumption promoted in EMHE that a beautiful, spacious home creates the best possible space for a family to flourish.

Although any episodes will fit Turner's pattern, I chose three examples from season four (2006–2007) because they represent different family configurations and regions of the country, and because that season is in the middle of the show's run. The three families are the Gilliam family, a widow and her children whose father died after a reaction to mold in their home in Armada Township, Michigan; the Ripatti Pearce family who live in Redondo Beach, California in a house unsuitable for the mother, confined to a wheelchair after being shot while performing her job as a police officer; and finally the Collins family of Murfreesboro, Arkansas, which includes two parents and their teenaged son who sustained brain damage as a three-year-old due to cancer, and five of his cousins who lost their parents in an accident. Each of these families has suffered a blow to their identity and ability to maintain a stable family life in a healthy physical environment, so each of these families, like all the EMHE families, fit the profile of the "deserving poor" – a profile that creates a foundation for the mythic structure of each episode of the show.

The mythic narrative of the extreme home makeover

Each episode of EMHE ritually enacted a "myth," to use the term in the sense articulated by Wendy Doniger (1998). Doniger's concepts of the "micromyth" – the bare bones of a myth, articulated by a scholar in a way that would never be engaged by a storyteller or television show – and the "macromyth"– another purely theoretical construct consisting of all the extant variants of the myth – can be applied more concretely in this case than Doniger can apply them in her comparative studies. This micromyth is told over and over each week: a deserving, virtuous family faces hardship and challenges, reaches out for help to the network, the host, and his crew who assemble a local team of experts and laborers, and are spirited away on a dream vacation; a house is destroyed and a new one built; and the family is happily installed in their new life. The macromyth, unlike Doniger's unwieldy history of religious examples, can be precisely catalogued. Because the show ran for a limited time and produced a limited number of episodes, all of them can be collected into a canon and examined as evidence for answers to questions about values, identity, narrative, and ritual (Doniger, 1998, 92).

Just as Doniger sees repetition and reiteration as inherent in stories that are categorized as "myth," Bruce Lincoln describes the repeated telling of a story as essential to the process by which memories, narratives, and identities work together to become a shared mythology. He describes how "we can observe a moment of triadic co-definition: … in which a social group, a set of ritual performances, and a set of mythic narratives produce one another" (Lincoln, 1996, 166). Each episode of EMHE shows an example of this triad: the participants, hosts, and television audience are the social group; the ritual performances are: the family ritually recounts its story, the home is ritually destroyed and rebuilt, and the host re-introduces the family to the new home; and the mythic narrative is the storyline of the family's struggle and salvation through the intervention of the network and the community, a myth that almost perfectly supports the neoliberal worldview. In that neoliberal perspective, the way to create a better society is through corporations joining with communities to help individual people or families gain a financial footing that will allow them to become productive members of the economy.

As Lincoln points out, different people relate to the myth differently, depending on their relationship to the social group in question. In terms of EMHE, the family actively creates its own mythology up to the point that they are selected for participation in the show; the hosts add the particular family to a cumulative mythology by creating the narrative of the show; and the audience watches and shares in the emotional journey of both, participating via the internet and through emotional reactions with the construction of the narrative as reflecting "reality."

The first iteration of the family's narrative comes in the second scene of the show. After a brief introduction, the first commercial break, and the show's logo, the scene shows the interior of the tour bus, where host Ty Pennington stands in the back, and the members of the team sit along the sides of the bus where they can look back at him or forward to a television screen. He introduces the team, then might mention something about the family, then rolls the "audition tape." This speech, combined with footage of the family, establishes why they deserve the team's help. It singles them out – "separates" them, in Turner's terms – from all the other deserving families who sent their audition tapes to ABC. It also establishes their "bona fides" as worthy of help and recognition by the community. For example, the father in the Gilliam family was a firefighter, representing a heroic figure in their community. In the case of the Ripatti Pearce family, both parents are police officers, one of whom, while making an arrest, was shot and lost the use of her legs. The Collins family took in five orphaned children, and their son, Mitchell, devoted his time and energy to raising money for sick kids.

In addition, audiences and the team view the families' horrendous living conditions for the first time. In the Gilliam family's case, the house itself caused the tragedy of the father's death and was uninhabitable due to toxic mold. In the case of the Ripatti Pearce family the home was simply not equipped to accommodate a wheelchair, which made being the mother of a toddler extremely challenging and added to the emotional and psychological burden of recovering from a gunshot wound. For the Collins family, the house was physically deteriorating as well as not providing adequate space for six children and their parents.

Once the team arrives at the home, they are guided through it by the family, and the narrative of hardship and heroism is repeated, but in this iteration the cameras follow them, and Ty and the team also question the family members about their personal interests and dreams. The narrative has particular poignancy as the hosts and audience get to see the history narrated in its physical location, echoing the emotional experience of a pilgrimage. The hardships the family has faced are reflected in the worn and uncomfortable conditions of the building and grounds.[1] While members of the family are telling their stories to the team, they are demonstrating that they have agency, and that they have worked hard to create a good life in the face of adversity, but this is the last time in the show that the family will control the action. All of this introductory material creates the premise that the family is deserving, and that its living situation may be terrible or reprehensible, but it is not their fault.

A third opportunity to recite the family's history comes later, in the context of triumph over adversity, represented by the presence of a new, perfect home.

The ritualized enactment of the myth: affect and emotion

The term "reality" in "Reality Television" (RTV) creates another point of overlap between television narratives and ritual. Both media (if we can posit that ritual is a form of media) fall into the category of performances that profess to be "true" as contrasted with those that are understood to be "false" or fictional. The quality of scriptedness in both ritual and RTV episodes is downplayed by both participants and audience. Each privileges the authenticity of emotion and experience as a measure of the success of the performance. As Bell points out in her discussion of Geertz's analysis of a "failed ritual," one measure of failure is that the performance of the ritual did not create the expected or desired emotional outcomes for the community (Bell, 1992, 33). In her research on audience reception of makeover reality television shows, Katherine Sender found that "audiences saw emotional realness as central to the authenticity of the shows" (Sender, 2012, 115). In fact, the viewers she interviewed recognized that particular emotions were linked to particular parts of the narratives (e.g. the made-over person cries as he thanks the "guys" from *Queer Eye for the Straight Guy*) and that the expression of emotion indicates the success of the makeover to transform the person beyond looks or products. "Some (viewers) saw emotional release as a sign that the makeover had been a deeply affecting process, necessary to achieve anything but the most superficial changes to the outer self" (Sender, 2012, 116). In EMHE, each segment of the show portrays the team and the family expressing the emotions that are expected for that segment. For example, on the bus, as the team members watch the audition tape, some of them are shown openly weeping. Then, when they arrive at the home and awaken the family, the mood is exuberant, but that mood shifts as the family brings the team into their house and shows them all of its problems and recounts whatever tragedy or hardship has happened to them in their past.

Seeing the family and the hosts display the emotions of sadness and grieving elicits sympathetic emotions in the viewing audience, which we are invited to make public by a banner displayed at the beginning of the episode exhorting us to "Share your reactions while you watch" by logging on to "EnhancedTV at ABC. com." The audience can become participants in the show by sharing their experiences of emotions and opinions in an online community during the show's airing. This acknowledgement of the presence of an audience emphasizes again the nature of Reality TV as real, as somehow "live" and instrumental, in a way that scripted television did not at the time. In addition, viewers are encouraged to "participate" by buying the same items featured in the show, or at least shopping at the stores (a practice that overlapped with scripted shows such as soap operas).

Beverly Skeggs and Helen Wood (2012) argue that a study of reality television must pay attention to the shows' relationships to affect. An analysis of the show as ritual relies on this approach as well, with the assumption that a primary effect of ritual itself is to create venues in which affect is directed into particular emotions. As they define it, "affects are pre-linguistic bodily experiences that are produced through the social encounter: they only have the potential for emotion, they are … intensities and resonances produced through the social encounter" (Skeggs & Wood, 2012, 149). In EMHE the bodily experiences are perceived and coded as highly ritualized by audiences and hosts, and often by the participating families themselves as well. As Skeggs and Wood argue, the power of affect is harnessed by these shows to help create "a period of intimate intensity, not indifference, in which connection is incited and produced … through a capitalist drive towards intimacy as a new way of extracting value in the political economy of television (and its multi-platform extensions)" (144). This commercial motive contrasts with the motivations ascribed to ritual actions, although both RTV and ritual use affect to encourage these moments of emotional intensity. In turn, this emotional reaction – which itself can be understood as the "product" being consumed by viewers – can then create a connection to the items and services showcased in each episode, thus encouraging viewers to participate in the transformative process through buying the same products and services for themselves.

Producers make sure that affect directs emotion throughout each episode, guiding participants and viewers through a range of prescribed emotions. In the sixth season's application form, the network gives extensive guidelines for making a successful audition video. The introductions, in bold print, read:

The key is you want the folks at ABC to fall in love with your family and that means revealing all the layers. We want to see your bubbly fun personalities when you are saying hello and good-bye and giving us the tour. We want to see you speak from your heart even if it means being emotional when you tell us your story. We need to know what it is like for you and your family when times are tough and when the tough times make you strong.

In the section on "Interviews" the advice continues: "Sit down and talk to the camera like an interview and tell us your story. Explain your situation, why you think you deserve a makeover. During this portion you want to be emotional, open up and ask for help" (Extreme Makeover, 2008). The producers make explicit the fact that they need a family that can express the proper emotions when faced with situations that created the affect required for the transformational process of the show.

The beginning segments of the show create, in sequence, conditions for the participants and team, as well as viewers, to experience all the emotions that are expected from the show: sadness during the screening of the audition video (in both respects discussed by Skeggs and Wood (2012, 150–155): an emotional response as well as a judgment of a person's situation), hope and determination in the verbal and physical affirmation that the team can help, and elation when the bus reaches the house and Ty calls the family out to meet the team. This cycle is repeated in the next scenes as well: sadness and hope expressed during the tour of the home, and elation when Pennington, as the god-like figure descended from the heights of Hollywood after the family's arduous process of petitioning (via video auditions), reveals the destination of their vacation. Finally, the pattern recurs when the roles are reversed and the hosts lead the family on a walk-through of the new house. This repetition reinforces the ritual aspects of the show. The recursive tendency is part of the "sequencing rules" that shape ritual performances as well as the process that Lincoln claims turns an idiosyncratic story into a myth (cf. Tambiah, 1985, 139).

The ordinary made extraordinary and the authority of ritual specialists

Bell, in her description of "ritualization," describes how an everyday task is performed in a specialized way that marks it as not ordinary but extraordinary: "ritualization is a way of acting that specifically establishes a privileged contrast, differentiating itself as more important or powerful" (Bell, 1992, 90). Thus an action that is ordinary in one setting is created as powerful in another setting by the act of ritualization. In the case of EMHE, we can see this throughout each episode starting when families are "awoken" by Pennington with his signature bullhorn – where on a normal day a clock radio might wake a person in the privacy of their own home, on this day, a celebrity is present on their front lawn acting as an alarm clock! Next, the renovation of a house is normally something carried out as a transaction between the homeowner and a contractor but in this case the process is accompanied by the presence of an intercessor (the show) and by a television crew. The actual building of a new house in this specialized, ritual, case comes about through the work of a huge crowd of volunteers from the community, where normally a much smaller crew of professionals would be paid to do the work. In the ordinary course of renovations most homeowners must endure a period of living in a disrupted environment as their home is repaired around them. In this case, the homeowners are treated to an expenses-paid vacation and avoid the inconveniences of renovation altogether. Even more, the vacation removes the family from the process of oversight and decision making, creating the unusual situation where a house is renovated without the direction of the people who own or live in the home.

These differences mark the events as different and ritualized, and also serve to reinforce a particular power relationship between the host/network and the family, a relationship that assumes a neoliberal ideal of private corporations helping individual families boot-strap themselves into the middle class. By removing them from the premises and supplying them with the perfect vacation, the family is constructed as passive recipients of the show's largesse. In Bell's terms, the host, exerting control over the "text" or narrative gains an authority that allows him to interpret the emotions, experiences, and needs of the family (Bell, 1992, 130–131). In the scene on the bus, for example, a scene repeated on every episode as ritual, it becomes clear that the spatial arrangement on the bus reinforces a particular power dynamic establishing the host as leader and controller of events. Pennington's physical position, at the back and standing, lends him a kind of authority as he is physically above the group, in addition to which he is portrayed as having both privileged knowledge, being the only one to have viewed the tape previously, and power, as he controls the remote.

The vacation gives the family a special status as winners – in many contests on television or otherwise the family vacation *is* the grand prize, after all – but it also serves to separate them ritually from the rest of the community during the house construction. The nature of the separation as a vacation serves to invert the status of the team and the family. The family, by definition because they live in a substandard home, occupies a place of low economic and social status. For example, the Collins and Gilliam families own homes that are either falling apart or toxic and do not have the financial resources to address the problems. Christina Ripatti has had a dramatic change of social status due to her sudden transformation from "able bodied" to a person who relies on a wheelchair for mobility and the help of others to negotiate everyday life, and who cannot work at her chosen profession or be the kind of mother she wishes to be, both strong markers of worth in American society.[2]

Pennington and the team, due to their status as television personalities, occupy a much higher social and economic rank than the family. However, during the vacation/construction phase of the process, the family is treated "as royalty" – given the opportunity to engage in the luxury of "doing nothing" as all the expenses for the trip are covered (often with a trip to Disneyworld, a resort owned by the same parent company as ABC, thus saving the show the costs of the trip) and all the logistics are taken care of, leaving them free to live as most Americans imagine the very wealthy live every day. The team, meanwhile, nominally assumes the low status of manual laborers, putting in extremely long hours using power tools and offering hands-on help with the construction of the new home, even if this "low status" job position is an acknowledged fiction. (The fact is that no matter how sweaty they are or how much they get paint on their coveralls, the team always has perfect hair and make-up, and in the case of the women, may even be sporting heels as they use their power tools! Pennington, however, has made a signature of his unruly and rumpled hair, so that serves again as a way to place him above the helpers on the team.) Inversions like this are characteristic of Turner's descriptions of the liminal part of rituals, and in particular initiation rituals.[3]

During the time the family is on vacation, members of the community, especially in the building industries but also in the professions of the family members if that is appropriate, come together as volunteers to complete the construction of the house in 106 hours. The process of building the house is shown intercut with scenes from the family's vacation in the case of the Ripatti Pearce family, and with scenes of special projects the individual team members take on in the other two families' episodes. In the Collins family episode, the crew collected pop tops and turned them in for money, which they used to buy toys for kids with cancer. The episode features Ty's trip to the hospital to give the toys away, a scene that is also shown to the family as they are on vacation. This activity, in which Pennington takes over the son, Mitchell's, work and performs it himself, including meeting the children in the hospital – a part of the process that has not been available to Mitchell himself – illustrates how the family is set apart and subordinated to the team and to Pennington. As Turner (1969) describes, during the liminal phase the initiates are often prohibited from speaking, or when they do speak are limited to a formal script. While this is not literally true for the EMHE families, it is true in effect. They receive video messages from Ty, showing and telling them of the progress in destroying their old homes, but they cannot speak back to Pennington with any response or with any directions for him to follow concerning how they would like their new home to look or function, effectively silencing them in the process of renovation.

In terms of affect, this segment of the show takes part in an "over the top" aesthetic, with the team shown reveling in the tearing down aspect, and exultant about the machines used to do it. The Ripatti Pearce home, for example, gave the producers a chance to use the couple's occupations to create a themed destruction segment. The LAPD SWAT team used explosives to blow off the front door, then ran into the home to "secure" it, and the entire following segment from one commercial break to the next is devoted to footage of the SWAT team using sledgehammers and other tools to demolish the interior, an armored vehicle with a battering ram to take out the exterior walls, and an excavator starting to take off the roof. In the bathroom, Pennington, who films the process on a handheld video camera that he frequently trains on himself, commiserates with Christina about how the bathroom has given her a lot of trouble. Well, he says, "don't worry about it because look at it now, now it's really got problems" as he videotapes the toilet after it has been smashed to pieces. This personification of the bathroom as an enemy receiving its just deserts supports a neoliberal program in that it directs the family's and audiences' feelings or affect of anger inspired by the suffering and injustice of Officer Ripatti's injury and subsequent substandard housing onto the house itself, which can be corrected through the project of buying a new one (or in this case being given a new one by a generous corporation), rather than looking for ways to change the conditions that caused the injury in the first place or looking to the government for assistance in rectifying the problem. The role of the state is erased from the story, as is the rest of the local community, aside from volunteers and corporations that donate time and money. The focus of EMHE is on healing and transforming an individual family, not the community itself (Palmer, 2007, 171). The path to this healing lies through the catharsis of demolition.

The show's production practices reinforce the relative statuses of host/team and the family, at the same time as they collapse time in a way that reflects the "play" with time that scholars like Eliade (1963) attribute to ritual. EMHE uses the standard RTV practice of editing each episode to switch from the "live action" shots of the family, hosts, volunteers, and the home itself, to the confessional one-on-one setting of an interview, in which the participant speaks to an invisible interlocutor. This narrative technique mimics standard documentary practice, where footage moves from documenting "in the field" to the "talking head" commentary of an expert. By adopting this cinematic convention from anthropological documentaries or television news reports, RTV not only reinforces the "reality" aspect of the show, but applies the authority given to the "experts" to its own hosts, in this case Pennington and his team. The members of the family are also given time to voice their reactions at the end of the show, thus demonstrating that they have moved into a position of higher authority as a result of the transformative experiences given to them by the show.

The new home shapes the new life

When the house has been completed the family returns (in a limo, usually, as they left – again a mark of the extraordinary nature of this process in comparison to the usual means of getting to the airport) and the entire crew of volunteers and staff is assembled to participate in the reveal. Pennington greets the family, reiterates how much they have struggled and suffered in their old house, and assures them that all of that is over. After this moment of reconnecting and rehearsing the narrative, he asks if they are ready and invites them to chant the mantra with him: Move that bus! Usually the crowd of volunteers has already taken up the cry, but it is the combined voices of Pennington and the family that prove instrumental in the ritual: only their voices have the actual power to make the bus move.

The reactions to the reveal vary from family to family of course, but usually they include tears, shouts of disbelief and joy, and frequently gasps of "Oh my God!" This part of the episode and of the process begins the final stage of the ritual. Once the house is revealed, the family is then led from room to room and shown how their new home both reflects their individual personalities, hopes, and passions, and how it is especially built to address whatever particular problems they faced in their old home. This process of leading them through the home gives the family its first chance to engage physically with the home and learn how the home is meant to shape their lives in spatial and physical ways. For example, the Ripatti Pearce home clearly illustrates this effect during the walkthrough of the house when Pennington and Christina are in her daughter's bedroom with Paul DiMeo, one of the designers on the team. DiMeo explains how a sling can help Christina move throughout the house and be down on the floor playing with her daughter, not needing the wheelchair or someone else's help. The show cuts to a shot of DiMeo as a "talking head" where he states: "one of the things I really wanted to achieve this week was bringing mother and daughter closer together. With the lift, with the crib, we're gonna see that relationship, nurture itself into a great mother-daughter relationship." This commentary implies that it is the physical environment that can create this kind of good mothering. And, the implication follows, without it the relationship was at risk of failure.

Objects in the house frequently become central to the team's expression of caring for the family, and this attention on the part of the team elevates the symbolic importance of those particular objects. An object from the family's life before the destruction of the home is preserved and transformed and then replaced in the new home to form a symbolic bridge to the past. This process means that the team cannot be accused of trying to "erase" the past, but in fact they seek to enshrine part of the past as a symbolic kernel of a more hopeful, and successful, future. For the Gilliams, for example, two items form the focus of a memorial reverence on the part of both the family and Pennington and his team. First, the daughter of the firefighter, David, created a garden featuring sunflowers in the backyard, which Pennington promises to preserve and to improve (although it is unclear if that promise is made to the daughter, or only to the audience). The second object is a bouquet of roses that David had given Maryann on their thirteenth wedding anniversary, and which she kept, dried, in their bedroom, the place where her husband passed away. In the scene where she guides Pennington through the house, just after she explains the roses to him, he sees a kind of shrine of photos and says that he "just realized, this is where he died." He says he is sorry and hugs Maryann, who is weeping openly. Then he tells the audience that it was hard being in the room where David had delivered the couple's baby and died less than a month later. In the new home, the roses are preserved, encased in glass and set on a mantel. Maryann's reaction to seeing them in the new bedroom evokes her husband's memory both in the bedroom and in the public spaces of the house, and she repeats that "he would be so proud." In her segment, speaking to the camera, she says "I just attribute that everything that was in David's heart was just put in there. I know as clear as day that that dream was this house. And looking at this house is, ah, part of my husband. It's beautiful" (Extreme Makeover, 2006, "Gilliam Family"). The connection between David and the house has been transformed from a negative one (he died in and because of the house) to a positive one: the house as shrine to his memory and an expression of his dreams and pride in his family. Likewise, one reaction shown by the Collins family is that the deceased parents of the five younger children, and especially their mother, would have loved the house, and are in some way present. Mrs. Collins says "I look around and I see, I see them in here too" (Extreme Makeover, 2007).

The same shrine-like reverence for the past is evident in the Ripatti Pearce makeover. After Christina has put her daughter to bed, and explored the new master bedroom with her husband, they move into the bathroom that has been custom made to accommodate her wheelchair. Pennington comes in while they are admiring the shower and its accessibility, and asks them to "take a look at these pictures … I wanted you to see that one picture because I know that would mean a lot to you because that was the day that you ran the marathon in the morning." Then her husband tells how they were running to support other officers who had been injured, and then "eight hours later, bam, it hit Christina." And she states that it is the last photo of her standing, something she may never do again. During the interview she says, "It's probably one of the most important pictures that we have in the house, for me" (Extreme Makeover, 2006, "Ripatti-Pearce Family"). In the scene in the bathroom, she is speechless and crying, and her husband tells Pennington it is good that the picture is there. Pennington explains that he chose to put it there because he knows it will motivate her to keep going, and ultimately to try to walk again. Using these objects from the families' pasts creates a powerful affective environment, encouraging the families to express emotions like grief, love, and hope. This ties their very first moments in the new house indelibly to those emotions and memories. The audience, too, sees and responds to these emotions, confirming the transformative power of the narrative.

This final segment of the show allows the participants to tell and interpret their narrative of struggle and hope one last time. In the Collins family episode, for example, Tanya McQueen, one of the members of Pennington's team, explains, "It's going to be so much easier for them in this new house. It's a dream for them, and it reminds them that people are good, and that every tragedy can actually have a happy ending" (Extreme Makevoer, 2007). Putting it that way makes it clear that the ritual has performed its function of transforming the family, which formerly could not achieve its full potential, into a new, more integrated, identity, ready to focus on its role as a contributing member of the community, as defined and celebrated by a neoliberal ideal. Just as Christina Ripatti is told that she can now focus on being a mom, and therefore embody a more valued identity than that of a "disabled" person, each family is given the ritual tools to re-envision itself as able to enact better a valued role or position going forward, with the help of a house, provided for them by a beneficent corporation and the unpaid labor of their generous neighbors, tailored to their self-identity and their special requirements, and filled with the good material items and tools that they need in order to succeed.

Conclusion

There are many possible approaches to analyzing this makeover reality television show, including other analyses that, like this one, include ritual, morality, ethics, and other religious concerns. EMHE presents strong symbolic images of gender, race, and family that I have not had space to explore in this chapter. For example, the presence of a SWAT team using militarized police equipment to "save" a family from its unsatisfactory home creates a very different image in today's media landscape of police attacks on African American people of all ages and genders and neo-Nazi marches in university towns like Charlottesville, Virginia, and even in 2006 it would have looked very different if the family in question had not been White. The use of state forces to reinforce institutionalized racism at the service of American capitalism forms a part of the neoliberal agenda that cannot presently be ignored, but was not prevalent in the daily news reports of 2006. For another example, one could also explore the way the show depicts what a "family" in America is, and see that in this context, although heterosexuality is the exclusive norm, all kinds of other relationships are accepted as fitting the definition of family: adoptive or foster relationships, grandparents, single parents, cousins, aunts, uncles, all are accepted as equally worth of the title "family" (Edwards, 2010). These topics can also be understood in the context of the initiatory nature of the structure of this show and other makeover shows like it, in which participants are separated from their old identities by experts and fitted with a new one.

In my analysis I have focused on how the weekly repetition in EMHE of the same story with different details represents a modern, televised form of American ritualization. It accomplishes important tasks of forming identity for the participants – both families and hosts – and presenting those identities to a broad general audience, thereby reinforcing the values implied or inherent in these rituals. These values exemplify the neoliberal ethos that society should rely on the market and private or corporate philanthropy to support people who have fallen through the cracks – especially those who have demonstrated their worthiness through their own service to others – and that material goods reflect and shape the morality of a family.

In the years leading up to the recession of 2008 the home owning and building industry boomed and, in the case of this television show, became the vehicle for expressing true belonging, the American Dream, and a way to successfully participate in America as a family. The show's justification of its participating families' worthiness implied that those who fell on hard times in America deserved a helping hand, but in order to truly regain their footing, their physical world needed an "extreme" process of destruction and renewal. Even if the producers, writers, directors, and host of the show had no conscious sense of it, they drew on the patterns of ritual practices as described by anthropologists to create and enact a narrative of initiation. The unique capabilities of mass media – in this case television combined with the internet – allowed this process of transition to be witnessed and vicariously experienced by millions of viewers on a weekly basis. By borrowing theories of anthropologists and applying them to media phenomena like *Extreme Makeover: Home Edition*, we can better analyze the emotional, symbolic, and perhaps even transformative power that reality television engages in our contemporary American society, and see why it is impossible to dismiss these shows as "just junk television."

Notes

1 For a full discussion of this aspect of the show see Askew (2011). However, Askew misses or ignores the idea that the "deserving" quality of the family is attributed not to the problems or disabilities they face, but to their status as "heroes" because of their profession (police, firefighters, military) or their own charitable involvement in the community, often including bringing awareness of their particular disease but often through direct actions that support those in need. Examples include rescuing animals, an art therapy program for kids with special needs, and many, many others.

2 The question of "Americanness" as discussed by Weber (2009, 46–48) can be applied easily to EMHE, especially in its featuring of homes in all 50 states, and depiction of the families as "ordinary Americans." Instead of contestants being brought to Hollywood, Hollywood comes to the families in the glamorous persons of Ty Pennington and his crew.

3 For a more class-based interpretation of this aspect of the show see Palmer's (2007, 168) analysis in which the team as "petit bourgeoisie" learn about "real people," and the "working class" learn "taste" – that is, how to have a beautiful house full of beautiful things to improve their lives.

References

Askew, Emily. "(Re)Creating a World in Seven Days: Place, Disability, and Salvation in Extreme Makeover: Home Edition." *Disability Studies Quarterly* 31:2(2011). http://dsq-sds.org/article/view/1590/1558.

Bell, Catherine. *Ritual Theory, Ritual Practice.* New York: Oxford University Press, 1992.

Doniger, Wendy. *The Implied Spider: Politics and Theology in Myth.* American Lectures on the History of Religions 16. New York: Columbia University Press, 1998.

Edwards, Leigh. "Reality TV and the American Family." In *The Tube Has Spoken: Reality TV and History*, edited by J.A. Taddeo and K. Dvorak, 123–144. Lexington: University Press of Kentucky, 2010.

Eliade, Mircea. *Myth and Reality.* W. Trask, translator. New York: Harper & Row, 1963.

Extreme Makeover. "Extreme Makeover: Home Edition Season 6 Family Application." ABC.com [PDF] 2008. http://a.abc.com/media/primetime/xtremehome/apply/2008_APPLICATION.pdf?v1

Extreme Makeover. Extreme Makeover: Home Edition. "The Collins Family." Directed by Jack Cannon. ABC, April 29, 2007.

Extreme Makeover. Extreme Makeover: Home Edition. "The Gilliam Family." Directed by Jack Cannon. ABC, October 1, 2006.

Extreme Makeover. Extreme Makeover: Home Edition. "The Ripatti Pearce Family." Directed by Jack Cannon. ABC, December 10, 2006.

Lincoln, Bruce. "Mythic Narrative and Cultural Diversity in American Society". In *Myth and Method*, edited by Laurie Patton and Wendy Doniger, 163–176. Charlottesville: University of Virginia Press, 1996.

Orne, Nicole. "Family Gets Dream House." *Brattleboro Reformer.* September 13, 2007. Reposted on "ABC: Extreme Makeover Home Edition." Phyl T. Macomber, T.H.E.P. A.C.T. website. Retrieved from http://aboutthepact.com/about-the-author/abc-extreme-makeover/

Palmer, Gareth. "Extreme Makeover: Home Edition: An American Fairytale." In *Makeover Television: Realities Remodeled*, edited by Dana Heller, 165–176. New York: I.B. Tauris, 2007.

Sender, Katherine. *The Makeover: Reality Television and Reflexive Audiences.* New York: New York University Press, 2012.

Skeggs, Beverly, & Wood, Helen. *Reacting to Reality Television: Performance, Audience, and Value*. New York: Routledge, 2012.

Tambiah, Stanley Jeyaraja. *Culture, Thought, and Social Action: An Anthropological Perspective*. Cambridge, Mass.: Harvard University Press, 1985.

Turner, Victor. *The Ritual Process: Structure and Anti-Structure*. Chicago: University of Chicago Press, 1969.

Weber, Brenda R. *Makeover TV: Selfhood, Citizenship, and Celebrity*. Durham: Duke University Press, 2009.

6

WHEN THE MOST POPULAR FORMAT REACHES THE MOST ATYPICAL COUNTRY

Reality TV and religion in Israel

Yoel Cohen and Amir Hetsroni

This chapter looks at the ways in which Judaism finds expression in reality shows in Israel. Three aspects are examined: reaction to the programs from religious leaders and religious communities; participation of religious people in the shows; and the appearance of religion-related topics in the programs.

Reality shows predominate the ratings chart in Israel, where nine of the ten most highly watched programs in 2014 were of this genre (Eurodata TV, 2016). The typical stance of Orthodox Judaism – the dominant Jewish religious stream in Israel – rejects the reality genre as a contemporary backdrop to the days of Sodom and Gomorrah (Engelman, 2009). Thus, the existence of religious motifs in Israeli reality programming is not taken for granted. However, a "marriage of convenience" has gradually evolved – an arrangement in which religious people are even willing to take part in the reality extravaganza – reflecting both the genre's predominance in popular culture in the third millennium and the growing presence of Jewish religion in popular programming in Israel (Dardashti, 2015). Furthermore, religious people – whether as viewers or program participants – do not seem bothered by greed and the search for wealth, and the qualifications which moral codes like Judaism may have about it.

Israeli television and religion

When it comes to the connection between religion and popular TV fare, Israel is not dissimilar from other Western states. It developed over the years into a modern Western state without neglecting its religious roots. While Israel is a democracy, it still strongly favors one religion: Judaism. The accommodation of religion finds expression in the country's legal system, including regulations that dictate the *modus operandi* of commercial TV channels. Stations are free to broadcast programming that caters to popular taste, but they are still required to devote a portion of air-time to religion. The outcome is often a hybrid wherein scandalous scenes – which in typical reality productions would be devoid of religion or dogma – are, in fact, clothed in an ideological frame. That religious Jews are easily recognized by their dress code (yarmulke for men; modest attire for women) and lifestyle (e.g. not smoking on Sabbath) makes their images even more visually salient.

The general attitudes held by the main religious Jewish communities in Israel toward television are a clue to their perceptions of reality television. The two main religious Jewish communities in Israel are *modern orthodox*, or national religious *("dati leumi")*, who account for 20 percent of the Israeli Jewish population, and the *ultra-orthodox* Haredim who account for nearly 10 percent (Central Bureau of Statistics, 2009).

Historically, the Haredim in Israel rejected television because as an entertainment platform it reflects promiscuous values – associated with love and sexuality outside of marriage – which are anathema to Judaism, and therefore inappropriate in the Jewish home, which draws on Torah for a framework. Over the centuries, Haredim have erected a cultural ghetto to ensure that secular media do not endanger the religiosity of the Jewish home. For example, when television was first introduced in Israel in 1968, Haredi leaders not only banned it but also carried out inspections of Haredi neighborhoods in an effort to locate TV antennae on roofs. Punitory measures included not accepting the family's children to a Haredi boys school or "Talmud Torah," or girls' high school or "seminar," or the endangering of a *"shidduch,"* an arranged marriage. Today, given that much content online is of a visual nature like YouTube, there are clues indicating that televised entertainment is not rejected by all Haredim in principle. Over the last fifteen years, a Haredi film industry has evolved with the production of films either with male actors or female actors – only for screening before male or female audiences respectively – comprising Torah-based, moral messages. These films are often shown during religious holidays (Vinig, 2011).

Unlike the Haredim, the modern orthodox community do not see an inherent conflict between Jewish religious identity and television. It reflects their desire to become full partners in the modern Zionist state. Rather than censorship *carte blanche*, this community believes in media literacy, with the individual modern orthodox Jew regarded as self-disciplined in matters concerning media exposure. Yet in practice, modern orthodox Jews also have their own qualifications regarding the portrayal of love and sexuality on screen. Reflecting its determination to overcome these obstacles, this community established in 1989 the Maale School of Film to train religious people in film production, partly in an effort to impose its imprint on the Israeli film fabric (Jacobson, 2004).

Earlier, when television began broadcasting in Israel in 1968, the National Religious Party campaigned unsuccessfully against broadcasting on the Sabbath, given that the use of electricity is regarded by Jewish religious law as "work" on the Sabbath day of rest. Later, in 2001, with the arrival of cable television in Israel, the religious political parties – both the National Religious Party and Haredi parties – passed a law in the Israel Parliament, the Knesset, banning cable and satellite channels from broadcasting sex channels. A court appeal by the franchise owners of the Playboy channel put an end to the ban. Over the years, religious politicians have made several attempts to restrict mainstream broadcast channels from airing shows that include sexual content (including episodes of *Survivor*), or to move the program's slot to a later hour so that younger viewers would not see it (as in the case of *Big Brother*), but these efforts were never successful because of the objections of the Israel Supreme Court and public television regulatory bodies.

Reality TV in Israel

The arrival of reality TV in Israel – like the arrival of TV broadcasting itself – was belated. The genre took off slowly. The first reality show to be broadcast in Israel, *The Mole*, lasted for only one season (2001) on Channel 2 and was considered a commercial flop, which put on hold the production of additional reality shows by three years. The next program, *Choose me, Sharon*, a local non-franchised version of *The Bachelorette*, was aired on Channel 2 in late 2004 and gained high ratings. While the show was not renewed – partly due to the fact that the American franchise owners threatened to sue the production company for copyright violation – its success indicated that international reality formats can succeed in Israel, as proven by the success of *Survivor* (aired between 2007 and 2016 on Channel 10 and since 2017 on Channel 2), *Running for a Million* (a local version of *The Amazing Race* that has been aired since 2009 on Channel 2), and finally *Big Brother* (aired since 2008 on Channel 2). Although Israel has become a capital of dramatic formats and game shows, local inventions of reality formats have been less successful in terms of ratings (Shahaf, 2014).

The Israeli public remained mostly indifferent to reality TV until the broadcasting of a local version of Israel's *Next Top Model* in 2006, which required contestants to take part in photo shots while scantily clad. This fact, together with the emphasis put on lean physiques as a key to success on the runway, triggered hundreds of complaints submitted to the network's ombudsman, newspaper op-eds, and even a parliamentary debate in the Knesset. On the one hand, some voices demanded censorship and even cancellation of the show because of its supposedly pro-anorectic message. On the other hand, producers insisted that the potential damage was too limited to justify any censorship. The discourse was generally concerned with the invasion of privacy, the lack of authenticity and stereotypical representations, and ignored questions of faith (Hetsroni, 2010). No academic research on religious dimensions of reality television in Israel has been published heretofore (see Cohen, 2012 for a summary of past research on media and religion in Israel). This chapter is intended to fill the void.

Religious leaders, religious communities, and reality TV

Rabbis have grave qualifications about reality programs because much of the content appears to infringe upon Jewish religious norms. Given the Haredi rabbinical ban on television per se, most of the discussion and reaction has come from rabbis in the modern orthodox sector. Surprisingly, there has been negligible discussion about reality TV among rabbis from non-orthodox religious streams like Reform Judaism and Conservative Judaism because, no less than their orthodox colleagues, the latter seek to embellish Jewish life in particular, and the public sphere in general, with a moral framework drawing upon Torah ethics.

Rabbinical criticism of reality TV shows relates predominantly to the fact that the genre reflects such values as competition, dishonesty, trickery, achievements drawn from physical strength, sexual prowess, and the sexploitation of women. Different branches of Judaism discuss at length the portrayal of sex and physical immodesty. The Israelite camp in the Wilderness in "which God walked shall be holy … that God should not see anything unseemly and turn Himself away from you" (Deuteronomy 23:15) is an allusion to nudity as impious. Moreover, the unseemliness results in the withdrawal of the Divine Presence (*shekhinah*). Although various branches of Judaism interpret sexual modesty differently, the general stance among Jewish religious streams is negative. Judaism forbids a man to look on a female immodestly attired; in the ultra-Orthodox community, this includes the uncovered hair of a married woman. Similarly, a man is forbidden to listen to a woman singer, lest he be sexually aroused; some in the modern Orthodox community permit listening to a female voice in particular if the song is prerecorded.

These restrictions raise profound artistic questions as to how intimate relations, which are the cornerstone of many reality shows, can be portrayed and expressed in a religiously acceptable manner. For instance, *The Bachelor* – one of the most globally copied reality formats – is essentially a show about "swinging," and is composed of mostly intimate scenes. It is difficult to envisage how religious women may be participants without compromising their religious standards. Indeed, during the program's second season, one woman who defined herself as "moderately religious" left the show after two episodes because she felt that she could no longer take part in what she called "the orgy."

Tzeniut, or modesty, is another Jewish value which Orthodoxy interprets as requiring a modest dress code, including long skirts and sleeves (for all women), head coverage (for married women), and limited exposure of the skin. Orthodox Jewish thinkers in particular suggest that by distancing oneself from illegitimate sensuality, one achieves personal sanctity. The human body in Jewish terms, argues Lamm (1997), is not an object of beauty, as it was in Greek culture, but rather a sacred object which, if anything, should be hidden from public exposure. *Tzeniut* has to do with honor, self-respect, or an awareness of one's self-worth. Just as the dignity of God is His very concealment, the dignity of the human individual – created in God's image – is in his obscurity. Obscurity, however, is not just in physical terms but in every sense, including a person's talent and wealth. Clearly, such values run contrary to the bragging and uninhibited behavior of reality TV show contestants like those on *Survivor* (Wilson, Robinson & Callister, 2012). Another contradiction between the demands of reality TV production and Orthodox Judaism that drew attention in Israel happened during the first season of

Models in 2006. A female contestant refused to participate in an implied nude photo session because it went against her convictions. She was given an "incomplete" grade on the assignment, but the judges decided not to disqualify her because "we are judging models for their abilities and for their faith." Media discussion after the incident justified the contestant's behavior (Hetsroni, 2010).

From a wide Judaic standpoint, another concern is about the need to divulge information about oneself. Religious Jews consider the need to disclose personal information on reality shows a major lacuna (Weimann, Cohen & Hirschmann-Shitreet, 2007). To understand why, reference may be made to Biblical sources. Leviticus 19:16 – in warning against not being "a talebearer among your people, or standing idly by the blood of your neighbour" – imposes substantial limits on the passage of information. Judaism looks negatively upon information about an individual being accessed by the public at large. The *Hofetz Hayim* (Ha-Cohen, 1873), an influential religious tome about the Jewish laws of speech, authored by Israel Meir Cohen, a prominent Haredi rabbinical figure in nineteenth-century Europe, went as far as to interpret this, and related Biblical verses, in ways which limit interpersonal conversation. He divided types of information communicated in interpersonal communication into a number of categories. Most severe is the divulging of secret information to the wider public that is intended or has the effect of damaging someone's reputation (*lashon hara*). Also forbidden, but with lesser severity, is the disclosure of even positive information about somebody (*rehilut*). Undoubtedly, a significant share of the dialogue in reality TV shows transgresses against the religious prohibitions of *lashon hara* and *rehilut*. A religious couple who took part in the second season of *The Amazing Race* commented in one of the episodes: "We close our ears when we stand next to other couples not because we do not like to hear what they say about us, but because God does not allow us to hear that."

Reality TV may take some comfort in the fact that if a participant willingly exposes information about himself or herself there is no transgression of religious law. This is rather like what some modern Jewish scholars argue: that a candidate for office in a democratic society understands his record will be exposed for public scrutiny, such as by the media, in an effort to enable citizens to reach a decision regarding his or her suitability for public office (Falk, 1999). One rabbi, Azriel Ariel (2001), articulated it as "*lashon hara* by consensus." Yet if a participant in a reality show divulges information about somebody else without his or her permission, it is tantamount to infringing the laws prohibiting *lashon hara*. Obviously, this often happens in reality shows.

Many of the criticisms raised by rabbinical critics of reality TV – modesty, privacy, speaking the truth, and the quality of speech – are interrelated. According to a liberal orthodox group of Israeli rabbis, Bet Hillel (2013), modesty (*tzeniut*) is a central value in Judaism whether in terms of physical clothing, or an individual's behavior and external characteristics. The Jewish objective in modesty is to locate an individual's inner character and develop it. Reality TV, by contrast, seeks to neutralize any value associated with either modesty or privacy, but instead advances self-publicity and even the humiliation of the individual. As one rabbi, Lior Engelman (2009), remarked: "A key difference between man and animal is in man's ability to be modest and conceal himself. Animals, by contrast, go naked as if on the day they were born but man from the day he ate from the tree of life, is covered in garments." Reality TV, therefore, illustrates the link in Judaism between the twin values of modesty and privacy. A separate yet related third value is the nature of speech. Judaism emphasizes the importance of using clean speech as well as avoiding slanderous speech. Some reality TV programs, by contrast – *Big Brother*, most notably – encourage a low level of speech, including cursing at fellow competitors. A fourth related value is speaking the truth. A confession draws upon truth; it plays a central role in a civilized society. While reality shows often emphasize authenticity and truth, their version of "truth" reduces it to technical facts and a source of humor (Hetsroni, 2010).

While most rabbis reject reality TV in its entirety, some do regard selective reality programs as legitimate sources of entertainment. One example was a contest series in 2016 with the goal of choosing a *"payten"* or synagogue cantor, broadcast on Channel 20, a new channel which seeks to incorporate programming with traditional Jewish values.

The questions which rabbis address about reality TV are not only whether religious Jews are permitted to watch the shows but also whether they are allowed to take part in them. Most orthodox rabbis forbid participation in reality shows because their content negates Torah values. "Participation in reality programs is regarded as a transgression because it contradicts the laws of modesty and the traditional values of a Jew's conduct," remarked Rabbi Shlomo Aviner (2015), who is identified with the "stricter" *hardal (haredi leumi)* sub-stream of modern-orthodoxy. Even the Bet Hillel group of liberal orthodox-inclined rabbis issued a Jewish law ruling in 2013 prohibiting participation in the programs "because the messages, and the principles on which the format is based, do not accord with Jewish values ... and by participating a participant in effect contributes to the competition's ratings." Another rabbi, Haggai London (cited in Goodman, 2016) opined that "the question of participation is in fact a more basic question: What is Judaism – a religion or a belief? While the former is merely a collection of practical laws to be adhered to, in the latter Judaism is a way of life, in which an inner world of a person – comprising feelings, thought and values – is opened." Even Rotzon Arusi (cited in Krasner, 2016), a respected liberal enlightened rabbinical figure in the modern-orthodox sector, said that "participation in reality TV is worse than living on safari or in a zoo. Though man is made in God's image, these people close themselves off for long periods, cut off from the outside world. They are photographed for all to see. I am surprised by how many people allow themselves to play cynically with their freedom – all for the sake of money." Arusi recommended avoiding watching the programs altogether. In practice, religious Jews watch reality programs less often than they watch the news (in contrast with secular Israelis), but even among religious viewers the more successful reality shows cross the 20 percent rating threshold (compared to 30 percent among secular viewers) (Eurodata TV, 2016).

The religious ban on watching reality shows and taking part in them leaves some room for exceptions. For example, Israel's largest modern religious youth movement, Bnei Akiva, passed a resolution in 2013 calling on its members "not to participate in 'inappropriate reality programs,'" thereby leaving the door open to "suitable" programming like the competition for a "*payten*" (synagogue cantor). A few rabbis note that when religious people participate in reality shows, they may, in effect, be "sanctifying God's name" (*kiddush Hashem*) by letting the secular Israeli or the non-strictly religious viewer become exposed to religious customs and their message (Churlow, 2011).

Far less clear is the attitude of rabbis towards the materialistic goals underlying reality TV. This broadly reflects Judaism's own dilemma of material benefit. While Judaism does not believe in asceticism, and favors materialistic benefit, it does so within certain confines (Lifshitz, 2004). After the Flood, Noah was told to leave the Ark with the animals so that "they may swarm the earth, and be fruitful and multiply upon the earth" (Genesis 8:17) – a clue towards enjoying the material pleasures of God's world.

Yet, there is a debate about whether Judaism is inclined towards socialism or towards capitalism. Scholars generally agree that Judaism does not have a single opinion that can be classified as "socialist" or "capitalist." Just like the other two monotheistic religions – Islam and Christianity – Judaism has features that support both sides. Sauer and Sauer (2007) summarize five principles of Judaism that are relevant here: Participation in the Creative Process (which means that Jews are not exempt from working even if they devote their time to learning the holy scriptures); Protection of Private Property (recall the story of King Ahab and Naboth Vineyard, where even the king of Israel was not allowed to confiscate land without fair compensation); Accumulation of Wealth (which means that Jews are allowed to inherit property from their fathers and that when a person dies his assets are not given to the state); Caring for the Needy (donating to the poor is a positive virtue); and Limited Government (tendency to prefer market economy). While the fourth principle has a socialist flavor, the other principles tend towards capitalism. Yet another is the Biblical edict, set forth by Leviticus 25:13, that in the Jubilee Year (the fiftieth year of the Jewish agricultural calendar), land wealth reverts back to its original owners – a clue that land is not the absolute possession of man, but belongs to God.

After the state of Israel was established in 1948, some religious politicians were inclined towards a more capitalist stance (Lifshitz, 2004), while some preferred socialism (Helinger and Londin, 2012). Perhaps because of a lack of consensus on the question of Judaism's attitude towards commerce, rabbis in their critique of reality television have not mentioned greed as a primal problem. Rather, the concern of rabbis with reality TV is elsewhere; reality TV is considered the antithesis of core Jewish values such as modesty, privacy, and family bonding. Reality TV, rabbis argue, has at best little or no moral message of social value. The challenge for Man is to control his animalistic instincts – popularly coined in religious circles as the "evil inclination" (Bet Hillel, 2013). The "appropriate" goals of life, from a religious Judaic standpoint, are to contribute to society, for man to have positive ties with his fellow man, to show kindness, and to espouse the idea that Man is created in God's image – all goals which are hardly the stuff of reality productions (Wilson et al., 2012). When the "actors" are real people, the danger, rabbis argue, is that values expressed throughout the programming will in the long term be imitated and seep into everyday society (Bet Hillel, 2013).

Religious content in reality programming in Israel

The attitude towards religion and spirituality in popular reality TV shows is generally positive. For example, a religious tenant in the first season of *Big Brother* was given permission to build a synagogue in the house. An antireligious tenant who objected to the idea, claiming that "this is a TV show and not a temple," was criticized by the voice-over of *Big Brother* for being inconsiderate. In another case, in the fourth season of *The Amazing Race*, when female contestants were asked to mud-wrestle while wearing swimsuits, a religious contestant was exempted without reservations. Such cases reflect a respected right to practice religious customs in Israeli reality shows. According to Hemo (2009), the attempts of reality TV producers to recruit religious contestants and allow them to practice exemplify the place of popular culture in a country where over half of the population define themselves as traditional or religious. In part, it may also reflect fears among TV executives of sanctions by regulatory bodies for not giving proper representation to religious people.

To understand whether or not reality programming in Israel truly represents the amalgam of religious faiths in the country, including Christianity (observed by 2 percent of the population) and Islam (observed by 17 percent of the population), the authors coded the participants in the three most successful shows – *The Amazing Race, Survivor,* and *Big Brother* – by their religiosity (secular, religious, ultra-religious) and demographics. The analysis included 437 persons who comprise the population of participants in seven seasons of *Survivor* (n = 154), five seasons of *The Amazing Race* (n = 121) and eight seasons of *Big Brother* (n = 162). Two hundred and twenty-one of these people (51.5%) were men and 430 (98.5%) were Jewish.

The analysis showed that 424 participants (97%) defined themselves as secular. Only thirteen participants (3%) defined themselves as religious/modern-Orthodox, and no one defined himself as ultra-Orthodox/Haredi. The largest share of religious participants (5.6%) appeared in *Big Brother*. *The Amazing Race* also included religious participants in 3.3 percent of the roles, but *Survivor* did not feature a single religious contestant. These gaps reflect differences in emphasis among the shows: *Big Brother* aims to offer a mosaic of Israeli society. This view is not restricted to the producers, but strongly shared by one-third of the viewers and partly held by another third (Barak, 2012). *The Amazing Race* is another show that attempts to feature a multicultural ensemble that represents different sects of Israeli society (Pollak, 2011). In contrast, *Survivor* is mainly a physical contest featuring skimpily dressed, well-built young adults – hardly a framework that attracts religious people to take part. In contrast with *The Amazing Race* and *Big Brother*, *Survivor* in practice lacks storylines that engage viewers with religious themes. However, even in *Big Brother* – the format which features the largest share of religious participants – their share (5.6%) is still significantly lower ($\chi^2_{(1)}$ = 69; P < .001) than their share of the Israeli population which hovers around 25 percent (Arian & Kaiser-Sugarman, 2009). This confirms a 2013 study of minorities in Israeli television, which found that the representation of religious people in reality shows is negligible (The Second Authority for Television & Radio, 2013). The ban imposed by mainstream Orthodox rabbis on participation in reality productions (see Aviner, 2015) could deter potential participants who follow their rabbis. Yet, even without a rabbinical ban, the typical content of shows that prioritize greed and lust (Escoffery, 2006) is hardly appealing to strictly religious Jews. The incongruence of religious lifestyle to the promiscuous atmosphere on reality shows is possibly another deterring factor, even when producers apparently allow religious contestants to practice and observe religious rulings (Hemo, 2009). The reservation of religious people also is reflected in rating charts: while approximately one-fourth of the adult Jewish population define themselves as religious-orthodox, their share of viewers of *Big Brother* (14%), *The Amazing Race* (16%) and *Survivor* (9%) is considerably smaller. *Survivor*, with its emphasis on bodily exposure and deceit, deters religious people more than other reality formats.

An examination of the breakdown of religious contestants by gender and religion reveals an underrepresentation of men; only 23 percent of the religious contestants are male. In terms of content, the deeply-rooted conception of women as weaker in their adherence to religiosity finds expression in plotlines. For example, in the eighth season of *Big Brother*, a religious tenant was often engaged in physical contact with another tenant, even though she was aware that this contact is prohibited by Jewish religious law (*halakhah*). The sinful tenant justified herself by saying, "Please forgive me, Lord, for not being strong enough to resist."

While the representation of non-Jews in Israeli reality shows goes beyond the scope of this chapter, the authors found an underrepresentation of Christians and Muslims. The share of Arabs in Israeli's population is estimated around 20 percent (Arian & Kaiser-Sugarman, 2009), but in the shows sampled for this chapter the share of Muslims and Christians was merely 1.6 percent none of whom were religious. This reflects the low place which minority non-Jewish faiths receive in the Israeli media (Cohen, 2005).

While romance is a recurring theme in reality shows (e.g. *The Bachelor* is about finding a lasting mate), the question of mixed marriages between Jews and Arabs has hardly been addressed in Israeli reality TV, partly reflecting that mixed religious marriages rarely happen in Israel. Only 0.003 percent of Israeli marriages feature Jewish-Arab partnerships. We found only one example of a mixed couple in *The Amazing Race*. This couple was strongly condemned by viewers and eliminated in an early episode. This condemnation mirrors a religious, as well as cultural, ban on mixed marriages (Pollak, 2011).

We also examined scenes where religion played a major role. These scenes can be grossly divided into two clusters: conflicts over "lifestyle" and ideological battles.

Examples that demonstrate the first cluster include a fight between religious and secular female contestants over whether it is appropriate to wear a bikini on an assignment (which appeared in *The Amazing Race*) and a disagreement about where to keep non-kosher food in a kosher kitchen (which appeared in *Big Brother*). An example of an ideological battle is a verbal argument between religious and a non-religious *Big Brother* tenants about whether one is allowed to pronounce the holy name of God – otherwise known as the Tetragrammaton, an acknowledgement that no word can capture the awesome, infinite power of the Creator (Deuteronomy 5:11). The reality genre also serves as a mirror of current affairs. The second season of *Big Brother*, for instance, featured a high-pitched debate between tenants on whether or not the Jewish nation is responsible for the "Canaanite holocaust" (the conquest of the Promised Land by the Israelites some 3,500 years ago and the slaughtering of the land's earlier inhabitants). This discussion was essentially similar to conflicts that have swept the political agenda regarding historical land rights of Jews and Palestinians in the land of Israel.

Conclusion

Although the content and representation of religious faith and customs in popular reality TV shows in Israel is marginal, the stance of the programming toward religion is generally positive in the case of Judaism, or absent in the case of Christianity and Islam. This is not radically different from the standpoint of other commercial TV genres in Israel towards religion (Cohen & Hetsroni, 2018).

Although religious viewers do not flock in large numbers to the programs, and despite the fact that popular public discourse about reality shows in Israel has not considered religion a major issue (Hetsroni, 2010), the subject of reality TV has raised a considerable amount of concern among religious leaders and rabbis. Perhaps the mainly negative attitude of prominent rabbis is at least in part responsible for the marginal appearance of religious participants on the programs which, in turn, may deter religious viewers from watching since they are unable to see "people like them." By corollary, the small number of religious participants explains, in turn, the relative scarcity of religion-related content.

References

Arian, Asher, and Ayala Kaiser-Sugarman. 2009. *Israeli Jews – a Portrait: Beliefs, Values, and Observance of the Jews in Israel 2009.* Jerusalem, Israel: Guttman Center of the Israel Democracy Institute.

Aviner, Shlomo. 2015. "Is it Worthy to Partake in Reality Shows?" *Ynet*, November 4, 2015. http://www.ynet.co.il/articles/0,7340,L-4720918,00.html

Ariel, Azriel. 2001. "Loshon HaRah B'Maarekhet Tzibnori Democrati" [Hebrew: "The Place of Social Gossip in the Public Democratic System"] *Tzohar.* 5–6.

Barak, Roee. 2012. "Seventy-Four Percent of Youth Admit: Reality TV Does Affect Our Behavior." *Globes*, March 6, 2012. http://www.globes.co.il/news/article.aspx?did= 1000730855

Bet Hillel. 2013. The Big Brother: Our View on Reality TV Culture. http://www.beithil lel.org.il/show.asp?id=57855

Central Bureau of Statistics. 2009. *Social Survey*. Jerusalem, Israel: Central Bureau of Statistics.

Churlow, Yuval. 2011. "Reality TV and 'Kiddush Hashem'" Beit Hamidrash. https://www. ypt.co.il/beit-hamidrash/view.asp?id=6645

Cohen, Yoel. 2005. "Religion News in Israel." *Journal of Media and Religion*, 4(3): 179–198.

Cohen, Yoel. 2012. *God, Jews and the Media: Religion and Israel's Media*. London: Routledge.

Cohen, Yoel, and Amir Hetsroni. 2018. "Religious Practices and Conversations on American and Israeli Prime-Time Television Programming." *Društvena istraživanj.* .

Dardashti, Galeet. 2015. "Televised Agendas: How Global Funders Make Israeli TV more 'Jewish'." *Jewish Film and New Media: An International Journal*, 3(1): 77–103.

Engelman, Lior. 2009. "Reality as a Phenomenon." Kipa. https://www.kipa.co.il//jew/print. asp?id=32189 (accessed March 25, 2009).

Escoffery, David. 2006. *How Real is Reality TV: Essays on Representation and Truth*. Jefferson, NC: McFarland & Co.

Eurodata TV. 2016. *One Television Year in the World*. Paris: Mediametrie.

Falk, Erika. 1999. "Jewish Laws of Speech: Toward Multicultural Rhetoric." *Howard Journal of Communication*, 10: 15–28.

Goodman, Yoram. 2016. "Reality Shows vs. Life Values." Parashat Hashavua. April 18, 2016. http://www.meirtv.co.il/site/content_idx.asp?idx=23533

Ha-Cohen, Israel Meir. 1873. *Chofez Hayim*, Translated by Zeev Pliskin [1975] *Guard Your Tongue: A Practical Guide to the Laws of Loshon Hara Based on the Chofez Hayim*. Jerusalem, Israel: Aish HaTorah.

Helinger, Moshe, and Yossi Londin. 2012. "The Socio-Economic Ideology of Religious Zionism in Israel." *Journal of Political Ideologies*, 17(1): 87–106.

Hemo, Michal. 2009. "Textual Mechanisms for the Representation of Israeli Identity in the 'Sof Ha-Derech 2' (End of the Road 2) Reality Show." *Media Frames*, 3: 27–53.

Hetsroni, Amir. 2010. "The Praise and the Critic of a TV Format: An Analysis of the Public Discourse Concerning Reality TV in Israel." In *Reality Television: Merging the Global and the Local*, edited by Amir Hetsroni, 151–162. Hauppauge, NY: Nova Science.

Jacobson, David. 2004. "The Maale School: Catalyst for the Entrance of Religious Zionism to the World of Media pProduction." *Israel Studies*, 9(1): 31–60.

Krasner, Efrat. 2016. "Rabbi Rotzon Arusi: The cage of Big Brother is Worse than the Safari." *Kippa*. January 24, 2016. http://www.kipa.co.il

Lamm, Norman. 1997. "Tzeniut: A Universal Concept." In *Haham Gaon Memorial Volume*, edited by Marc D. Angel, 151–161. New York: Sepher-Hermon Press.

Lifshitz, Yosef Yizhak. 2004. "Jewish Economic Law." *Tekhelet*, 17: 63–89.

Pollak, Uri. 2011. "Viewers Boycott on the Amazing Race because of the Participation a Jewish-Arab Couple." *Kippa*. November 1, 2011. http://www.kipa.co.il

Sauer, Corrine, and Robert M. Sauer. 2007. "Jewish Theology and Economic Theory." *Religion and Liberty*, 17(1): 4–6.

Shahaf, Sharon. 2014. "Homegrown Reality: Locally Formatted Israeli Programming and the Global Spread of Format TV." *Creative Industries Journal*, 7(1): 3–18.

The Second Authority for Television and Radio. 2013. The Absent and Present on Prime-Time Programming: Follow-Up Study. Research Report. Jerusalem: The Second Authority for Television and Radio.

Vinig, Marlyn. 2011. *Orthodox Cinema*. Tel Aviv, Israel: Resling.

Weimann, Gabriel, Jonathan Cohen, and Michal Hirschman-Shitreet. 2007. Reality Shows in Israel: Between Real and Imagination, between Innocence and Manipulation and between Public and Private. Research Report. Jerusalem: The Second Authority for Television and Radio.

Wilson, Christopher, Tom Robinson, and Mark Callister. 2012. "Surviving Survivor: A Content Analysis of Antisocial Behavior and its Context in a Popular Reality Television Show." *Mass Communication and Society*, 15(2): 261–283.

7

ALL-AMERICAN CANCELLATION

Spectacle and neoliberal performativity in *All-American Muslim*

Melinda Q. Brennan

The case study of an event, the cancellation of *All-American Muslim*, is a uniquely interesting example of the neoliberal project of cultural assimilation and consequential backlash, come together in The Learning Channel's (2011–2012) reality television series and its cancellation. Between July 2011 and February 2012 *All-American Muslim* was introduced, aired, faced backlash, had a robust email campaign launched against advertisers supporting the show, raised a national debate about anti-Muslim racism in the U.S., and ultimately was cancelled.[1] The arc of this event frames this chapter, as well as the ways that religious and political performativity mark national debate over "the Muslim question" in the U.S.[2] In a climate perpetually stamped by the date September 11th, 2001, spectacle continues to erupt around Muslims and Islam in the U.S.[3] The spectacle of the cancellation, however, is the facet of the event that reveals a ritual performativity: political patriotism built on the back of religion. The rigid regulation of a political script, right versus left, enforces the expectation that debates in the public sphere will manifest in that way (Butler, 1990, 25). The reactionary discourse – the performativity of backlash – manifests the hostility that pre-exists the newest row. Thus, the compulsion to fulfill the script forces religion to emerge as the ground upon which backlash engages. Beyond the confines of the program, Evangelical Christian activists, corporations pulling advertising, and liberal celebrities boycotting those corporations, each enacted a different performative American nationalism. Despite contrary purposes and political stances, each performative act revealed a shared sense of what animated controversy as well as an elusive unfinished project requiring intervention, determining what is real.

All-American Muslim was a short-lived reality television show, docu-series or docudrama produced by TLC, which aired eight episodes between November 13, 2011 and January 8, 2012. Filmed primarily in Dearborn, Michigan, a location known for having the most intense demographic concentration of Muslims in the

U.S., the series fit neatly into TLC's diversity narratives. *All-American Muslim*'s storylines pivoted on five families of Lebanese-American descent and Shi'a faith, and despite a limited pool of diversity within even a single Muslim community in America, the show espoused "access" to "authentic, real-life characters," and their "diverse experiences" while "negotiat[ing] universal family issues" (Poniewozik, 2011b). The family focus of the show functioned as familiar and unchallenging territory to address "misconceptions" about Muslims, ostensibly to diminish Islamophobia by exposing the ordinariness of the intimate, everyday lives of Midwestern Muslims. Representing benign Americanness as appropriately assimilated was key to producing unchallenging subjects for consumption (Poniewozik, 2011b; Tucker, 2011).

Somewhere between representing ordinariness across difference and the fetishization of less familiar types of difference, one can find TLC's commitment to portraying stories about underrepresented communities in the U.S., in this case the racialized religious difference of Muslim Americans.[4] The quotidian versions of gender roles and family in *All-American Muslim* enraged some members of the Evangelical Christian religious right, who were ultimately credited with the cancellation of the show. These activists and their far-right political supporters argued that rather than illustrating stark gender, familial, and religious differences that were incompatible with American life, TLC championed Muslim Americans that were "nominal," and not appropriately devout (Geller, 2011). Far-right and Evangelical Christian activists, organized through the Florida Family Association, argued that the series was deceptive in its representational choices and generalizing of Muslims as American, already assimilated, and authentically Muslim all at once. In essence, Muslims needed to be represented as problematic characters to be feared, and any other representation was dishonest and unpatriotic.

The ordinariness also spurred on liberal defenders and redeemers of the show during the anti-bigotry backlash against the cancellation.[5] The two sides, the Evangelical Christian and far-right activists of the Florida Family Association, and celebrities Russell Simmons and Mia Farrow, entered into a well-worn public encounter, a ritual of political performativity. The spectacle of the cancellation reiterated a religious nationalism, in this case Evangelical Christian nationalism, which triggered a liberal reaction against religious nationalist politics. Rather than term this interaction religious versus secular, it is more fruitful to consider the way the presence of religion shapes a public political interaction, and thus, cascading forms of performativity.

While Simmons and Farrow pushed back against what they perceived as bigoted or racist arguments against Muslims being equated with terrorists, an Islamophobic narrative to be sure, their desire to voice critiques on a national stage was an intentional reiteration of their liberal political personas. Their engagement with the issue on the basis of anti-bigotry or anti-racist performativity distances them from a political standpoint they actively disidentify with, Evangelical Christian nationalism, not via a secular stance; instead, they work to identify themselves through an anti-racist and anti-xenophobic perspective (Muñoz, 1999). Simmons and Farrow maintained that the backlash against the show skirted overt racism, making the backlash not only racist, but dishonest; they also argued that exclusionary arguments on the basis of difference are un-American themselves. Thus, tropes of dishonesty and reality circulated not only through Evangelical Christian religious right activists' discourse, but also through liberal celebrity anti-bigotry and anti-racist backlash, with the shared stakes a vision for American nationalism.

Backlashes

That radicalness infuses "the ordinary" in this tiered backlash event is quite telling – radicalness becomes a performative measure of national engagement and patriotism. The representation of Muslim people in the U.S. is a radical idea for some, including the Florida Family Association, an idea dependent on a narrow and Christian vision for what is permissibly American. For the Florida Family Association and others, "Islam" and "Muslim" are conceptualized and judged as radical or fundamentalist religious beliefs, cultural norms, faith and cultural practices, ideology, and behavior (Elver, 2012). The Florida Family Association's activism pivots on disidentificatory critique, strengthening their relevance and nationalist vision on the backs of a universalized Muslim peril. The very doing of Florida Family Association's critique substantiates the original terms of the debate: Muslims are exceptional, and require an exceptional amount of attention. In this case, the questions of whether Muslims are to be feared and what representation of Muslimness is more honest, and therefore, more real, are accepted terms of the debate by all actors in the spectacle. What is most interesting, however, is the repetitive push-pull visions for nationalism, all of which engage with religion and questions about authenticity determining what is "more real." In these formulations of nationalism that collapse and stereotype, questions of authenticity stand in for "what or who can be trusted" to represent the world as *one wants it to be* rather than *as it currently exists*. As the *New Yorker* described the convoluted logic, "the truth is false if it does not look the way one thought it would. It is seized by the fear of a bland Muslim" (Davidson, 2011). Thus, TLC's project in *All-American Muslim* begins a tiered wave of performativity that shifts as energy transfers from one backlash to another. What begins as a vision of nationalism that includes Muslims but represents Muslimness as a negotiated American identity, continues beyond the show into the public debate about the "real" value of the show. Thus, the characters of the series substantiate the framing of "Muslim American" as an always incomplete activity of choosing, readjustment, assimilation, and fear. For example, Amy Winter, General Manager of TLC at the time *All-American Muslim* ran and was cancelled, issued a press release that highlighted the always incomplete identity work of Muslim Americans, "Through these families and their diverse experiences, we will explore how they blend their values and traditions with everyday life in America, providing insight into their culture with care and compassion" (Poniewozik, 2011b). The work of "blending" ostensibly religious (and ethnic) "values and traditions" puts Muslim Americans at odds with an unmarked, and thus homogenously white Christian "everyday life in America," whereby identity work like "blending" would not be required. The TLC statement ends by reiterating the gap between universal American issues and the specificity of Muslim life, the careful alterations, balance, and compromise required to maintain a state of being recognized as *Muslim American*, "ALL-AMERICAN MUSLIM shows how these individuals negotiate universal family issues while remaining loyal to the traditions and beliefs of their religious faith – and how they simultaneously defy the assumptions and stereotypes prevalent in today's society" (Poniewozik, 2011b). Thus, cast members' performative identity work on the show does several things at once: (1) it substantiates that there is a way to be Muslim American, though it takes careful work to balance national and religious requirements, (2) it crystalizes the universal as American and not Muslim, while solidifying Muslim as the Other needing to "blend" or assimilate to American norms, and (3) it acquiesces to the terms of Islamophobia, by accepting the requirement to disprove that difference is troublesome.[6]

Despite the series operating within existent frameworks, frameworks that are not anti-racist and in fact support the continued Othering and essentializing of racia-lizeable populations, it was not enough to protect the show from becoming a target. For example, being recognized as Muslim or mistaken for Muslim has frequent negative consequences, including hate crimes. Such violence emanates from a mixture of xenophobia that is anti-immigrant and isolationist, racist and supports ethno-centric nationalism, and imagines America as a white Christian nation. Thus, cast members of *All-American Muslim* are not only religious Others, but racialized Others, represented and intelligible through a multicultural framework.

The multicultural and diversity focus of TLC's framing attracted critical attention because even these weakly political, and clearly neoliberal choices required the construction of positive associations with Muslims in America. *All-American Muslim*, as described by Amy Davidson Sorkin (2011) in a *New Yorker* article, committed a perilous error: "simply by depicting Muslims as 'nice' Americans, a show became too controversial for [advertisers] to engage with." This means that Muslims, a racialized religious identity and community, are always already disturbing by their very public presence. Worse still, by TLC crafting a positive depiction of Muslim American life, the Florida Family Association and prominent Islamophobic pundits Pamela Geller and Robert Spencer were able to partially dodge charges of overt racism because they did not target and demonize the Muslim cast members of the show. Instead, these religious and far-right activists confidently and obliquely argued that Muslims' existence in the U.S. is antithetical to safety and security, a national political issue, as well as for *devout* Muslims to be considered a general danger, which they maintained the members of the cast were not. Such a peculiar argument is at once white Evangelical Christian nationalism and xenophobic protectionism.

The second tier of backlash, by liberal celebrities, framed their objection to the email campaign to defund *All-American Muslim* through direct charges of "Islamo-phobia" by Russell Simmons and an under-defined "bigotry" by Mia Farrow (Hughes, 2011; Hibberd, 2011). The non-specificity of Farrow's charge of bigotry underscored the multiculturalism-diversity framing of *All-American Muslim* itself. Early in the controversy, the Florida Family Association targeted Lowe's, the home improvement retailer, to drop its advertising buy from *All-American Muslim*. Once swayed by the Florida Family Association's email campaign supported with signal boosts from the well-established Islamophobic pundits Pamela Geller and Robert Spencer, Lowe's began a domino effect amongst other advertisers, despite liberal celebrities, non-profit political action groups, and elected democratic representatives' continuing charges of bigotry, racism, and Islamophobia. Russell Simmons, in particular, focused his critique of Lowe's actions as un-American, "There are American principals [sic] at stake here. ... This country is built on religious freedom. This is the kind of hate that tears this country apart" (Hibberd, 2011). Simmons' performativity, partial outrage, multicultural pluralist nationalism, and neoliberal opportunism, vaguely deployed liberalism in his public critique of Lowe's. His partiality established his rejection of advertisers' withdrawal of support, without broader or less individualistic concerns, namely a critique of systemic racism within capitalism, or the racisms of the Florida Family Association. His entrance into the public fray was individualist in focus: what Lowe's did wrong, what the Florida Family Association did wrong, and what he could make out of the situation for his own ends. Despite the crowning controversy and bad press for corporations dropping their advertising buys, the email campaign started by the Florida Family Association achieved its goal. In sum, over one hundred marketers pulled their advertising dollars from *All-American Muslim* throughout the duration of the cancellation spectacle. Vague arguments about nationalism and multiculturalism did not engender enough support to sway corporate interests away from avoidance of national controversy about religion and race.

A few things are consistent across contrary vectors of rhetoric surrounding the cancellation of *All-American Muslim*: (1) the characters in the show were deemed too ordinary to be interesting or worthy of vitriol, (2) the show's treatment of the political import of mainstream representation of Muslim life is underwhelming or ill-fitting, judged as either not political enough or too political, and (3) the role of gender expression, gender roles, and gender in familial relationships in the show is pivotally important in determining authenticity of Muslimness in America. Whether based on multicultural liberalism or white Evangelical Christian nationalism, each discursive trajectory followed all three of these tenets, and much of the political performativity operated through approaches to authenticity.

Authenticity

Doubt and accusation swirled around the concept and enactment of authenticity – authentically religious, authentically representing Muslims, authentically representing reality – during the cancellation spectacle of *All-American Muslim*. The Florida Family Association did not take aim at the cast members of *All-American Muslim*; instead, they focused their critique and subsequent email campaign on advertisers through a peculiar vector of Islamophobia: charges of inauthenticity and misleading the public, or put another way, dishonesty about Muslims as a threat to America. They argued that the show was not authentic in its representation of Muslim life, specifically accusing producers of excluding "extremist" Muslims from the cast, equating "extremist" with "faithful" Muslims, thus labeling all devout Muslims as dangerous and incompatible with American life. Cast members became in tolerable to the Florida Family Association, Pamela Geller, and Robert Spencer, because they were too American, too assimilated, and not religious enough. To this point, the Florida Family Association (2012) described the problem with *All-American Muslim* in these terms: "[it is] propaganda designed to counter legitimate and present-day concerns about many Muslims who are advancing Islamic fundamentalism and Sharia law. The show profiled only Muslims that appeared to be ordinary folks while excluding many Islamic believers whose agenda poses a clear and present danger to liberties and traditional values that the majority of Americans cherish." The parsing of "ordinary folks" from "Islamic believers" re-entrenches xenophobic nationalism, as does "traditional values that the majority of Americans cherish" – a Christian moral majority's needs defining and outweighing an Other constructed as threatening, both ideologically and physically. To be Muslim, in this Evangelical Christian religious right discourse, is to be a faithful fundamentalist in a way that consolidates their own political power and ideological strength, rather than raise questions of the symmetry of fundamentalisms and the place of religion within the contemporary American public sphere.

Religion became the platform for postmodern theatrics, as successive Evangelical Christian and liberal backlashes raised political performativity to the height of spectacle. Liberal responses to the Evangelical Christian backlash were an opportunity for neoliberal progressive performativity. Advertising buys for *All-American Muslim*, and TLC more generally, quite literally became the metric for tolerance. Ad dollars were interpreted as shrinking tolerance, a rejection of Muslims and Muslim Americans alike, as if corporate queasiness about controversy was equivalent to not only "tacit acceptance" of Muslim difference, a multicultural-diversity measure of tolerating difference, but of something more and direct, such as active anti-racist politics (Decena, 2008). As celebrities like Russell Simmons accused Lowe's of falling to opportunistic bigotry, he, too, offered to fill the void in the advertising buy with commercials for his own products, specifically a prepaid Visa card. Liberalism, in this moment of spectacle, was deeply imbricated with capital and public displays of outrage. Simmons' multiple interviews and tweets were not the beginning of a national conversation about a post-September 11th, 2001 climate of creeping and increasing Islamophobia, the democratic principles related to practicing religious belief or ritual, or a more general conversation about racism and xenophobia in the U.S. Instead, Simmons' performative outrage seized upon spectacle for capital gains, grasping at the collective emotion of outrage, to be harnessed for economic profit.

The public engagement with *All-American Muslim* underscores a neoliberal script emerging during the spectacle of the cancellation: the Evangelical religious right against racialized and racial minoritized groups, performativity of righteous indignation on both "sides" played out in the public sphere in real time as the series continued to air, with advertisers operating as the hall-monitors of risk and timing, deciding if conversations about religion, race, and racialization in the real world should be aired on a reality television show.

Neoliberal (real) citizenship

Formations of "proper citizenship" operate through a careful balance of racialized religious difference in the show, as American Muslims negotiate their particular formation of difference for a market of viewers. Their identity work and everyday negotiation of their marked status(es) function within a "neoliberal mandate" as attractive enough and intelligible enough to be viewable (Weber, 2009, 38). Identity work, whether within familial relationships, heterosexual couplehood, or through the eyes of a single cast member, is commodified labor. Neoliberal citizenship, an individualist ladder of self-actualization and improvement, intermixed with familial bonds and roles, provides comparative ground for viewers to find the daily rituals of world-making as much an American project as faith practices (Weber, 2009). The reality of the show offers a vague correspondence to individualist neoliberal labors of audience members. A thin membrane separates one labor from the next – the fourth wall. The power of reality television was assumed as an everyday aspect of American life *by both sides* of the debate; the value of a reality show was too great to represent Muslim American life, too great to be cancelled and not available for consumption of tolerated difference.

Laura Brown's (2005, 81, 82) feminist account of women in reality television comes to two conclusions: first, "These people are real," and second, "because [reality television] purports to be real, it is powerful in ways that fictional television cannot be." Therefore, the importance of reality television is greater than a single character on a television show, or series, as the construction of real people demonstrates a truth related to their representation. When documented proof exists that Muslim people *are American*, it is the *real* that is the *threat*. When people on a show, and by extension, an entire group are constructed as a threat (Islamophobia), not only is that group constituted through their representation, but also the specter of threat is reinstantiated as real. *All-American Muslim* was created, in part, to address a lack of familiarity with Muslims that breeds Islamophobia. Therefore, the show can never outpace its own rationale: the cast members are real, and they are real to viewers because of Islamophobia. It is a puzzle; what is elided is the real; what is real is threatening; people are real and fictitious and dangerous all at once. Put another way, the show was "'dangerously' [real] positive" (Poniewozik, 2011a). This story of cancellation has far less to do with actual people than with public space being made for the representation of American Muslims to look normal, ordinary in their Americanness. The Evangelical Christian backlash argument rests, perhaps uneasily, on the shared notion that reality television is seen as an entrenched part of American entertainment and spectatorship. Thus, any concentrated appearance of Muslim people, particularly as the focus of a show, will draw a significant amount of negative attention. The power of the real functions to make television into America: demographics and fears collide in a powerful representation of American life. The threat is *real* Muslims who are already American.

Neoliberalism is particularly important to this analysis given the backlash against *All-American Muslim* was meant to defund it. It was a matter of removing the advertising support for the show in order to get the show cancelled. And that is what happened. Those who worked to have the show defunded wrote emails to make advertisers so uncomfortable that they would back out of supporting TLC and/or *All-American Muslim*. Their efforts were not directed at TLC to remove the show from their lineup, but rather to eliminate the capital that created the public space for Muslims to seem ordinary in contemporary reality television America. Blocking "troubling" representation by choking off capital was the goal of the Evangelical Christian backlash by the Florida Family Association. However, the tactic of publically attacking capital to cancel a show, and by extension, a particular representation of reality, was also deployed to remove Bill O'Reilly from Fox (Grynbaum and Maheshwari, 2017). Neither of these campaigns elicited a lasting national conversation about religion or sexism, respectively. Instead, the neoliberal focus on capital and individual wrongdoing sidestepped the opportunity for national debate about inequality and oppression.

Waves of performativity

The following four examples of rhetoric about the cancellation reveal that however seemingly different their purpose, these messages carry forward a performativity that instantiates predictable responses across deep divides in the political sphere: Evangelical Christian, corporate self-interest, and liberal. As one wave of performativity hits another it may change argument, but not the agreed upon tenets, including a focus on authenticity as determinative of reality.

Example 1: Misleading progressivism as a method of cloaking threats against the nation. Pamela Geller (2011), guesting on *World Net Daily* wrote, "The fact is that the show specifically situates itself as a response to 'Islamophobia' – this was clear from the opening moments of the first show. But it is severely misleading, because it doesn't deal with the kind of Muslims who would ever have caused anyone any concern in the first place." Geller's far right performativity reveals the desire for a form of nationalism that is xenophobic and isolationist, which constitutes a desire for real (read: radical) Muslims on national public display. Islamophobia is denied in this response, even though *All-American Muslim* was produced to address exactly that construct: a Muslim to be feared, a pervasive stereotype that is defined through an unassimilable difference. *All-American Muslim* is a failure because it does not deliver the kind of Muslims who would be interesting and politically relevant to watch. The value of difference in this response is not in producing the real; instead, it is in the desire for the hyperreal, the stereotype, a construction that flattens the richness of Muslim lives into descriptors like "extremist," "fundamentalist," or "terrorist." The difference must be excessive, dangerous, imperiling to the nation, specifically a white Christian nation. If there are ordinary Muslims in America, they are not interesting enough to have a show dedicated to their normalness. The production of *All-American Muslim* becomes offensive, in part, because it is beneath the notice of those who desire "radical" or "fundamentalist" Muslims on national display. But, if there are Muslims in America who are the "dangerous Muslims" desired by the far right, required for a partnered coterminous outsider–insider, a reality that supports the call for an unrequited white Christian nation, then perhaps that would be worth watching. If only to hate watch.

Then, the only "real" Muslims are those who pose a threat to the U.S. Therefore, nationalism is deemed the solution to *looking racist*. Pamela Geller, in this instance, is caught out not by doing overt racism, but by her insistence that the show was misleading because *All-American Muslim* does not represent the world as it is; rather, the show represents fake Muslims. But, another element undergirds Evangelical Christian and far-right arguments – gender. What is the political function of gender in Islamophobic rhetoric? And how does gender operate as the crux of a neoliberal redemption narrative?[7]

In many of the cancellation news stories, the gender expression of the women of the show illustrates radicalism, as if any modest covering is deemed radical, or progressive via the freedom to choose to cover, or the "diversity" of gender expressions of faith illustrates progressivism. Diversity of gender expression in one family seems to captivate journalists of various stripes and commentators. For example, Poniewozik (2011b) writing for *Time* mentioned "sisters who are polar opposites (one who wears a headscarf and prays daily, the other has tattoos and is married to an Irish Catholic)" as a sign of the diversity of Muslim life, even in a single family. In both of these cases, gender operates as the moment of activation or denial of Islamophobia. Women, and their bodies, become central to determining the authenticity of Muslim representation. Difference, the gendered performativity of faith, stands in as a shibboleth of authenticity – the presence or absence of a hijab or other modest covering indicates diversity in the latter, and radicalism in the former.

Another example, one much more incendiary, authored by the Florida Family Association (2012), "Many woman were shown wearing hijabs and many who were not, but the program did not show what happens if one of the hijab-wearing women decides to take it off. Such conflicts would conflict with The Learning Channel's agenda to inaccurately portray Muslims in America. … [T]he show fails to mention many Islamic believers' demeaning treatment of women or great disdain for non-Muslims (infidels)." Gender operates in these accounts as Islam. Muslims, trapped as permanent outsiders to American life, are granted or denied assimilable status opportunities depending on how the women of the show are read. If the women are positioned to illustrate diversity within Muslimness, then read progressive. If women, by their gender expression and faith practices, are unassimilable because of their choice to cover or an imagined "forced oppression," then they become the very hallmark of cultural difference. This is tantamount to what miriam cooke (2007) terms the "Muslimwoman," a dramatic flattening of subjectivity and agency of Muslim women as powerless and oppressed objects that bear the full weight of cultural difference in the West. This disproportionate representational weight determines not only authenticity, realness, or threat, but also "goodness." Because of the paradoxical attention paid to women's bodies, faith symbols and gendered practices of faith, rhetoric from the right and left articulates the value of *All-American Muslim* through a morality tied to citizenship. As Sahar Selod (2014) and Sunaina Maira's (2009) critiques suggest, "good Muslims" don't look like Muslims; "bad Muslims" might or might not have visual signs of their difference. Gender becomes a site of totalizing confusion, a vector of such intense meaning that no definitive interpretation can emerge.

Example 2: Boycott operates as a site of performative liberal politics, bereft of critical dialog about systemic racism within capitalism. Kimberly Potts (2011) wrote for *The Wrap*: "California state Senator Ted Lieu called the Lowe's ad pull 'stunning bigotry' while actor-celebrities Mia Farrow and Russell Simmons called for people to boycott Lowe's after dropping *All-American Muslim*." It is clear that the senator and celebrities see Lowe's lack of support as an endorsement of bigoted Islamophobic sentiments. What is not clear, however, is the way in which bigotry is addressed by boycott, or the way that endorsement, as a literal financial measure, undoes Islamophobia. Lowe's punishment is yet more attention paid to its decision to pull their advertising buy from *All-American Muslim*; what is not addressed in these comments is the way in which capital protects itself, relaying self-interest towards a refusal to discuss racism in the U.S. The call to boycott is framed as an authentic and impassioned objection, and is interpretable itself as action against bigotry, specifically, racism. However, objection to systemic racism is elided in the individual focus on Lowe's as perpetrator, which mirrors the individualistic project of identity formation in the show. The criticisms by Senator Lieu and others, however earnest, are attempts to strengthen a multicultural-diversity approach to difference that is easily, and cyclically, commodified. Lieu, Farrow, and Simmons did not critique *All-American Muslim* for commodifying "palatable" Muslim life for reality television, nor did they call for all advertisers who pulled their spots to be subject to boycott. Their public outcry emerged as individualist doings of liberal politics, to hold a single entity responsible, all while the more difficult conversation about how racism operates within capitalism was elided. Racism, then, was an open-ended vector of performative politics, just as gender was in the first example – a method of elision and individualist exercise.

Example 3: Naomi Schaefer Riley (2012) writing for the *Wall Street Journal*:

> The TLC network announced that it will cancel the reality show "All-American Muslim" due to low ratings. Critics had complained that the show whitewashed the problem of Islamic radicalism in the U.S. by not portraying Muslim extremists, which led major sponsors such as the retailer Lowe's to drop their support. But the show's producers were closer to portraying reality than critics asserted. The story of Islam in America today is a story of rapid assimilation and even secularization, not growing radicalism.

In this case, "whitewashed" stands in for "assimilated" and certainly "just like you [white Christian Americans]." Reality television can be interpreted as *the truth*, not as a social construct, but as a reality that we can perceive by choosing to view a program, a window into another life. This is only because "these Muslims" have "assimilated" – which makes them literally visible, as reality television people. The specter of "Islamic fundamentalism" inhabits this response – in order to be visible, one must assimilate away from racialized religious difference, and in order to be viable for visibility, one must be a radical to have enough entertainment value to be commodified.

Example 4: Lowe's official response addressing the public outcry following their decision to pull advertisement support, per the *Wall Street Journal*:

> As you know, the TLC program "All-American Muslim" has become a lightning rod for people to voice complaints from a variety of perspectives – political, social and otherwise. Following this development, dozens of companies removed their advertising from the program beginning in late November. Lowe's made the decision to discontinue our advertising on Dec. 5. ... [W]e have a strong commitment to diversity and inclusion, and we're proud of that longstanding commitment. If we have made anyone question that commitment, we apologize.
>
> *(Riley, 2012)*

Diversity and inclusion are multicultural buzzwords, used to express literal tolerance and support for a plurality of opinion, inclusive of bigotry and racism from the Florida Family Association. Corporations do not want to be embroiled in political turmoil as a brand, and do not want to be subject to boycotting. As capital refracts its own interests within its defensive choice of words, the palatability of difference becomes central to financial risk assessment. As the right and the left engage in a predictable battle formed through the rigid expectations of a well-worn political script, religion emerges as a primary organizing structure to the debates, as does the "doing" of backlash.

Reality television points us to deep nationalist desires, across political divides. The real is obscured through claims of authenticity and assimilation, negotiation and familiarity. The refusal to accept Islamophobia as real rests on the requirements for Muslim visibility: to be an excessive, dangerous, imperiling entity. To discuss Islamophobia and accept it as a credible concern is to "do harm" to a national discourse about safety and security in a post-September 11th, 2001 political landscape. When one doesn't want to discuss the intersectional realities of Islamophobia, that is, race and religion, and often gender's activating effects, it can be easily elided by discussing racism or terrorism instead. But without gender – and in particular veiling as an expression of foreign or familiar expression – to visibly define how "ordinary" or "excessive" Muslimness is, there can be no narrative that redeems nor one that impugns in totality. However, while the real remains an uncatchable and incomplete judgment, the very debates that perpetuate a need for assessment of authenticity reveal remarkably shared terrain across the political and ideological spectrum. Within spectacle resides unquestioned ground and shared tactics to control capital and representation, without accountability to national dialogue.

Notes

1 Viewership for *All-American Muslim* dropped steadily after airing the first episode; broad seasonal declines and declines across TLC shows occurred at the same time, making *All-American Muslim* a steady show for the network overall. *All-American Muslim* episodes are available via YouTube. Andrew Wallenstein, "'Muslim' TV ratings dive amid media frenzy," *Variety*, December 21, 2011, http://variety.com/2011/tv/news/muslim-tv-ra tings-dive-amid-media-frenzy-1118047824/.

2 Judith Butler, *Gender Trouble: Feminism and the Subversion of Identity* (New York: Routledge, 1990), 24–25. My thinking about "the Muslim question" is through Wendy Brown's theorization of "the Jewish question" and "the woman question." Wendy Brown, *Regulating Aversion: Tolerance in the Age of Identity and Empire* (Princeton: Princeton University Press, 2006), 48–77.

3 For an example of the collapse of specific events to a totalizing symbol of "9/11" see Véronique Bragard, Christophe Dony, and Warren Rosenberg eds., *Portraying 9/11: Essays on Representations in Comics, Literature, Film and Theatre* (Jefferson: McFarland & Company Publishers, 2011).

4 The racialization of religious groups has been well theorized and studied across critical ethnic studies, sociology, and legal theory. Steve Garner and Saher Selod, "The Racialization of Muslims: Empirical Studies of Islamophobia," *Critical Sociology*, vol. 41, no. 1 (2014); Jasbir Puar, *Terrorist Assemblages: Homonationalism in Queer Times* (Durham: Duke University Press, 2007); Jaideep Singh, "A New American Apartheid: Racialized, Religious Minorities in the Post-9/11 Era," *Sikh Formations: Religion, Culture, Theory*, vol. 9, no. 2 (2013); Hilal Elver, "Racializing Islam Before and After 9/11: From Melting Pot to Islamophobia," *Transnational Law & Contemporary Problems*, vol. 21 (2012).

5 Liberal defenders of *All-American Muslim* included elected democrats and liberal celebrities. A more comprehensive list of involved defenders and redeemers was compiled by the *LA Times*. Shan Li, "Lowe's faces backlash over pulling ads from 'All-American Muslim'," *LA Times*, December 13, 2011, http://articles.latimes.com/2011/dec/13/business/la-fi-lowes-m uslim-20111213. Given the focus on neoliberal spectacle, this chapter focuses on celebrities' public commentary, rather than all liberal defenders and redeemers of *All-American Muslim*.

6 Benedict Anderson, *Imagined Communities: Reflections on the Origin and Spread of Nationalism* (New York, Verso, 2006); Will Kymlicka, *Multicultural Citizenship: A Liberal Theory of Minority Rights* (Oxford: Clarendon Press, 1996); Edward Said, *Orientalism* (New York: Vintage Books Edition, 1994). My thinking about these themes is informed by Anderson's discussion of nationalism, Kymlicka's discussion of minority rights, and Said's critique of Orientalism.

7 For gender as an analytic in studies of Islamophobia, see: Alia Al-Saji, "The Racialization of Muslim Veils: A Philosophical Analysis," *Philosophy & Social Criticism*, vol. 36, no. 8 (2010); Paul Amar, "Middle East Masculinity Studies: Discourses of 'Men in Crisis,' Industries of Gender in Revolution," *Journal of Middle East Women's Studies*, vol. 7, no. 3 (2011); Louise Cainkar, *Homeland Insecurity: The Arab American and Muslim American Experience After 9/11* (New York: Russell Sage Foundation, 2009); Sunaina Maira, "'Good' and 'Bad' Muslim Citizens: Feminists, Terrorists, and U.S. Orientalisms," *Feminist Studies*, vol. 35, no. 3 (2009); Jasbir Puar and Amit Rai, "Monster, Terrorist, Fag: The War on Terrorism and the Production of Docile Patriots," *Social Text*, vol. 20, no. 3 (2002); Puar, 2007; Saher Selod, "Citizenship Denied: The Racialization of Muslims in American Men and Women post-9/11," *Critical Sociology* vol. 41, no. 1 (April 2014); Jasmin Zine, "Unveiled Sentiments: Gendered Islamophobia and Experiences of Veiling among Muslim Girls in a Canadian Islamic School," *Equality and Excellence in Education*, vol. 39, no. 3 (2006).

Bibliography

Al-Saji, Alia. 2010. "The Racialization of Muslim Veils: A Philosophical Analysis." *Philosophy & Social Criticism* 36(8): 875–902.

Amar, Paul. 2011. "Middle East Masculinity Studies Discourses of 'Men in Crisis,' Industries of Gender in Revolution." *Journal of Middle East Women's Studies* 7(3): 36–70.

Anderson, Benedict. 2006. *Imagined Communities: Reflections on the Origin and Spread of Nationalism*. New York: Verso Books.

Bragard, Véronique, Christophe Dony, and Warren Rosenberg, eds. 2011. *Portraying 9/11: Essays on Representations in Comics, Literature, Film and Theatre*. Jefferson: McFarland & Company Publishers.

Brown, Laura S. 2005. "Outwit, Outlast, Out-Flirt? The Women of Reality TV." In *Featuring Females: Feminist Analyses of Media*, edited by Ellen Cole and Jessica Henderson Daniel, 71–84. Washington, DC: American Psychological Association.

Brown, Wendy. 2006. *Regulating Aversion: Tolerance in the Age of Identity and Empire*. Princeton: Princeton University Press.

Butler, Judith. 1990. *Gender Trouble: Feminism and the Subversion of Identity*. New York: Routledge.

Cainkar, Louise. 2009. *Homeland Insecurity: the Arab American and Muslim American Experience After 9/11*. New York: Russell Sage Foundation.

cooke, miriam. 2007. "The Muslimwoman." *Contemporary Islam* 1(2): 139–154.

Davidson Sorkin, Amy. 2011. "The Attack on 'All-American Muslim." *New Yorker*, December 13. http://www.newyorker.com/news/daily-comment/the-attack-on-all-american-muslim.

Decena, Carlos. 2008. "Tacit Subjects." *GLQ: A Journal of Lesbian and Gay Studies* 14(2–3): 339–359.

Elver, Hilal. 2012. "Racializing Islam Before and After 9/11: From Melting Pot to Islamophobia." *Transnational Law & Contemporary Problems* 21: 119–174.

Florida Family Association. 2012. "The Learning Channel Officially Cancels All-American Muslim. Supporters' Emails to Advertisers Made the Difference." http://floridafamily.org/full_article.php?article_no=108.

Garner, Steve and Saher Selod. 2014. "The Racialization of Muslims: Empirical Studies of Islamophobia." *Critical Sociology* 41(1): 9–19.

Geller, Pamela. 2011. "All-American Muslim Hides the Truth About Islam." *World Net Daily*, November 15. http://www.wnd.com/2011/11/368197/.

Grynbaum, Michael and Sapna Maheshwari. 2017. "Fears of Revolt by Consumers Felled O'Reilly." *New York Times*, April 20. https://www.nytimes.com/2017/04/20/business/media/fears-of-revolt-by-consumers-felled-bill-oreilly.html?mcubz=1.

Hibberd, James. 2011. "Russell Simmons Blasts Lowe's for Pulling 'Muslim' Ads." *Entertainment Weekly*, December 10. http://ew.com/article/2011/12/10/russell-simmons-lowes-muslim-reality/.

Hughes, Sarah. 2011. "Russell Simmons, Kal Penn Offer Support to 'All American Muslim' After Lowe's Pulls Sponsorship." *Washington Post*, December 13. https://www.washingtonpost.com/blogs/celebritology/post/russell-simmons-kal-penn-offer-support-to-all-american-muslim-after-lowes-pulls-sponsorship/2011/12/13/gIQAdqwerO_blog.html?utm_term=.fdabdc2407b7 – comments.

Kymlicka, Will. 1996. *Multicultural Citizenship: A Liberal Theory of Minority Rights*. Oxford: Clarendon Press.

The Learning Channel. 2011–2012. All-American Muslim. Television. Shed Media.

Li, Shan. 2011. "Lowe's Faces Backlash Over Pulling Ads From'All-American Muslim.'" *LA Times*, December 13. http://articles.latimes.com/2011/dec/13/business/la-fi-lowes-muslim-20111213.

Maira, Sunaina. 2009. "'Good' and 'Bad' Muslim Citizens: Feminists, Terrorists, and US Orientalisms." *Feminist Studies* 35(3): 631–656.

Muñoz, José. 1999. *Disidentifications: Queers of Color and the Performance of Politics*. Minneapolis: University of Minnesota Press.

Poniewozik, James. 2011a. "All-American Muslim Meets an Un-American Advertising Pullout." *Time*, December 12. http://entertainment.time.com/2011/12/12/all-america n-muslim-meets-an-un-american-advertising-pullout/.

Poniewozik, James. 2011b. "The Real Muslims of Dearborn: TLC Announces Islam Reality Show." *Time*, July 21. http://entertainment.time.com/2011/07/21/the-real-muslim s-of-dearborn-tlc-announces-islam-reality-show/.

Potts, Kimberly. 2011. "Mia Farrow, Russell Simmons Urge Lowe's Boycott After Muslim Ad Drama." *The Wrap*, December 12. http://www.thewrap.com/tv/column-post/mia-fa rrow-russell-simmons-urge-lowes-boycott-after-all-american-muslim-ad-drama-33526.

Puar, Jasbir. 2007. *Terrorist Assemblages: Homonationalism in Queer Times*. Durham: Duke University Press.

Puar, Jasbir and Amit Rai. 2002. "Monster, Terrorist, Fag: The War on Terrorism and the Production of Docile Patriots." *Social Text* 20(3): 117–148.

Riley, Naomi Schaefer. 2012. "Defining the 'All-American Muslim': The Story of Islam in America today is a Story of Rapid Assimilation and Even Secularization." *Wall Street Journal*, March 22. http://online.wsj.com/article/SB100014240527023046364045772 97371335370072.html.

Said, Edward. 1994. *Orientalism*. New York: Vintage Books Edition.

Selod, Saher. 2014. "Citizenship Denied: The Racialization of Muslim American Men and Women Post-9/11." *Critical Sociology* 41(1): 77–95.

Singh, Jaideep. 2013. "A New American Apartheid: Racialized, Religious Minorities in the Post-9/11 Era." *Sikh Formations: Religion, Culture, Theory* 9(2): 115–144.

Tucker, Ken. 2011. "'All-American Muslim' on TLC: 'Muslims, They're Just Like Us!'" *Entertainment Weekly*, November 13. http://watching-tv.ew.com/2011/11/13/all-am erican-muslim-tlc/.

Wallenstein, Andrew. 2011. "'Muslim' TV Ratings Dive Amid Media Frenzy." *Variety*, December 21. http://variety.com/2011/tv/news/muslim-tv-ratings-dive-amid-media- frenzy-1118047824/.

Weber, Brenda. 2009. *Makeover TV: Selfhood, Citizenship, and Celebrity*. Durham: Duke University Press.

Zine, Jasmin. 2006. "Unveiled Sentiments: Gendered Islamophobia and Experiences of Veiling Among Muslim Girls in a Canadian Islamic School." *Equity & Excellence in Education* 39(3): 239–252.

PART III

Niche markets

8

SISTER WIVES

The Protestantization of Mormon polygamy

Myev Rees

Few religious movements in America have generated as much passion, controversy, and bewilderment as the one founded by a young man named Joseph Smith. The Mormons are, in their own words, a "peculiar people," marked by an innate sense of difference both claimed and imposed.[1] The most infamous marker of that difference never fails to grip the American popular imagination. Polygamy, or the Principle of Plural Marriage, fractured the Mormon community almost as soon as Smith received the revelation in the early 1930s.[2] Although the Church of Jesus-Christ of Latter-day Saints (LDS) abandoned the practice in 1890, the specter of polygamy haunts the mainstream Mormon Church. Much to the LDS' dismay, those loyal to "the Principle," persist in myriad splinter groups, and just like their nineteenth century counterparts, they never fail to inspire lurid curiosity among the "gentiles."[3]

American popular interest in Mormon polygamy has been especially fervent in the last twenty years. In 2003, Jon Krakauer published his best-selling *Under the Banner of Heaven: A Story of Violent Faith*, a chilling history of Mormon polygamy's darkest moments (Krakauer, 2003). Shortly thereafter, in 2004, Warren Jeffs, head of the polygamous sect the Fundamentalist Church of Latter-day Saints, captured headlines when he was charged with a host of crimes related to rape and child sexual abuse. In 2006, HBO's fictional depiction of Mormon polygamy, *Big Love*, debuted to rave reviews. In 2007, Oprah featured one of Jeffs' polygamist compounds, on her show. Jeffs' Yearning for Zion Ranch was then raided by the FBI just a year later, generating more headlines and inspiring Oprah to return for a series of shows. After the raid, some of Jeffs' victims penned popular memoirs and their success inspired a new genre of sadomasochistic "polygamy fiction."[4] Almost all of these depictions of Mormon polygamy reflected and reified the practice and those who live it as dangerous, totalitarian, and violent and failed to address the spectrum of Mormon polygamist groups or what polygamy scholar

Jannet Bennion calls the rather "boring" lives of most Mormon polygamists (Bennion, 1998).

Then came *Sister Wives*. In 2010, TLC decided to jump on the Mormon polygamy bandwagon – but with a very different point of view. Like the fictional family from HBO's *Big Love*, the stars of *Sister Wives* were hiding in plain sight. The Brown family was living plural marriage while "passing" for monogamists in Lehi, Utah. That is, until they "outed" themselves on national television. When the show debuted, the Browns were long-time members of a progressive Mormon polygamist sect called the Apostolic United Brotherhood (AUB), sometimes called the Allred Group. The AUB is wholly unlike the FLDS (Jeffs' group). Although most members keep their marriages private for legal reasons, they are fully integrated in mainstream monogamist culture, and women in the AUB have a level of autonomy and influence parallel to women in the mainstream LDS Church.[5] Despite their long-time affiliation, the Browns never mentioned the AUB on the show.

The Browns, prior to getting a reality show, were a rather typical AUB family, though they are a far cry from stereotypical media depictions of Mormon polygamists. Kody Brown, a handsome sports-car-driving advertising salesman, is disarmingly goofy and puckish. When the show debuted, Meri, Kody's first wife, was studying psychology and working as a social worker. Janelle, one of the two breadwinners in the family, was maintaining a demanding but fulfilling professional life and crediting polygamy for making it possible, and Christine was pregnant with her sixth child and working happily as the primary caregiver for the family's collective thirteen children. Robyn was about to join the family as Kody's fourth wife, and she was bringing three children from a previous, monogamous marriage with her.

The children attend public school, and state universities. Their sons play football, and participate in R.O.T.C. Their young daughters take ballet lessons. The Browns celebrate holidays together, take vacations together, and even go to family therapy together. Their polygamy presents unique challenges, like the jealousy that arose for the other wives when Kody married the beautiful, and much younger and thinner Robyn. But the Browns also deal with the same prosaic upsets most American families face – washing machines that break at the worst time, sibling rivalry, and the challenge of carving out time for "date nights," times four. In short, the show depicts them as generally content people (but with enough inter-personal drama to keep audience interest), with all the markers of white, hetero-normative, middle-class American culture. Or as Christine put it, "we're just a normal family" (*Sister Wives*, "Meet Kody and the Wives," 2010).

Jannet Bennion (2012), Derek A. Jorgenson (2014), and Moya Luckett (2013) have all ably examined many of the tactics the Browns use to create and deploy normalizing narratives and thereby gain acceptance. For example, the Browns mobilize post-feminism's claim that women's empowerment comes from their ability to make individual choices, like the choice to live polygamy. They exploit disarming gender tropes by depicting poor Kody as the henpecked husband of not just one, but four hormonal women. They co-opt LGBTQ-rights language like "coming out," while simultaneously advocating conservative "family values" like modest dress and pre-marital abstinence. Finally, they showcase their participation in late-capitalist materialism with the cars they drive, the oversized tract-homes they eventually build, and the beautiful (monogamist) weddings they throw for their daughters.

Existing scholarship on *Sister Wives* has focused on how the Browns use consumer consumption, gender, post-feminism, and the banality of everyday life to endear themselves to viewers. All of which is worthy of analysis. However, many examinations of *Sister Wives* assume that the Browns are trying to down-play their religious difference by signalling their full participation in mainstream, white, middle-class American culture. That is part of what *Sister Wives* does, but I argue that something more radical and complex is also happening. The Browns are not just trying to distract audiences from their polygamy, they are trying to convince them of its nobility.

The Browns seem to understand that if they are going to successfully convince viewers they are "just a normal family," they need to radically recast Mormon polygamy as not only compatible with, but *exemplary* of, the dominant religious narratives in American history and culture. By examining the creative and unexpected ways the Browns align themselves with historically accepted religious identities, and distance themselves from historically distrusted religious identities, we can see those authorizing narratives at work. *Sister Wives* is a kind of laboratory wherein the power dynamics at work in American religion both past and present can be observed.

Sister Wives is simultaneously a reality television show and part of something eternally consequential and holy for the Browns. The Browns are not just staging a public relations campaign for polygamy acceptance, they are bearing a testimony. Kody writes in the family's 2013 book, *Becoming Sister Wives: The Story of an Unconventional Marriage*, "… we have a testimony that this is what God wants us to do, and that it will make us better people" (Brown, 2015: 48). For Mormons (polygamist and mainstream LDS), *testimonies* are given by the Holy Ghost as a witness to spiritual knowledge. Bearing a testimony is to declare that one has come to a divinely given epistemological state. It is to *know* a Truth that has been revealed individually by the Spirit.[6] For Kody Brown, that Truth is that polygamy is the order of Heaven, and that God has called him to live it. Kody, and his wives, are enmeshed in a dialectical relationship with divine beings, and in a history populated by countless others who have been jailed or killed for bearing such a testimony. It is important to note the spiritual work the show is doing for the Browns as well as examine it in the contexts of American pop-cultural discourse and media studies. Only then can we get a multi-dimensional understanding of what *Sister Wives* might mean for the various discourses with which it is engaged.

Polygamy and persecution

Given the profound challenge it presents to traditional American Protestant imaginations of the family, it is easy to assume that polygamy was the primary reason for early Mormon persecution. Undoubtedly, the Mormons suffered for the Principle, but Mormon "otherness" is not reducible to one practice. A strong sense of Mormon difference existed well before Smith's revelation on polygamy (Moore, 1986: 27–32). Polygamy became the lightning rod for anti-Mormon sentiment, but the storm had been brewing for years. What is more, the Mormons were not the only ones rethinking the institution of marriage.[7]

The early to mid-nineteenth century was a time of extraordinary religious and social creativity and innovation in the American North East. Prophets and charismatic religious leaders were popping up across upstate New York and experimental religious groups like the Oneida Community and the Shakers were also experimenting with family structures, and reimagining the intersection of spirituality and sexuality.[8] At the same time, early feminists were challenging the existing laws that governed marriage by arguing that the institution amounted to white slavery.

After the Civil War, polygamy galvanized anti-Mormon activists, but in the antebellum period, the bloody conflicts between the Mormons and their neighbors in Ohio, Missouri, and Illinois, had nothing to do with plural marriage. As the Mormons moved west from Ohio to Missouri in the late 1830s, Smith began issuing revelations that set his people squarely at odds with the American project. The Mormons were undemocratic, communitarian, and they placed their prophet's revelations over the rule of law. Smith was establishing a political kingdom of God on Earth, smack in the middle of the western frontier. He organized militias and distributed arms, suppressed the freedom of the press, and even mounted a campaign for President of the United States. Smith may not have actively courted his community's persecution, but his brash rejection of democratic values, his claims to divine authority, and his willingness to take up arms did eventually cost lives, including his own.

Violence broke out everywhere the Mormons settled. In 1838, five years before the revelation on polygamy was recorded, Governor Lilburn Boggs of Missouri signed his infamous Executive Order 44. It read, "Mormons must be treated as enemies, and must be exterminated or driven from the state if necessary for the public peace – their outrages are beyond all description" (Boggs, 1838). The Missouri order is a testament to Smith's unabashed defiance and his community's loyalty to his radically countercultural vision of a new Zion. In one generation, the Mormons went from fellow white American Anglo-Protestants, to enemies of the state who needed to be "exterminated." As Boggs' order shows, Mormon polygamists have been historically distrusted and demonized not simply because they are polygamists, but also because they are *Mormon*.

The Browns are aware of the long history of Mormon persecution. They also know that despite LDS efforts over the last century, Mormons of all stripes face suspicion and ridicule.[9] The religious questions Mitt Romney received during his bid for the Presidency in 2008 made Mormon otherness plain.[10] As did the massive success of the musical, *The Book of Mormon*, which casts Mormon theology and practice as comically absurd. If the Brown's goal is cultural acceptance, it would be counterproductive to center what they share with mainstream LDS Mormons. To fulfill their mission, the Browns need to distance themselves from their Mormon-ness and say *shibboleth* to mainstream America. The surest way to do that, is to follow the example of countless other persecuted religious minorities in the US: start acting more like Protestants.

Good religion, bad religion

The Browns' tactics rely heavily on what religion scholars sometimes refer to as the "good religion/bad religion" paradigm (Orsi 2005; Moore, 1986; Smith, 2004). More a continuum than a binary, the "good religion/bad religion" paradigm as a legitimizing narrative shapes both the academic study of religion and how religious people interact and understand themselves in relation to others. "Good religion" in the contemporary United States has a distinctly Protestant grammar. It is a "belief system." It is private, textual, intellectual, individual, rational, compatible with capitalism, and regulated by the ethical criterion that emerged out of Western Enlightenment philosophy. "Bad religion" is visceral, ritualistic, tribal, embodied, sensual, anti-capitalist, bound up with the state, beholden to autocratic leaders, and attuned to the whisperings of unseen beings (Orsi, 2005: 12).

The contemporary American definition of "good religion" originates from Enlightenment notions of the "secular" state. Perhaps counterintuitively, the "best" of "good religion" is often called, "the secular." However, "the secular" has never been the neutral *absence* of religion, but the expression of hegemonic religious systems so ingrained as to become, at times, illegible as religion at all.[11] This is what Tracy Fessenden called "public-Protestantism" (Fessenden, 2007: 7).

This is to say that we often do not see the most powerful religious systems at work in our normalizing narratives. The more powerful they are, the less obvious they appear. As evidence, Catherine Albanese points to the myriad historical examples of religious minorities in America, from Catholics, to Jews, to Mormons, gaining cultural acceptance (or at least, stemming violent persecution) by conforming to Protestant norms, "although many times they were unaware of it" (Albanese, 1992: 395). From mixed-gender seating in American Reform synagogues to the Catholic Americanist controversies of the 1890s, "adapting to American norms" has long been synonymous with "acting like Protestants."[12]

But "Protestantism" in America is not a monolithic, ahistorical, or static set of beliefs and practices. It is a constructed category that cannot be separated from other similarly constructed hegemonic forces like nationalism, male privilege, hetero-normativity, white racial dominance, and consumer capitalism. As a result, the concept of "good religion" is bound up with economic, racial, and gender con-structs. It is also subject to political and historical contexts. "Good religion" in the contemporary United States is not just a product of Jeffersonian republicanism or Enlightenment philosophy. It is a designation that is always being made and remade. Although public-Protestantism remains the metric against which all other religions are measured in the United States, it takes on different nuances in response to other cultural forces from which it cannot be divorced.

The polygamous pilgrim

Although the Browns use terms like "religion" and "church," they use them less often than one might expect. Rather, the Browns favor the heavily Protestant term, "faith." The use of the term "faith" individualizes and intellectualizes their religious convictions and distracts from any association with institutional powers, ritual practices, prophets, or hierarchies. It harkens to the Pauline doctrine, later reified by Martin Luther and John Calvin, of justification by faith, or sola fide.

When Kody looks into the camera and says, "my faith tells me this [polygamy] is right" or "my faith is between me and God. I only answer to Him," he is staking his claim on Protestant ground.[13] He could easily say something like, "Heavenly Father revealed the Principle of Plural Marriage to the prophet Joseph Smith" or some variation thereof. This would be accurate, but unmistakably Mormon language. Kody Brown wants to be understood and accepted by the dominant American Christian culture and so, knowingly or not, he positions himself not as follower of a nineteenth-century prophet from Palmyra, New York, but as an inheritor of the sola fide principle of the Reformation. Like Luther, Kody is claiming to be justified by faith. Perhaps more importantly for most viewers, he is speaking a language they would recognize, if perhaps subconsciously, as "good religion."

One could argue that the emphasis on faith is just as Mormon as it is Protestant. Mormons do, after all, use the word faith. However, the Browns (along with TLC producers) avoided anything overtly Mormon until the show established a considerable fan base. Even thereafter, Sister Wives avoids mention of basic pan-Mormon concepts like the priesthood, ritual sealing, temple endowments, or sacred undergarments. Joseph Smith was only mentioned once in the first season and rarely after that. The Book of Mormon was not mentioned in the first season at all, although the Browns do mention "the Bible" several times – again signaling their Christianity, but not their Mormonism.

In fact, one of the few times the Browns bring up Joseph Smith, they do so to display their discomfort with celebrating him too much. In the third season, the family abandons their annual celebration of Joseph Smith's birthday (which happens to fall two days before Christmas) – a custom inherited from Christine's family. Although the Browns celebrated the prophet's birth every year prior, Kody explained to viewers that he never liked the tradition because it felt too close to "idolatry" – that is, "bad religion." Instead, the Browns celebrated Hanukah. Janelle, referencing the Gospel of John 10:22, explained, "Jesus honored the festival of light, this isn't a universal part of our faith, but something we've embraced as a family to enhance our Christian experience."[14]

Truth be told, their decision aligned with orthodox LDS doctrine. Much to many Jews' discomfort, claiming the mantle of Israel is a foundational part of Mormon identity. What is more, few LDS members mark Smith's birthday.[15] But for viewers unfamiliar with the intricacies of Mormon theology and culture, the Brown's decision could have easily been interpreted as a distancing, if not a rejection of the Mormon prophet. The Browns are Christians. They follow *Jesus'* example, and are devoted to their *faith*. They do not celebrate Joseph Smith.

To underscore this Protestantized identity, the Browns actively refer to the Puritan mythos as they use the show to appeal for "religious freedom." When the Browns outed themselves on television, they understood that doing so meant that the state of Utah could take legal action against them. Utah's anti-polygamy laws are uniquely stringent. Though bigamy is illegal in all fifty states, Utah law also criminalizes maintaining more than one marriage-like relationship at a time. Although the law is rarely enforced today, in the past, the state used the anti-polygamy laws to separate families, imprison and fine polygamous husbands, and even take custody of polygamists' children.

After *Sister Wives* aired in 2010, the Lehi police department announced that they had begun investigating the Browns. The results of the investigation were later turned over to the Utah Attorney General. The Browns did not wait for the Attorney General's response. They quickly moved their family of twenty-two to Las Vegas, Nevada. They packed up in a matter of days and fled in the middle of the night, leaving their house, their jobs, and even their pets behind (in the care of family and friends). Whether the Browns' dramatic haste was necessary is questionable, but nevertheless *Sister Wives* viewers were presented with footage of a family in apparent panic because of the repressive actions of state power.

The episodes chronicling their move are thick with dramatic references to religious persecution at the hands of a church-state. Kody claims the Puritan cause during the move outright. As they are about to leave Utah, he states, "I just want religious freedom ... Las Vegas is my Plymouth Rock" ("Gambling on the Future", May 22, 2011). Interestingly, Kody does not claim the legacy of Joseph Smith, Brigham Young, or the scores of Mormon men and women who fled west in what would become known in Mormon parlance as "the Exodus." Rather, he places himself in the footsteps of William Bradford and John Winthrop. Las Vegas is not his Salt Lake Valley, it is his *Plymouth Rock*. The Browns are rejecting the mantle of the religious outsider, and even the cherished Mormon identity of the pioneer, and claiming instead the celebrated, privileged, and American Protestant trope of the Pilgrim.

To reinforce the persecuted pilgrim image, Kody explains to viewers that the harsh Utah polygamy laws have everything to do with the power the LDS wields in Utah politics and its own discomfort with its polygamous past.[16] The Browns are meticulously careful not to directly impugn the LDS, insisting with almost naive earnestness that they have no quarrel with the Church, and only wish the Church had no quarrel with them. "We just want to be a family," Christine pleads.[17] But the Browns do not need to point fingers, they only need to keep subtly invoking the institutional ("bad religion") vs. individual ("good religion") battle at the heart of American Protestant identity, and make sure that they are perceived as on the right side.

Kody's charge that the Church of Jesus Christ of Latter-day Saints was complicit in his family's "persecution" has some merit. In 1890, under considerably political and social pressure Wilford Woodruff, then President and Prophet of the Church of Jesus Christ of Latter-day Saints, issued a manifesto that ended the official Church practice of polygamy. Yet the stain of polygamy remained – in part because the Woodruff manifesto was clearly more capitulation than revelation.[18] Over the twentieth century, the Church tried to redeem its public image by cracking down hard on polygamist holdouts. It summarily excommunicated anyone found to be living polygamy and lobbied for a series of strident anti-polygamy laws from which the Browns would later run. In a dramatic reversal, Utah quickly became the hardest place in America to be a polygamist.

By linking the LDS to the state, the Browns are reenacting the Protestant project. They are rejecting the established authoritative Church, which they cast as hypocritical and corrupted by political power. They are heeding their individual religious calling and fleeing religious persecution to the "Plymouth" of Nevada. Finally, they are telling their story as a reiteration of the Puritan Call, making the Protestant appeal for "religious freedom," and thus claiming the holiest of American mythos as their own.

More like Methodists

We can see how the Browns tactfully juxtapose themselves in relation to LDS power systems again in a more recent season of *Sister Wives*. In 2015, Madison Brown, the college-age daughter of Kody and Janelle, attempted to the join the mainstream Church of Jesus Christ of Latter-day Saints. Madison has been very vocal throughout the series about her desire not to live plural marriage. Her parents supported her choice again and again, reiterating on camera that polygamy is not for everyone. This support further endeared the Browns to fans. They reified the individualism and self-determination that undergirds American public-Protestantism. But Madison's individual choice was ultimately thwarted, not by her polygamous parents, but by the Church she sought to join. After completing the requisite tasks for conversion, the First Presidency (the highest governing body of the Church) informed Madison that they were denying her baptism, unless she was willing to publicly denounce her family.

Madison did not take the denial quietly. "The LDS church rejecting me for my parents' choices was one of the most devastating things I have been through," she tweeted (@MaddiR_Brown, October 11, 2015). In the *Sister Wives* episode chronicling the event, Madison is visibly upset and angry, so much so that she impugns the Church's very claim to Christianity, "This is the Church of Jesus Christ of Latter-day Saints" she insisted, "and Jesus Christ wouldn't be doing this … I don't know if I want to [join the LDS] now, because if they want me to publicly denounce my family, why would I want to be a part of your church?"[19] Madison also expressed these sentiments on social media, where she noted that her bishop, and her stake president, who both knew her personally, supported her conversion. The denial had come from the First Presidency, the inaccessible top of the Church hierarchy that does not usually concern itself with baptism requests.[20]

Fans were overwhelmingly supportive. In fact, much of the support also suggested that the Brown's acceptance-via-Protestantization strategy was working. Fans roiled against the LDS leaders and praised the Browns for insisting on their "right to worship God in their own way." One viewer wrote, "oh sweetie you dodged a bullet! Thank goodness you didn't get on that crazy #hypocritetrain!" Another wrote, "I feel 4 u, that must hurt. Blessing in disguise tho, the LDS 'religion' is not biblical or of God. Keep your eye on HIM." Yet another wrote, "the Methodist church welcomes you."[21]

Media coverage echoed the fans' support. Headlines like "*Sister Wives* Daughter Heartbroken by Rejection from Mormon Church" appeared in celebrity gossip magazines like *In Touch*. The picture was clear: here were the Browns, accepting, independent seekers of religious freedom, being harmed by a powerful church that rejects sincere believers for political reasons and pits family members against one another. Remarkably, what the fans and magazines seemed to overlook was that the Browns *are* Mormons. The Methodist community may welcome Maddie Brown, as the fan indicated, but she would not likely feel at home in a denomination that does not recognize one-third of her scripture, and does not share her understanding of the Godhead, the afterlife, and the nature of salvation. Fans offered comfort by denouncing the "non-biblical," "crazy," bad religion the LDS represents. But Maddie Brown is a Mormon, even if she is not a member of the mainstream LDS Church. That fact seemed lost on many viewers. In their minds, she seemed more like a Methodist.

Religion as lifestyle

Warren Jeffs is the autocratic leader of a religious cult with sexual secrets and closed compounds, but the Browns have opened their doors to America. The Church of Jesus Christ of Latter-day Saints is an *organized religion* that demands obedience from its followers, but the Browns are a seemingly unaffiliated *individual* family exercising their freedom to worship. In reality, Jeffs' FLDS and the Church of Jesus Christ of Latter-day Saints are a world apart. But on *Sister Wives*, both have hierarchies, secret rituals, and powerful prophets claiming to speak for God. They are both *religions*. In contrast, the Browns have a *lifestyle*. The term *lifestyle* appears in the content of nearly every episode of the first two seasons. It even makes a prominent appearance during the opening sequence of every episode. As the camera pans across Meri, she says in voiceover, "I believed in living this lifestyle, it just makes each of us better."

The Browns use of *lifestyle* exemplifies how public-Protestantism and other hegemonic forces, like free-market capitalism, are bound up with one another. The term *lifestyle* connotes identity-formation via consumer choice. It is used to sell cars, computers, candles, diets, and self-help books and magazines.[22] When you buy a Mac computer, or a Tesla, or a Hummer, you are not just buying an object, you are buying an identity, a *lifestyle*. By couching their religion in familiar late-capitalist language, the Browns provide viewers with a framework through which to interpret their version of polygamy: it is like being a "Mac person."

Lifestyle not only provides a cognitive framework for viewers, it morally relativizes polygamy as a practice. *Lifestyles* are about *fit*, not fixed notions of right and wrong, or orthodoxy and heresy. When a religion becomes a *lifestyle*, it loses its teeth. It is no longer an exclusivist truth claim, a moral schema, or a cosmology. It becomes a product for sale – one among many available options, all of which are equally valid, but only some of which will appeal to your unique needs and wants. By using *lifestyle*, the Browns create a way viewers can personally reject polygamy, without morally or spiritually denouncing it, or them, as wrong or heretical.

Lifestyle also conforms to the public-Protestant demand that religions be individually chosen, and rational, rather than tribal and mystical. American public-Protestantism bristles when, as Robert Orsi describes it, "the transcendent breaks into time" (Orsi, 2016: 48). Yet, for Mormons, that is exactly what happened in Palmyra, New York on March 26, 1820, and many times thereafter. *Lifestyle* conceals the supernatural, embodied, ritualistic, and magical foundations of Mormon theology and practice. It stands in direct contrast with *testimony*. *Lifestyles* are chosen by rational beings; they are not revealed by prophets, or provided by the Holy Ghost.

By bowing to the public-Protestant discomfort with transcendence, the Browns are not only undermining the validity of their own religious experience, they are reifying the notion that religion – bodily, visceral, supernatural, "bad" religion – is incompatible with modernity. The myth of a "secular modernity" is dangerous as it underscores colonial, racist, and sexist constructions of religious "others" by casting them as anti-modern and therefore, inferior. Incidentally, it is also largely responsible for the suspicion and mockery Mormons routinely endure. Public-Protestantism tolerates the miraculous, as long as it comes with the patina of antiquity.

Conclusion

All of this then begs the question: did it work? Did the Browns' methods of aligning themselves with dominant American religious narratives lead to greater acceptance? Did the Browns get the legitimization and normalization they hoped for? Yes, and no. It is notable that more Americans seem to be warming to polygamy. A 2015 Gallup poll found that the percentage of Americans who consider polygamy morally acceptable more than doubled in the last fifteen years.[23] The percentage remains small, but the growth is statistically significant. Given that the last fifteen years have also seen the reemergence of polygamy in popular culture, it is tempting to fall into the *post hoc ergo propter hoc* conclusion that these mediated depictions are influencing viewers' opinions of polygamy. Such temptations must be resisted. Media effects on public option are impossible to accurately measure, and there are myriad cultural and political discourses that could be influencing those numbers.

That said, *Sister Wives* has spurred a legal battle that could have significant consequences. After the Browns' panicked move to Nevada, they sued the State of

Utah for violating their constitutional right to privacy. In December 2013, a Utah judge sided with the Browns and ruled that the anti-polygamy laws criminalizing cohabitation between consenting adults were in fact, unconstitutional. *Sister Wives* successfully defeated a law that plagued Mormon polygamists for over a century. The result was that polygamous families in Utah could publicly identify as such without fear of legal action. Children in polygamous families could claim their parents and their siblings without risking their fathers' arrest. That freedom, however, was short lived.

In April 2016, a federal appellate court overturned the Utah judge's ruling, citing that the Browns did not have grounds to sue the state since the state did not actually take legal action against them. The Browns left Utah preemptively and voluntarily, and therefore they were not technically victimized by the law. Legal battles over Utah's undeniably reactionary anti-polygamy laws are ongoing. For now, the Browns seem committed to continuing their narrative acrobatics in the hope of legitimizing their family in the court of public opinion. Whether or not they are ever successful, and whatever happens in the actual courts, *Sister Wives* will continue to provide a method for seeing the often-obscured power dynamics at work in American religious discourse.

Notes

1 The use of the phrase "peculiar people" is a reference borrowed from the King James Translation of Exodus 19:5, "Now therefore, if ye will obey my voice indeed, and keep my covenant, then ye shall be a peculiar treasure unto me above all people" and 1 Peter 2:9 "Ye are a chosen generation, a royal priesthood, a holy nation, a peculiar people." It is a mantel various religious communities have also adopted, but it is a title the LDS often claims as its own. See, Bednarowski (1989), Wilford E. Smith (1992).

2 Although the exact date is unclear, a letter to Brigham Young penned by William Phelps in 1961 indicates that Smith discussed plural marriage with Phelps in 1931. Similarly, Smith's ninth wife, Mary Elizabeth Rollins Lightner, in a 1905 letter to Emmeline B. Wells, stated that Smith discussed his plan to take her as a plural wife with her in 1931 when she was twelve, though she was not sealed to him until 1942. Officially, the revelation concerning plural marriage was recorded by Smith's scribe, William Clayton in 1843. On the same day Joseph's first wife, Emma Smith, was told. She rejected the revelation completely. Brigham Young and the Church did not go public with the practice until 1852.

3 In common Mormon parlance, non-Mormon's are referred to as "gentiles" (even if those indicated are Jews). This language stems from the Mormon claim to the people Israel. For more see: Bushman (2005), Shipps (1985).

4 Examples of Memoirs include: Jessop and Palmer (2007), Wall and Pulitzer, (2009); Musser and Cook (2013). Examples of "polygamy fiction" include: Lynch Williams (2009), Ebershoff (2009), Dominguez Greene (2009).

5 There are several organized polygamous Mormon sects, along with a smattering of more disjointed groups and independent families. For more on these various groups and what differentiates them from one another see: Bennion (1998).

6 The term *testimony* does a lot of heavy lifting in Mormon theology and practice. In both the LDS and polygamous groups like the AUB, bearing testimony is ritualized in a specific testimony meeting, which is usually preceded by a period of fasting. Often testimonies simply rearticulate Mormon doctrine, however they can also be sites of controversy.

7 For more see: Barringer Gordon (2002), Hanks (1992), May (1997), Moore (1986).
8 See: Albanese (2007), Bednarowski (1989), Moore (1986).
9 The LDS Church has a dedicated office of public relations called the Public Communications Department, which reports directly to the First Presidency. It has been
   responsible (in its various forms) for radio, TV and now internet campaigns since the
   1930s. The most recent endeavor is the "I Am a Mormon" campaign, which tries to
   combat the image of the Church as populated by white, milk-toast, young men in
   short-sleeves, by showcasing members of the Church from various racial and cultural
   backgrounds.
10 Romney did not lose the election because he is a Mormon, but he was forced to answer
   questions about his Church and his religion few other candidates faced – particularly
   white, male, wealthy candidates. Attempting to settle the issue of his religious otherness
   once and for all, Romney delivered a speech on December 6, 2007 at Texas A&M
   University. The speech was widely compared to JFK's 1960 speech to Evangelical leaders assuring them his Catholicism would not interfere with his ability to execute the
   duties of President. In the 2016 presidential election, Mormon otherness was invoked
   again when Fox News commentator Lou Dobbs accused third party candidate Evan
   McMullin of being a "Mormon Mafia Tool." Dobbs' comment was panned by liberals
   and conservatives alike, but it remains telling that McMullin's Mormonism is what
   Dobbs chose to attack.
11 See: Asad (2003), Berger (1970), Callahan (2009), Chidester (2005), Modern (2001),
   Seales (2013), Stark (1999).
12 See: Fisher (2008), Sarna (2004).
13 Sister Wives, "Meet Kody and the Wives," 2010; "Browns Out of Hiding," 2011.
14 "Sister Wives Separation," 2012.
15 Mormons are often accused of worshiping Joseph Smith. The fact that Smith's birthday
   is coincidentally close to Christmas, thus producing the unfortunate name, "Smithmas,"
   only adds to that characterization.
16 "Gambling on the Future," 2011.
17 "Gambling on the Future," 2011.
18 Between 1880 and 1890 a landslide of federal legislation came down from Washington
   aimed at breaking the Mormon theocracy in Utah territory. Woodruff understood that if
   Utah was ever going to attain statehood, or if his community was ever going to maintain
   control of its land and its finances he was going to have to cast polygamy aside. Tellingly
   Woodruff's manifesto is not a condemnation of polygamy. Rather it states that Mormons are required to live by the laws of the land in which they live. It is not worded as
   revelations customarily were and there is considerable debate over whether Woodruff
   ever intended it to be canonized as such. The manifesto was not adopted as revelation in
   the Doctrine and Covenants until 1908. Although the manifesto placated federal law
   makers, prominent men in the Mormon hierarchy continued the practice of polygamy
   for years after the manifesto was issued. What is more, Woodruff's document has only
   ever applied to earthly life. Despite the contemporary Church's vehement denounce-
   ments of plural marriage and those who practice it, LDS doctrine still holds that a man
   can be sealed (married eternally) to more than one wife. If a man is sealed to one wife
   and is then widowed, he may be sealed again for all eternity to a second wife, meaning
   that in the Celestial Kingdom, the marriage will be polygamous. This provision is not
   extended to women. This remains a difficult and opaque aspect of LDS temple procedure. Some Mormon women are not aware of this doctrine and only learn of it as it
   becomes relevant to their lives. See Reiss (2016a, 2016b).
19 "Just Trying to Stay Afloat," 2015.
20 See Tweets under @MaddiR_Brown, October 11 and October 13, 2015.
21 Tweets by @brookes2qtkids, @_LoriHall, @MargieDTCSC, October 11, 2015.
22 For more on religion, consumerism and lifestyle see, Chidester (2005); Einstein (2008),
   Lewis (2010), Lofton (2011).
23 Newport, 2015.

References

Albanese, Catherine L. *America: Religions and Religion* (Belmont: CA: Wadsworth) 1992.

Albanese, Catherine L. *Republic of Mind and Spirit: A Cultural History of American Metaphysical Religion* (New Haven: Yale University Press) 2007.

Asad, Talal. *Formations of the Secular: Christianity, Islam, Modernity* (Stanford, California: Stanford University Press) 2003.

Barringer Gordon, Sarah. *The Mormon Question: Polygamy and Constitutional Conflict in Nineteenth Century America* (Chapel Hill: University of North Carolina Press) 2002.

Bednarowski, Mary Farrell. *New Religious Movements and the Theological Imagination in America* (Bloomington: University of Indiana Press) 1989.

Bennion, Janet. *Women of Principle: Female Networking in Contemporary Mormon Polygyny* (New York: Oxford University Press) 1998.

Bennion, Janet. *Polygamy in Primetime: Media, Gender, and Politics in Mormon Fundamentalism* (Waltham, MA: Brandeis University Press) 2012.

Berger, Peter. *A Rumor of Angels: Modern Society and the Rediscovery of the Supernatural* (New York: Anchor Press) 1970.

Boggs, Lilburn. Missouri Executive Order 44, October 27, 1838.

Brown, Kody, Meri, Christine, and Robyn. *Becoming Sister Wives: The Story of an Unconventional Marriage* (New York: Simon and Schuster) 2015.

Bushman, Richard. *Joseph Smith, Rough Stone Rolling: A Cultural Biography of Mormonism's Founder* (New York: Alfred A. Knopf Press) 2005.

Callahan, Richard J. *Work and Faith in the Kentucky Coal Fields: Subject to Dust.* (Bloomington: Indiana University Press) 2009.

Chidester, David. *Authentic Fakes: Religion and American Popular Culture* (Berkeley: University of California Press) 2005.

Dominguez Greene, Michele. *Keep Sweet* (New York: Simon and Schuster) 2009.

Ebershoff, David. *The 19th Wife* (New York: Random House) 2009.

Einstein, Mara. *Brands of Faith: Marketing Religion in a Commercial Age* (London; New York: Routledge) 2008.

Fessenden, Tracy. *Culture and Redemption: Religion, the Secular and American Literature* (Princeton: Princeton University Press) 2007.

Fisher, James T. *Communion of Immigrants: A History of Catholics in America* (Oxford: Oxford University Press; revised edition) 2008.

Hanks, Maxine. *Women and Authority: Remerging Mormon Feminism* (Salt Lake City: Signature Books) 1992.

Jessop, Carolyn and Laura Palmer. *Escape* (New York: Broadway Books) 2007.

Jorgenson, Derek A. "Media and Polygamy: A Critical Analysis of Sister Wives," *Communication Studies*, 65:1, 24–38, 2014.

Krakauer, Jon. *Under the Banner of Heaven: A Story of Violent Faith* (New York: Anchor Books) 2003.

Lewis, Reina, "Marketing Muslim Lifestyle: A New Media Genre," *Journal of Middle East Women's Studies*, 6: 3, Special Issue: Marketing Muslim Women, Fall, 58–90, 2010.

Lofton, Katherine. *Oprah: The Gospel of an Icon* (Berkeley, CA: University of California Press) 2011.

Luckett, Moya. "Playmates and Polygamists: Feminine Textuality in Big Love, Sister Wives and The Girls Next Door," *Feminist Media Studies*, 14: 4, 2013.

Lynch Williams, Carol. *The Chosen One* (New York: St. Martin's Griffin) 2009.

May, Dean L. "One Heart and Mind: Communal Life and Values among the Mormons," in *America's Communal Utopias*, Donald E. Pitzer ed., (Chapel Hill: University of North Carolina Press) 1997.

Modern, John Lardas. *Secularism in Antebellum American* (Chicago: University of Chicago Press) 2001.

Moore, R. Laurence. *Religious Outsiders and the Making of Americans* (New York: Oxford University Press) 1986.

Musser, Rebecca and M. Bridget Cook, *The Witness Wore Red: The 19th Wife Who Brought Polygamous Cult Leaders to Justice* (New York: Grand Central Publishing) 2013.

Newport, Frank. "Americans Continue to Shift Left on Key Moral Issues," Gallup News, May 26, 2015. http://www.gallup.com/poll/183413/americans-continue-shift-left-key-moral-issues.aspx.

Orsi, Robert. *Between Heaven and Earth: The Religious Worlds People Make and the Scholars Who Study Them* (Princeton, NJ: Princeton University Press) 2005.

Orsi, Robert. *History and Presence* (Cambridge, MA: Harvard University Press) 2016.

Reiss, Jana. "Mormon women fear eternal polygamy, study shows," *Religion News Service*, July 20, 2016a.

Reiss, Jana. "Polygamy Lives on in Mormon Temple Sealings," *Religion News Service*, August 3, 2016b.

Sarna, Jonathan D. *American Judaism: A History* (New Haven, CT: Yale University Press) 2004.

Seales, Chad. *The Secular Spectacle: Performing Religion in a Southern Town* (Oxford: Oxford University Press) 2013.

Shipps, Jan. *Mormonism: The Story of a New Religious Tradition* (Urbana: University of Illinois Press) 1985.

Sister Wives, "Gambling on the Future," May 22, 2011.

Sister Wives, "Just Trying to Stay Afloat," October 4, 2015.

Sister Wives, "Meet Kody and the Wives," September 26, 2010.

Sister Wives, "Polygamist Party," April 17, 2011.

Sitzer, Carly. "Sister Wives Daughter Heartbroken By Rejection from Mormon Church," *InTouch*, October 13, 2015.

Smith, Jonathan Z. "Religion, Religions, Religious," in *Relating Religion: Essays In The Study of Religion* (Chicago: University of Chicago Press) 2004.

Smith, Wilford E. "Peculiar People," in *The Encyclopedia of Mormonism*, Twentieth Century Mormon Publications, Harold B. Lee Library, Brigham Young University (New York: Macmillan Publishing Company, 1992) 1072–1074.

Stark, Rodney. "Secularization RIP," *Sociology of Religion* 60:3, Autumn, 249–273, 1999.

Wall, Elissa and Lisa Pulitzer. *Stolen Innocence: My Story of Growing Up in a Polygamous Sect, becoming a Teenage Bride, and Breaking Free of Warren Jeffs* (New York: Harpers) 2009.

9

PARANORMAL REALITY TELEVISION

Audience engagement with mediums and spirit communication

Annette Hill

Introduction

Reality television is a term that describes a mixture of fact and drama. We cannot understand reality television in isolation, but part of wider social and cultural phenomena, including production practices, communicative modes, and audience practices. As an inter-generic space reality television occupies the world space of observable phenomena, the dramatic space of entertainment, and the entertainment space of constructed studios and locations (Corner, 2014 cited in Hill, 2015, 9). Reality television also plays with the spaces in between information and entertainment, authenticity and performance, truth claims and deception. As such, reality television makes visible its own mediation process; it can offer reflections on reality in late modern society.

This argument about reality television as an inter-generic space is explored through a critical analysis of empirical qualitative research on audiences of reality television based on mediums and spirit communication. Paranormal reality television continues a long tradition of representations of the extraordinary in popular culture. In *Paranormal Media* (Hill, 2011), previous work on this genre highlights the connections between new communication technologies and spirit communication; mediums have long been associated with the performance of spirit communication through their participation in and through the telegraph, photograph, film, radio, telephone, television, and digital media. Mediums represent charismatic religious figures who claim they can communicate with the spirits of the dead, offering messages to the living, and signifying spiritual belief in an afterlife. Mediums are mainly associated with spiritualism, an alternative religious movement established in the nineteenth century in Britain and America that draws on an eclectic range of Eastern and Western religious and philosophical writings. Paranormal reality television borrows from earlier historical examples in alternative and mainstream culture, such as Victorian magic lantern shows, or public demonstrations of mediums. For this chapter, the representation of mediums in paranormal reality television offers a useful site of analysis for the performance of spirit communication and audience engagement with unorthodox religious beliefs.

The audience research is drawn from a wider study (Hill, 2011), using focus groups, interviews and participant observations with over 250 participants, ranging from sceptics to believers. The approach is a popular cultural ethnography, and the research extends beyond texts or genres to offer empirical data regarding audience responses to the representation of mediums in a range of reality television, and their personal experiences of mediums and psychics in tourism, live events, and public demonstrations. One participant said: 'If you want to be a medium in media you've got to be extra, extra special' (34-year-old female nurse). Her comment was rare, as the majority of participants in the study claimed the opposite – mediums in the media were not special at all. There was a high degree of scepticism from audiences towards the profession of mediums and the issue of trust and authenticity within the psychic industry (see Koven, 2007, for example). This position of distrust was heightened by appearances of mediums and psychics in reality television, pro- grammes that often mixed the world space of ghost hunting with the entertain- ment space of artificially constructed locations and studios. Here, then, reality television as an inter-generic space for fact and entertainment invites audiences to think through concepts of authenticity and deception in paranormal reality televi- sion, in the profession of mediums and spirit communication, and people's spiritual experiences in their everyday lives.

For critics such as Trezise (2008), the performance of mediums is an example of a neo-Foucauldian approach to reality television, where the political ideology of late capitalism and neoliberalism is represented in the genre; audiences who watch these programmes, or participate as members of the public, are complicit in the commercialisation of television and paranormal beliefs. However, when speaking with viewers of these kinds of programmes assumptions that audiences are naively trusting of mediums, and their religious and political economic messages, are chal- lenged by audiences themselves. Audience research offers another interpretation of paranormal reality television, where viewers are intensely critical of the commercial framing of mediums in reality television, and sceptical of claims to authentic spirit communication in the shows. Such critical engagement is also extended beyond the moment of reception to the everyday lives of audiences, who use paranormal reality television as a resource to reflect on their own experiences of mediums and psychics and their hopes and uncertainties about alternative spiritual beliefs.

In the inter-generic space of reality television the ambiguous nature of fact and entertainment opens up a reflexive space for audiences to question the value of their spiritual experiences in late modern society. The argument put forward here is that critical engagement with paranormal claims in popular culture is a pathway to understanding the cultural meanings that shape contemporary spiritual experi- ences. Similar to Ammerman's (2013) research on spirituality in everyday life, and Winston's (2009) discussion of television drama and religious speculation, this research avoids polarisation between religion and spirituality by analysing the personal and collective cultural experiences of audiences. It argues for research that addresses the intersections across spirituality, popular culture and personal and social experiences (see Mazur and McCarthy, 2010). The ambiguity of what is real within reality television connects with a sense of uncertainty with regard to alternative religious beliefs and what this means to audiences in their search for spiritual experiences that they understand as proof of life after death.

Reality television as inter-generic space

Bignell suggests thinking about reality television as 'a nodal point at which different discourses within and outside television culture have temporarily come together in an unstable conjunction' (Bignell, 2005, 171). This is a useful position to take for reality television as it resists a single identity, adopting multiple aesthetics and appealing to various audiences living in different regions and cultures. Paranormal reality television is a container for a range of diverse programmes, series, formats, and events in which elements of tabloid news, investigative journalism, documentary, sports, crime drama, melodrama, soap opera, and horror mix together. For Corner (cited in Hill, 2015, 9) 'reality television is a new kind of inter-generic space rather than a genre.' In the book *Reality TV* (Hill, 2015), the idea of reality television as an inter-generic space is explored in more detail across a range of content and audience engagement. In this case, paranormal reality television draws on subvariants of other genres across factuality, serial drama and entertainment television. Generally speaking there are three kinds of spaces for this subgenre: the world space of mediums represented in real life situations, such as meeting with bereaved persons in their homes, for example *Long Island Medium* (TLC, USA 2011–); the dramatic space of mediums represented in television series, in particular drama documentaries or crime reconstructions, where real life mediums and their experiences are dramatised as a true story, for example *Psychic Detectives* (Court TV, USA, 2006–); and there is the entertainment space of television series where mediums are placed in artificially constructed settings, such as a television studio or a ghost hunting event filmed for television, for example *Psychic Challenge* (Zodiac 2005–).

World space of reality television

For the world space of reality television, there are examples from the earlier days of the genre in the 1990s, such as live public participation programmes like *Crossing Over with John Edward* (Sci Fi, USA, 1999–2005) which involved a medium giving live readings with members of the public. The programmes usually contain participants who are performing as themselves in recognisable social roles, such as a professional medium, or a grieving family member. Mediums in reality television as world space connect representations of the paranormal with a medium's professional and private life, related news articles and online content, and with real life experiences of the paranormal. What is significant is that these reality series can include a narrative of disbelief within the scripted storyline; a celebrity medium will address fakery scandals in their show and branded social media, or make reference to and sometimes appear in anti-paranormal reality programming such as *Penn & Teller: Bullshit!* (2003–2010, USA Showtime) and Derren Brown's *Fear and Faith* (2012, UK, Channel 4). Public debates about scepticism of paranormal claims are incorporated into personal branding and PR management for celebrity mediums; *Hollywood Medium With Tyler Henry* (E!, USA 2014–) promotes the medium as a 'regular millennial' with unusual abilities, who offers advice to audiences about how to spot a fake psychic.[1]

A recent example of the world space of reality television is *Long Island Medium* on TLC. According to the official website for the series 'Theresa Caputo is an average mom from Long Island in every way except one: she talks to the dead.'[2] The series brands itself on the authentic experience of the star: 'Theresa spends her days with her loving family and helping individuals connect to the spirits of their departed loved ones. This is not her job … this is her life.'[3] The show attracts a primarily female demographic, with ratings of around 2.5 million viewers.[4] A typical episode of the seventh season running in 2017 includes Caputo conducting group readings to help a family contact their dead relative, and performing private readings with clients and celebrities. A combination of organised readings with clients, and 'surprise' readings where Caputo will drop in and do an on-the-spot reading, on Wall Street for example, make the representations within the show connect with representations of the real world. What is interesting is that the real world is often depicted in places where there are disbelievers, highlighting a spiritual journey where ordinary people become convinced of spirit communication. As Koven (2007, 200) notes, there is an *a priori* assumption of scepticism produced within paranormal reality television that invites critical viewers to remain open to the possibility of paranormal claims. Caputo has been accused of fakery, there are amateur videos on YouTube purportedly showing her cold reading, and the series deliberately addresses such scepticism in the narrative of the show; there is a storyline in season seven (episode eight 'Is the Gift Real?') where Caputo under-goes a brain scan to prove her psychic powers. Here, we see the real world space of reality television include scripted factual entertainment that fuses with the real life of a professional medium and public criticism of their claims to authenticity.

Trezise's research on the performance mode of mediums in the reality series *Crossing Over* illuminates the combination of entertainment and emotional engagement by audiences with the series, and the real world space of Edward as a charismatic medium. 'As a live event, Edward offers memory traces that link the alleged spirits of deceased relatives to audience members via a process of data validation' (Trezise, 2008, 103). Trezise argues: 'this moment is essential to under-standing how the trace generates memory as affect … the embodied authenticity of memory as social discourse' (ibid.). There was some controversy surrounding Edward in 2001 concerning a special show with relatives of the victims of the terrorist attacks in America on 9/11 (Sci Fi did not air this episode). For Trezise, this kind of reality television trades on trauma and grief for commercial gain. In this example the real world space of reality television transgresses entertainment and factuality in such a way that trauma is used as a driver in the market in emotions within popular culture.

Dramatic space of reality television

The real world space of reality television crosses over into dramatic spaces, mixing reconstructions with real crimes in series concerning paranormal investigators. This type of programming borrows heavily on drama documentary traditions; this is a hybrid genre that uses actors, dramatised stories and reconstructions, scripting the narrative and relying on aesthetics commonly associated with crime drama, melo-drama, or horror, to tell a true life story (Paget, 1998). This kind of paranormal reality television uses reconstructions and interviews with real persons. Emotional identification with the professional medium, law enforcement and the victims' point of view is important. The affective structures for dramatised true crime series highlight traditional family values, a strong sense of justice and morality, a respect for the law and legal system, and a narrative drive for resolution and/or justice for the victims and their families.

Psychic Detectives shows on the niche digital channel Crime and Investigation in the UK, a small channel that makes various reality crime series about police investigations and famous criminal cases and legal trials. On the official website they brand the channel as 'CI is dedicated to true crime stories, because fact is darker than fiction.'[5] The series has seven seasons, and advertises itself by comparing this reality television with popular paranormal drama: 'When detectives run out of time and out of luck where do they turn? No longer the sole realm of the *X-Files*, psychic detectives now aid police in their most perplexing cases.'[6] The series borrows from the popularity of paranormal and crime drama such as *The X-Files* (Fox, USA 1993–) about FBI paranormal investigations, or *Medium* (CBS, USA, 2005–2011) based on the real life medium Allison DuBois. Viewers are in no doubt that this true crime paranormal series has aspirations of dramatic appeal; each episode deals with a true crime, using reconstructions with actors, interspersed with interviews and voice over from the lead detective and medium involved with the investigation of a missing person or murder case.

Entertainment space of reality television

A third kind of reality content includes the entertainment space of programmes set in specially designed studios, houses, or locations. These programmes are often formats and have proven to be very successful business models in the development of reality television for cross-media content. This type of series is usually described as entertainment to signal the reliance on production, where a certain amount of scripting and producer intervention will inevitably take place. These series contain participants as contestants who are both performing as themselves and competing in a reality contest, and although there are entertainment aesthetics, there are usually claims to reality in the series in the form of the use of professional mediums or parapsychologists.

Psychic Challenge (Zodiac, 2005) is a formatted competitive reality series that is based on a nationwide search for people with psychic powers. The format was launched in the UK on the commercial Channel 5 in 2005 and has since been shown in fifteen territories, including *America's Psychic Challenge* on Lifetime, and a version in Russia which has aired for ten seasons on TNT.[7] The format follows a typical narrative for competitive reality television, such as *Survivor* (CBS, USA, 2000–), with a host and expert judges who devise different challenges for the participants who compete for a place in the semi-finals and finals, where one person wins a cash prize and the title of number one psychic. The challenges the psychics are given weave real life scenarios with the constructed space of the format. For example participants are taken to the real life locations of a crime and asked to conduct a psychic walkabout, reporting information that is relayed through video cameras to the victims and/or witnesses of these crimes. Each time a participant makes a statement that corresponds with the real crime a 'key fact' banner runs across the screen; this is a hit for the psychic. These challenges end with an emotional encounter between the participant and the victims/survivors, sometimes involving a psychic reading and spirit communication. Such manufactured moments offer both verification of psychic abilities by members of the public within the entertainment space of the show and are bite-sized promotional videos for sharing on social media.

A style of programming that crosses over between the entertainment, dramatic and world space of reality television is ghost hunting shows. A series like *Ghost Adventures* (Travel Channel, USA, 2008–), on the Travel Channel, manages to combine elements from the real world of paranormal investigations and historical facts about locations, the dramatic space of stories, folklore and legends about haunted locations, and the entertainment space of an artificially constructed 'lockdown' investigation, with a presenter, expert parapsychologists, and manufactured tests; all of these elements create a structured narrative for each episode of these ghostly adventures. On the official website, the brand of the series illuminates the mixture of participants, production crew, location and factual and dramatised aesthetics that make it a hybrid reality show: 'paranormal investigators ... travel to a haunted destination where they meet with locals, eyewitnesses and experts to piece together the haunted history of each site. They then begin a dusk-to-dawn "lockdown" investigation, using the latest scientific gadgets ... in an effort to uncover the truth behind each haunted mystery.'[8] The dusk-to-dawn lockdown, and the mystery to be uncovered in each episode, frame the show within dramatic and entertainment genres, referencing horror and crime drama, whilst the scientific gadgets, key evidence, and truth claims frame the show within factual genres, referencing documentary and reality programming. A recent example of celebrity ghost hunting includes *The Lowe Files* (A&E, USA, 2017), which features celebrity actor Rob Lowe and his two sons on a paranormal road trip. The entertainment space of celebrity culture merges with the performance of the Lowe family on the road and the real world space of the locations for the investigations.[9] In such a way *Ghost Adventures, The Lowe Files* and long running series *Ghosthunters* (Sy Fi, USA, 2004–2016), or *Most Haunted* (Living TV, UK 2002–10; Sky Go 2013; Really 2014–) construct and negotiate the inter-generic space of reality television across factuality and entertainment.

Values and reality television

A generic analysis of reality television also needs to address the values associated with representing the paranormal, including the production values in the craft and creative industries, economic values in the business of television, and also moral, public and cultural values (Bolin, 2011). This is where further research on issues of knowledge and power, gender representation, race and ethnicity, and social class, amongst others, need to be considered alongside production and reception contexts. *A Companion to Reality Television* (Ouellette, 2014) maps some of the further research that has been done, and still needs doing, on the social, political and cultural values, and value judgements, of reality television.

There are two dominant discourses within academic writing regarding the values of reality television and audiences. Lunt (2014) sums up the two perspectives as situated in different value positions about popular culture. One position comes from neo-Foucauldian theories of governmentality, drawing on the influential work of French theorist Michel Foucault and his ideas regarding power and surveillance by state institutions. In this view of reality television, the 'contours of modernity' are a neoliberal project and critiques of neoliberalism and reality television highlight how the media 'construct, constrain and shape conduct' (Lunt, 2014, 512–13). Given the historical background to reality television in 1980s Great Britain and America, this critical approach has been dominant in writings on this genre. Lunt notes how the politics of Thatcher and Reagan became 'a harbinger of a broader political ideology of neoliberalism' and academic writings criticised the 'conditions for the neoliberal political subject in which individualism is expressed through mutual competition in an enterprise culture' (ibid.). The viewer became inextricably caught in a 'system of subtle control beyond the state such that conformity resulted in the game of life rather than through adherence to authority and traditional norms of conduct' (Lunt, 2014, 513). Work by Andrejevic (2004), amongst others, critiques the neoliberal project in popular culture, calling for resistance to this subtle control over citizens, viewers and users.

Another position comes from 'liberal theories of late modernity in which new agencies were identified as potential rationalisation of the lifeworld or as part of a new reflexive agency reflecting life political movements' (Lunt, 2014, 512). This alternative interpretation of reality television draws on writings of sociologist Anthony Giddens (1991) on late modernity and the reflexive project of the self, and the later writings of Habermas (1996) in which earlier thinking on political agency and public life is repositioned in relation to progressive rationality in everyday life.

In this work, truth, aesthetics and morals form a normative basis for liberal society; institutions associated with science and the law encompass spheres of truth that are dispersed into society, culture and everyday life. For Lunt, reality television can play a role in reflection and critical engagement, and the production of knowledge about identity, or morality, based on life experience. Such a reading of reality television disrupts a neo-Foucauldian interpretation of paranormal programming, offering an alternative perspective that places more agency with audiences and offers a means for popular culture to have pro-social value in everyday life.

There is a politics of representation for reality programming about mediums that can be located within broader critiques of a neoliberal ideology explicit in lifestyle and reality television in America. Trezise argues there is a neoliberal politics within the construction of the market in emotions within these series:

> During the course of a reading, a viewer can expect to narrate, guess, watch or confess, for example. This is not simply a signposting of differing emotional responses, but is much more significantly a process of playing out relationships to the cultural commerce of appearance itself.
>
> (Trezise, 2008, 103)

Similar to other arguments about reality television and the free labour of audiences (Andrejevic 2004), Trezise suggests that there is a social acceptance of the commercialisation of paranormal beliefs in popular culture.

Set within this critique of reality television are value judgements of audiences who watch this kind of programming and are complicit in the politics of representation and neoliberal ideology. In relation to audiences, Jermyn critiques fears about the influence of reality television on so called vulnerable viewers (women, working class, young viewers); 'the paternalistic and conservative impulses behind this critique' need to be carefully scrutinised when we consider actual audiences for these programmes (Jermyn, 2007, 15). As Jermyn notes assumptions about the female viewer as vulnerable and 'even hysterical in her engagement' (18) need to be challenged by audience research. Similar arguments have been made about women's beliefs in religion and their vulnerable engagement with popular culture (Winston, 2009). She argues that women like to watch reality crime as a strategy for managing their fears, showing 'a reconfiguration of their engagement with the genre that endows them with agency rather than vulnerability' (Jermyn, 2007, 18). In the next section audiences discuss their strategies for value judgements, and managing scepticism and belief about the paranormal within the inter-generic space of reality television.

Critical engagement

There is a double negative to value judgements about reality television and paranormal matters. First, reality television is shorthand for trash entertainment and has low cultural value with audiences, even with those viewers who like to watch this kind of factual entertainment (see Hill, 2015). Second, mediums and psychics are controversial figures, especially professionals who choose to work within the media. In an empirical study of audiences for paranormal reality television the research shows how the mediation of mediums in reality television invites a default critical engagement by audiences, generating reflections on discourses of authenticity and deception within the commercial television industry and paranormal professions (see Research note below).

In Koven's research on *Most Haunted* he describes a 'matrix like relationship among supernatural belief traditions, the television show, and those watching that show' (Koven, 2007, 183). He refers to the idea of legend tripping; part of the experience of going on a ghost hunting event, or participating in a televised live paranormal investigation, is to balance scepticism and belief, neither taking a strong position of uncritical belief, or active disbelief, but remaining open to the possibility of a paranormal experience. Koven suggests that for reality television there is an inbuilt scepticism of the reality genre and paranormal beliefs. He argues participants and audiences for *Most Haunted* have an ambivalent experience, engrossed in the ghost hunting narrative and investigation and at the same time remaining sceptical of claims to authenticity and evidence within the series. In such a way, paranormal reality television challenges both the truth claims within the reality genre – is it real? – and the truth claims within paranormal investigations – is this evidence of a haunting?

The real world space of reality television is a resource for critical engagement with the reputation of a TV medium. For example, one medium in Britain was part of a high profile scandal involving alleged fraud in their participation in *Most Haunted*. This male viewer, and practising psychic, commented in an interview:

> it's enough to put anybody off ... he plays to the audience ... There is another medium and I must admit, I watched the first time thinking I bet she is one of these frauds, but I must admit, bloody hell, she comes across as really good ... Other people come and say that she is similar to me, because sometimes I can do that ... it's stuff that really goes really deep, oh my god.[10]

Fakery scandals framed the personal branding of this TV medium; his name became shorthand for over-the-top, highly produced performances. One viewer couldn't even remember this medium's name but referenced them as a signifier for fraudulent mediums: 'I always believe the least about the mediums. The guy that used to be on TV, he was possessed all the time, just ridiculous' (21-year-old male student). Another viewer commented: 'he's got worse and worse. He always does all these funny little voices. What are you doing? ... I think that everybody thought he can't do it, it's not real, and he is actually ripping people off' (32-year-old female interpreter). These value judgements about the mediation of mediums highlight an intense critical engagement with their performance within reality television.

Some viewers in this study not only watched with a critical eye, but also went to live demonstrations to further enhance their critical skills. One woman went to see a studio recording of a medium's live show.

My nan passed away, so, I just was thinking, you know, maybe I could get to speak to my nan ... I couldn't understand why we had to wait for an hour and half before we were brought in the show ... Everything that's going on in the cafe beforehand, people are talking about what they brought, there are people who are asking ... people with all this information and then the next minute that information was used in the show ... When you're actually there, he's talking to you, he gets a sniff of it, and goes away and comes back and tells you the story that you just told him. For the person that he was telling the story to it is great, it's comforting, there is a positive message, fair enough. But for people who are bit sceptical, I don't know, I just worked it out ... I am telling everybody what he's going to say ... I am quicker than him. Might be dead people speak to me, who knows [laughs]? It's clever editing, put altogether in one piece it looks like he is psychic.

(32-year-old female interpreter)

Her interpretation of this medium as a fraud was based on real world observation during pre-recording, listening to others in the production cafeteria, and forming an opinion based on what she knew of hot and cold reading techniques as evidence of deception.

This critical engagement of the mediation of mediums signals scepticism of the performance of psychic abilities. These viewers commented:

I mean there is a website of bad psychics and if you look on it, it will tell you they've been caught and cheat you.

(34-year-old female mother)

How would you explain that one that we watched the other night? They sorted out everything that happened, who did it, and everything like that before the police knew everything about it.

(56-year-old female homemaker)

Some people probably do have a gift, but when it comes to TV then it's more for money ... If you go on TV, and you want thousands of pounds doing the same thing, you should be doing it for nothing. It's supposed to be a gift ...

They are really, I think, true mediums, if they are not for profit, and they tell you things you don't know. If you want to have a one to one sitting with a TV medium it would cost you about £200. A one to one sitting in a spiritualist church with mediums, you get the same sort of thing if they are any good, and it will cost you about £4.

(34-year-old mother)

If I lost my son, I know I'd try to find him. And they charge all this money, and if it's on telly they get all this adoration from the crowd who are clapping like seals. They should do it for free.

(56-year-old female homemaker)

The real world space of reality television is used to critically engage with the truth claims of a medium, such as websites about how to spot a bad psychic. The commercial imperatives of the television industry also frame their modes of engagement; for example, the expectation that reality television will script a positive resolution in order to ensure the attention of an audience, the economic incentives for TV mediums to capitalise on their success and charge high prices to vulnerable consumers, and the will to believe of television audiences easily manipulated by the industry. The image of the crowd clapping like seals signifies an uncritical audience taken in by the spectacle of a televised medium demonstration.

Critics of reality television point out that the genre has become successful in part because of the way it trades on an emotional, or affective, economy; this includes highly emotional performances of participants and the way these performances are used to emotionally engage consumers (see Kavka, 2012, Ouellette, 2014, Hill, 2015 amongst others). Emotional economics is part of a broader marketing trend in various industries, like sports or tourism, which utilises the emotional invest-ment of consumers in a product or experience. Value judgements about reality television and mediums shift back and forth between cynicism about the emo-tional economics of reality television and the potentially positive experiences of real life medium demonstrations. The public and commercial spaces of reality television frame negative engagement by audiences, whereas the private and non-commercial spaces of mediums frame positive engagement by people in their everyday lives.

Such positive and negative modes of engagement can be seen in people's reflections on the mediation of mediums:

> My grandmother is a medium, supposedly, I don't know. She came to stay and my mother was watching *Most Haunted*, and she sat down and watched with her. Coming from somebody who is living as a medium and somebody who believes she has a gift passed down ... half way through, she said it's a bunch of crap.
>
> *(20-year-old unemployed male)*

This viewer switched between negative engagement with reality television and positive engagement with ordinary people 'living as a medium.' The absence of economics, the reference to a gift, the ordinary way in which their grandmother dismissed the theatrics of mediums on reality television all suggested ways in which the truth claims of mediums were related to their performance in private spaces. As this viewer noted:

> It is very difficult, when things are in front of a camera there is money involved, and it's very difficult. How far would they go and try to get more fame and money? That's why I am cynical about that. You go to see someone privately, that's all right.
>
> *(34-year-old female senior youth worker)*

In another example the small details made the viewer question her personal experience: 'I went to one medium, right. All she said was "I've got your husband here, he is showing me food … he loves his food and he loves gravy." He hated gravy' (56-year-old female homemaker). The matter of fact recounting of this experience points to the significance of everyday details in value judgements about encounters with mediums.

What we see in audience engagement with television is the cultural identity work involved in reflections on spiritual beliefs, including metaphysical reflections on our own role in shaping religious experiences (see Winston, 2009). For example:

> When my grandmother passed away, she was really, really the first person I have ever been close to. Not long after she died, I got the name of a medium … I do believe, but I don't know why I believe …
>
> *(20-year-old female construction worker)*

> I have a couple of people who were close to me who died … A friend of mine booked an appointment, and I think she is mad because what do you expect to hear?
>
> *(19-year-old male student)*

> Some of them I met were OK. Whatever they are, it's really weird.
>
> *(20-year-old female construction worker)*

> You really want to believe, you really want to believe anyway, and –
>
> *(19-year-old male student)*

> I don't know, you are right, you are really right, but it's kind of, I don't know why I did it, but sometimes I find there is something.
>
> *(20-year-old female construction worker)*

The difficulty of even describing the process – 'I do believe, but I don't know why I believe' – suggests a complicated experience of rational and irrational feelings. Audiences engage with discourses of authenticity and deception within the paranormal professions, and at the same time reflect on their own role in the process, where participation in an encounter with a medium helps shape the experience overall. In such a way the affective and cognitive work of engagement with popular culture and spirituality highlights the centrality of ambiguity to metaphysical reflections; to question truth claims and also remain open to the possibility of spiritual experiences – 'sometimes, I find there is something.'

Reflections on paranormal reality television

The inter-generic space of reality television creates tensions in how audiences engage with paranormal programming. The crossovers between factuality and entertainment are broadly categorised as the world space of mediums represented in real life situations; the dramatic space of mediums represented in television series, in particular drama documentaries or crime reconstructions; and the entertainment space of television series where mediums are placed in artificially constructed settings, such as a television studio or a ghost hunting event filmed for television. Most of the examples of these types of programmes are from the commercial sector, in particular subscription channels and video on demand distribution platforms, including television containing cross-media content. The commercialisation of paranormal reality programming indicates successful niche content for branded channels and websites looking to attract consumers who are open to paranormal beliefs.

Claims to authenticity within the genre and the paranormal professions are questionable within the context of the political economics of the television industry. The world space of reality television is used as a resource by audiences to question the truth claims within the genre; websites aimed at sceptics, newspaper articles debunking mediums, are all information sources for audiences to assess the discourses of authenticity and deception within paranormal reality television. Mediums in turn also use the real world space of reality television to counter such criticism, incorporating scientific tests in their show, using their own social media to offer an alternative interpretation of paranormal claims. For the dramatic space of reality television, the truth claims of the genre and its participants are explicitly within an entertainment setting, inviting audiences to engage with the storyline and performance of the actors and/or mediums in the series. This means that audiences are less critical of these dramatised reconstructions than other kinds of reality programming. The entertainment space of reality series specifically created for television offers multiple modes of engagement for audiences; they can be sceptical and negatively engage with these competitive reality, or structured reality series, and they can also look for the moments of authenticity within the staging of a paranormal investigation (see Hill, 2011). The real world space of reality television also crosses over into these other kinds of paranormal programming, adding counter narratives, and alternative facts, to the representation of mediums and psychics in this genre.

Paranormal reality programmes encompass key debates on the politics of representations of gender, ethnicity, or religion, commercial imperatives, and cultural and social values surrounding this entertainment genre. Debates also include criticism regarding the representations of the paranormal, transgressing boundaries between fact and entertainment, making truth claims that are difficult to prove by parapsychologists conducting scientific investigations. There are concerns that misrepresentations of reality are not only deceptive, but also politically framed with neoliberal values, or containing racial and gender bias. The factual and dramatic spaces of reality television raise questions about the rational and emotional impact of popular culture on audiences and their spiritual and religious beliefs.

Audiences are aware of a cynical use of their openness to believe in the paranormal to generate ratings and profit. But in the reception spaces of reality television, there is intense critical engagement with the economic, social and personal value of this kind of popular culture. Popular factual entertainment about mediums and psychics has a role to play in inviting audiences to critically engage with the blurring of boundaries between factuality and entertainment in reality TV, the framing of authenticity and deception in the performance of mediums, and the power dynamics between professionals and ordinary people in the television and paranormal industries. Critical engagement with the mediation of mediums highlights how audiences construct and negotiate the intergeneric space of reality television, and at the same time reflect on their experience of alternative spiritual beliefs and what this means to them as they live with uncertainty and hope about the existence of an afterlife in late modern society.

The concept of engagement offers a rich analysis of the shifting modes of cognitive and affective engagement with popular culture and religion. The centrality of ambiguity in paranormal reality television invites audiences to rational interpretation of alternative religion and evidence to support paranormal beliefs, and at the same affective and emotional responses to the possibilities of spirit communication. This sense of uncertainty affords audiences the double identity of critic and cautious believer. In relation to alternative religious beliefs such a sense of uncertainty connects with broader contexts of late modern society where reflexivity and subjectivity are part of people's search for spiritual experiences. The dynamic processes of engagement offer significant pathways for thinking through and feeling around what is spirituality in contemporary life.

Research note

An empirical study of audiences for paranormal reality television was conducted in 2008–2010. The approach used in this research was informed by audience research in media and cultural studies. This approach understands cultural practices as the things people do with television representations that are situated in social contexts and culturally specific to place, space and time. The research adopted a popular cultural ethnography, extending beyond texts or genres to cultural experiences. The fieldwork included individual and group interviews, semi-structured focus groups, household in-depth interviews, and participant observation in Britain. The sample included participants with a range of positions, audiences of paranormal drama, reality TV, films, photography and the web, from sceptics to believers, to those in between. Over a hundred men and women aged 18–65+ took part in focus group interviews, 15 individual and expert interviews were conducted, 27 households interviews took place with 70 participants, and there was participant observation of ghost hunting events with approximately 70 participants. The data and analysis informed each other and led to a specific approach that combines qualitative media audience research with critical social and cultural theory (see Hill, 2011 for detailed information on the audience research, including sampling, research design and analysis).

Notes

1 See official E! website: http://www.eonline.com/now/hollywood-medium-with-tyler-henry, and Agius, 2017.
2 See official TLC website: https://www.tlc.com/tv-shows/long-island-medium/, accessed 12 July 2017.
3 See official TLC website: https://www.tlc.com/tv-shows/long-island-medium/, accessed 12 July 2017.
4 See official TLC press release for the ratings for 2016 series six (ibid.).
5 See official website for digital channel CI: http://www.crimeandinvestigation.co.uk/content/about-us, accessed 12 July 2017.
6 See official website for digital channel CI: http://www.crimeandinvestigation.co.uk/content/about-us, accessed 12 July 2017.
7 See article in *Broadcast*: http://www.broadcastnow.co.uk/news/international/psychic-challenge-picked-up-in-chile/5036945.article, accessed 12 July 2017.
8 See official website for the series: http://www.travelchannel.com/shows/ghost-adventures, accessed 15 July 2017.
9 See Lowry, 2017.
10 Interview with author, London, 22 April 2008.

References

Agius, Nicola. 2017. 'The Trick to Spotting a Fake Psychic', Digital Spy, 24 May 2017, http://www.digitalspy.com/tv/reality-tv/feature/a829111/fake-psychics-hollywood-medium-tyler-henry/, accessed 12 July 2017.

Ammerman, Nancy. 2013. 'Spiritual But Not Religious? Beyond Binary Choices in the Study of Religion.' *Journal for the Scientific Study of Religion* 52(2): 258–278.

Andrejevic, Mark. 2004. *Reality TV: The Work of Being Watched*. Maryland: Rowman and Littlefield.

Bignell, Jonathan. 2005. *Big Brother: Reality TV in the Twenty-first Century*. Basingstoke: Palgrave Macmillan.

Bolin, Göran. 2011. *Value and the Media: Cultural Production and Consumption in Digital Markets*. London: Ashgate.

Giddens, Anthony. 1991. *Modernity and Self-identity: Self and Society in the Late Modern Age*. Cambridge: Polity.

Habermas, Jurgen. 1996. *Between Facts and the Norms: Contributions to a Discourse Theory of Law and Democracy*. Cambridge: Polity.

Hill, Annette. 2011. *Paranormal Media: Audiences, Spirits and Magic in Popular Culture*. London: Routledge.

Hill, Annette. 2015. *Reality TV: Key Ideas*. London: Routledge.

Jermyn, Deborah. 2007. *Crime Watching: Investigating Real Crime TV*. London: I B Tauris.

Kavka, Misha. 2012. *Reality TV*. Edinburgh: Edinburgh University Press.

Koven, Mikel J. 2007. 'Most Haunted and the Convergence of Traditional Belief and Popular Television.' *Folklore* 118(2): 183–202.

Lowry, Brian. 2017. 'Rob Lowe Turns Ghost Hunting into Family Affair on A&E', CNN Entertainment, 1 August 2017, accessed online 7 September 2017, http://edition.cnn.com/2017/08/01/entertainment/the-lowe-files-review/index.html?utm_source=CNN+Media%3A+Reliable+Sources&utm_campaign=eaf2b38ec6-EMAIL_CAMPAIGN_2017_06_06&utm_medium=email&utm_term=0_e95cdc16a9-eaf2b38ec6-84749969.

Lunt, Peter. 2014. 'Reality Television, Public Service and Public Live: A Critical Theory Perspective.' Ouellette, Laurie, ed. (2014). *A Companion to Reality Television*. London: Wiley Blackwell: 501–515.

Mazur, Michael and McCarthy, Kate. 2010. *God in the Details: American Religion in Popular Culture* (second edition). New York: Routledge.

Ouellette, Laurie, ed. 2014. *A Companion to Reality Television*. London: Wiley Blackwell.

Paget, Derek. 1998. *No Other way to Tell It*. Manchester: Manchester University Press.

Trezise, Bryoni. 2008. 'Ambivalent Apparitions: The Pop-Psychic Art of the TV Medium John Edward.' *Performance Research*. 13(4): 100–110.

Winston, Diane, ed. 2009. *Small Screen, Big Picture: Lived Religion and Television*. Waco, Texas: Baylor University Press.

10

CONJURING SPIRITS IN A NEOLIBERAL ERA

Ghost reality television, Third Wave spiritual warfare, and haunting pasts

Sean McCloud

Randy Ervin was a mail carrier in the mid-1970s in rural Standish, Michigan. He moved into an old home that his father – a contractor – was rehabbing. One day, while working in the basement, Randy and his father discovered human bones jutting out of the dirt floor. Investigation revealed that the house was built on an Indian burial ground. This discovery set off a chain of events in which Randy began experiencing strange phenomena, including seeing dark shadows and having lights and radios turn on by themselves. His curiosity led him to the public library, where he checked out a book of spells and started "dabbling in the occult" by performing rituals. In doing this, Ervin unwittingly invited demons into his home and life, resulting in much hardship. Manifestations of dark figures and poltergeist activity in the house increased and Randy decided to seek religious help. He met with a liberal Protestant minister who listened to his concerns and then ended the conversation by telling him that there are no such things as demons. Becoming ever more tormented and desperate, Ervin then asked a "white witch" to come to his home and banish the evil spirits. The witch's ritual failed and the demons dramatically chased him and Ervin out of the home. The horror finally ended when Ervin was introduced to a beautician who was also a lay deliverance minister. She asked Randy to give his heart to Jesus, evicted the resistant demons residing within him through prayer and a large cross, and later blessed his home. Speaking in the present as a born again Christian, Ervin warns people not to dabble in the occult and witchcraft, because "it will open a door you cannot close."

Ervin's story follows the typical chronological trajectory of most evangelical narratives about individuals who move from "occultism" to evangelicalism. It also features elements found in many contemporary horror films. But the tale's presentation was not publically presented in the form of evangelical conversion narrative or B-movie horror film. Instead, it was featured as a 2006 episode of a ghost reality television show called *A Haunting*, a Discovery Channel/TLC/

Destination America series that combines first person interview accounts with acted out scenes to relate stories of hauntings, possessions, and supernatural harassments. While not all episodes of *A Haunting* feature such explicit evangelical plots, many involve Roman Catholic and evangelical elements such as demons, exorcisms, and deliverance rituals. This is not unusual. Ghost reality television and some forms of American religion share supernatural motifs and themes.

This chapter compares ghost reality shows and the revenants they conjure to those summoned and vanquished in Third Wave spiritual warfare, a contemporary Protestant evangelical movement focused on removing demons from human bodies, material objects, places, and regions of the world. Specifically, I juxtapose two episodes of the A&E series *Paranormal State* with demon deliverance narratives from spiritual warfare handbooks. While these two media forms and their producers obviously differ in some ways, they share narratives in which individuals and locations suffer hauntings that have been fomented by concealed pasts and "unfinished business." In this way, I suggest, both ghost reality television and Third Wave spiritual warfare provide narratives asserting that the past – even in a neoliberal era that often plays down the role of history and material conditions – still haunts the present, conjuring current maladies and requiring acknowledgment.

Ghost reality television and the haunted present

Despite occasional scholarly assertions that we live in a disenchanted world, American culture continues to be infused with supernatural entities such as ghosts, angels, and demons. The moniker "the haunted present" describes this vibrant and increasingly visible interest in the supernatural and paranormal, as seen in everything from surveys to television series and purchasable ghost-hunting kits. Polls suggest that between one-third and one-half of all Americans are either certain or think it probable that ghosts exist (Lyons, 2005; Alfano, 2009; Bader, et al., 2010). An even larger number (68 percent), "completely" or "mostly" agree that angels and demons are active in the world (Heimlich, 2009). One 2013 Yougov poll suggested that a majority of Americans believe that the devil and his evil spirits could possess people (Jagel, 2013). Tuning into television suggests a consistency of interest over time, as reality programs such as *Paranormal Lockdown*, *Paranormal State*, and *Ghost Adventures* have replaced television dramas from the 1990s such as *Touched by an Angel* and *The X-Files*. Both polls and media offerings suggest a continuing American fascination with things that go bump in the night (Hill, 2010).

Since the middle 2000s, there have been nearly 50 ghost-related reality series on American cable television. More than a dozen of these could be found – either with new episodes or repeats – on expanded cable during a single week in the summer of 2017. The two recurrent program styles entail amateur (and amateur-like) video camera footage of night time hunts and staged revenant re-enactments interspersed with interviews of the haunted. Some shows, such as *Ghosthunters*, feature little discussion of what most viewers would think of as "religion," while in others, such as *Paranormal State* and *A Haunting*, it plays large roles. Those interested in ghost tourism can watch *Scariest Places on Earth* on the Travel Channel. Viewers with more specific paranormal tastes might pick the college hauntings program *School Spirits*. *The Haunted Collector* features possessed objects ranging from false teeth to dolls, while Animal Planet's *The Haunted* specializes in the supernatural torments of pets and their owners. *Ghost Brothers, Ghosts in the Hood, My Ghost Story: Caught on Tape, Ghosts of Shepherdstown, Paranormal Lockdown, Celebrity Ghost Stories, Haunted Highways, Long Island Medium, Kindred Spirits*, and *Psychic Kids: Children of the Paranormal* illustrate just a few of the other viewing pleasures for those interested in spirits familiar and unfamiliar, good and evil.

While these ghost-hunting reality shows vary, a dominant aesthetic in many of them is one of slow wane. In *Paranormal State, The Haunted, Dead Files*, and others, the settings are small rural towns in Pennsylvania, Indiana, North Carolina, Kentucky, and Alabama. The population is dwindling, the paint is peeling off the 1920s bungalow housing stock, and the leafless trees suggest a perpetual autumn. The victims are usually working-class individuals and families being harassed by forces beyond their everyday vision and reach. The decay and dilapidation ramp up when the cameras turn away from individuals' homes and toward larger structures and institutions. Ghost hunters traipse through abandoned and condemned factories, hospitals, prisons, and schools, their infra-red cameras and digital recorders ready to capture a fading image or faint sound of a livelier past. The detail of every haunting is different. Sometimes the spiritual culprit is an abusive father who refuses to go to hell; other times they are the ghosts of slaves who are angered that their history of suffering has been ignored. But while the specifics vary, the stories are also very similar in that they feature something "uncanny," something the psychoanalyst Sigmund Freud described as "nothing new or foreign, but something familiar and old – established in the mind that has been estranged only by the process of repression" (Freud, 2003: 148). The haunted present ambivalently suggests that the spirits of history, family, community, and institutional structures cannot be discarded but continue to haunt the present. In the contemporary period, supernatural entities signal a "return of the repressed" in which, to quote the scholar Judith Richardson, "things usually forgotten, discarded, or repressed become foregrounded, whether as items of fear, regret, explanation, or desire" (Richardson, 2003: 3). In the case of the haunted present – a neoliberal one in which the effects of history are frequently played down in favor of imagining individuals as completely autonomous and divorced from their pasts – the repressed that returns seems to be history itself, with all of its familial, social, and material entanglements.

The Third Wave

In terms of contemporary hauntings, revenants are not only found on television. In one particular form of contemporary evangelicalism, not ghosts but demons are of primary concern. This is because Third Wave theology denies the existence of ghosts and asserts that such spirits are really demons in disguise. The "Third Wave" is a term coined by former Fuller Theological Seminary Professor Peter Wagner in

1988 (Wagner, 1988). The name described what he and some of his colleagues viewed as a new evangelical movement of the Holy Spirit – the latest in an historical succession with two previous "waves," the birth of Pentecostalism at the turn of the twentieth century and the charismatic movement of the 1960s and early 1970s.

Most of the movement's founders and major figures are North Americans based in the United States, including Peter Wagner, Cindy Jacobs, George Otis, Jr., Ed Murphy, and Chuck Pierce. Some of the movement's largest publishers and organizational structures are based in Southern California, reflecting the connection between the region and the larger evangelical conservative movement, a history that has been recently traced by the scholar Darren Dochuk (Dochuk, 2011). At the same time, interviews with current and former participants suggest that the movement is well-represented throughout the United States, with members performing spiritual mapping in rural Michigan towns, delivering individuals and their possessions from demons in North Carolina, performing intercessory prayers on behalf of others in Maine and Texas, and staking the land for Jesus in suburban Colorado. Third Wave evangelicalism is also deeply involved in and largely dependent upon mission fields outside the United States, in countries such as Guatemala, Nicaragua, Singapore, Papua New Guinea, and other locations in Africa, South America, and Southern and East Asia (Jorgensen, 2005; O'Neill, 2010; DeBernardi, 1999; Holvast, 2009). The "dependence" suggested here lies in the importance of international mission fields for the development of Third Wave demonology, which views all non-evangelical religions as Satanic because they are believed to promote "contact with, worship of, homage to, and even use of spirit beings other than the one true God" (Murphy, 2003: 499). In other words, all non-evangelical religious figures – ranging from the Buddha to the Virgin Mary – and religious objects and sites – from Native American jewelry and African statuary to Shinto temples and Masonic Lodge buildings – are viewed as either actual demons or the abodes of demonic presence.

The "spiritual" and "material/natural" worlds are tightly intertwined in Third Wave theology. "The natural," writes the Guatemalan pastor and Spiritual Warfare Network area coordinator Harold Caballeros, "is only a reflection of the spiritual, and a connection between them always exists" (Caballeros, 1993: 124). The majority of Third Wave evangelicals are Pentecostals, Charismatics, and neo-Pentecostals who hold to a belief in divinely imparted "gifts of the spirit," citing – among other things – I Corinthians 12 and 14 and Acts 2: 1–4 to suggest that Christians have the divine ability to heal, prophesize, speak in tongues, and cast out demons. Because of this, activities and experiences such as speaking in tongues and dancing in the spirit provide physical "proof" of the realities of the spirit world. Physical experience as proof is so crucial that some Third Wave theologians suggest that biblical interpretation must be evaluated and judged through experience. The deliverance counselor Ed Murphy, for example, writes that "correct biblical interpretation is that interpretation which is most consistent with experience," and that "theology which is contradicted by experience, or at least brought into question, is theology that needs to be reexamined" (Murphy, 2003: xii). One of the clusters of experiences given significant weight in Third Wave evangelical theology is that of encounters with demons on earth.

Demons play a crucial role in Third Wave evangelicalism. Third Wave practitioners' interests in demons are, to quote the phrase that historian Walter Stephens used to describe European demonologists of the Middle Ages, "inseparable from their theological concerns, not an eccentric sideline" (Stephens, 2002: 9). As spiritual beings who regularly take on a physical presence in the material world, demons do several kinds of work in the Third Wave imaginary. First, they provide a very material and spatially located form of theodicy, explaining why certain places, objects, and people have been – and continue to be – witness to tragedy and sin. Events and phenomena as variant as plane disappearances in the Bermuda Triangle, the 2010 Haitian earthquake, haunted houses, generational alcoholism in families, and financial crises are all explained via some combination of human sins and demonic activities. Second, demons are the focal point of attention and attack in spiritual warfare. Because Satan and his evil spirits stand between the individual and her salvation through Jesus Christ, expelling demons from people, objects, and places is a goal upon which a large portion of spiritual warfare practices are based. Third, and most broadly, in asserting the reality and even physical presence of demons, one simultaneously asserts the reality of the entire Third Wave theology of God, Satan, and the spiritual world. To put it simply, without the demonic, there would be no Third Wave spiritual warfare.

Third Wave spiritual warfare and ghost reality television

Hauntings fill Third Wave spiritual warfare manuals. The storylines resemble those found in programs such as *Paranormal State, The Haunted, Psychic Kids, My Ghost Story*, and most of the other dozens of syndicated ghost reality television shows. The only difference is that, in Third Wave tales, what seem like ghosts are actually always demons. The close parallels suggest that the influence is mutual, with explicitly religious elements and pop/folk supernatural motifs blending together to create common tropes. In phrasing it like this, I am making a distinction between elements that are part of religious social formations (Jesus, "born-again" conversion experiences) and motifs and themes that have no direct connection to specific religious movements (ghosts). At the same time, I don't think it is useful, as a scholar, to distinguish "religious" from "nonreligious" supernatural themes and elements. Such boundaries are often based on conventional and institutional definitions of religion and fail to acknowledge that one could as easily recognize any supernatural motif/narrative as being "religious." Such boundary marking depends upon subjective definitions of religion, which are more interesting and useful for scholars to analyze than engage in.

In terms of haunting motifs, Third Wave writer Alice Patterson, for example, relates a typical tale. After moving into a new house in 1979, Patterson began waking up in the middle of the night. When she entered her house's front bathroom, she was overcome by fear. Some neighbors eventually informed her that the previous owner had committed suicide in that bathroom. In response, Patterson writes:

> John and I prayed through the house. We applied the blood of Jesus all over it, especially in the bathroom. We commanded every evil spirit – especially suicide, death, and fear – to get out in the name of Jesus ... That's a pretty minor occurrence, but it validates the concept that demonic entities can inhabit a specific location.
>
> *(Patterson, 2010: 148)*

In its broad outlines, this sounds like any other ghost story. The exceptions, of course, have to do with the praying, the blood of Jesus (a Pentecostal practice dating to the early twentieth century) and the nature of the entity in the bathroom. In terms of the latter, the main difference between Patterson's account and one you might see on ghost-hunting reality television is that, for Third Wave evangelicals, there are no such things as ghosts. Theologically, what is haunting the house is not the ghost of its former owner but a demon.

At the same time, a significant number of ghost reality programs actually do include stories about demons, curses, and the occult. On *Paranormal State*, Ryan Buell and his ecumenical paranormal team of Catholics, Wiccans, and psychics have numerous episodes in which they investigate demonic spirits (Buell and Petrucha, 2010). And demons appear regularly on shows such as *A Haunting, The Haunted, Paranormal Witness, Ghost Adventures,* and *Psychic Kids: Children of the Paranormal*. Third-Wave intercessor Rebecca Greenwood mirrors a theme in these shows when she describes how a demon harassed her daughter regularly at 3:00 a.m. (Greenwood, 2011: 13). Paranormal investigators on both television and the internet refer to this as the "haunting hour" or "devil's hour," when evil spirits are strongest. The belief stems from a legend that it was at 3:00 in the afternoon when Jesus died on the cross. This hour, the moment furthest from that act of salvation, is thus prime time for evil. And so we see the merging of Christianity and folk beliefs.

Spiritual warfare handbooks and ghost reality television share a number of other motifs, particularly surrounding children. Both ghost hunters and Third Wave intercessors agree that children in general are especially adept at sensing spirits. It is a theme seen not just in child-centered programs such as *Psychic Kids*, which focuses on "training" children to accept and control their abilities to see and communicate with spirits, but also on *Paranormal Witness, The Haunted, Paranormal State,* and other shows. Greenwood argues, "the children who begin seeing or hearing in the spirit realm and dreaming dreams at young ages are those the Lord has gifted in prophecy, intercession, and discernment." (Greenwood, 2011: 15) Ghost reality shows have less to say about prophecy, but do suggest that discernment of spirits may be more common among kids. Similarly, both warn readers/viewers that your child's imaginary friends could be evil spirits. Third Wave intercessor Cindy Jacobs, for example, cautions readers that imaginary friends might be "a spirit guide trying to attach itself to your child – not just the child being cute" (Jacobs, 2001: 199). Greenwood even suggests that children must repent for having an imaginary playmate, since it could be a demon. Other shared tropes include the reality of demon-inspired human shapeshifting, astral projection, and the dangers of disturbing occult altars and sites without proper spiritual defences (Jacobs, 2001: 87, 130). Such themes and plots float freely between Third Wave spiritual warfare, paranormal television, and folk/popular legends, influencing and blending into each other so much as to become variations on the same story.

Haunting pasts in *Paranormal State* and Third Wave demonology

Paranormal State, which aired on A&E from 2007 to 2011 and continues in reruns today, tracks the work of the Penn State-based Paranormal Research Society led by Ryan Buell. The opening frames of each episode feature white lettering on a black background while an ominous soundtrack of atmospheric reverberation, feedback, and white noise plays. "These are the real stories of Penn State's Para-normal research Society," the first frame states. "Each year," the second continues, "PRS receives hundreds of reports of paranormal activity … only responding to the most severe." The sounds grow louder as the final frame appears, "This is one of those cases."

Each episode follows the same format. The research team, which features a Catholic, a Neopagan, and several religiously unidentified members, discuss the case they will be investigating, interview the people involved, and then engage in two nights of investigation of the paranormal activity site (most frequently someone's house). They call the night-time reconnaissance "dead time." Most frequently, and unlike shows that focus on technological ghost hunting devices such as *Ghost Adventures* and *Ghost Hunters*, their dead time explorations usually yield little beyond a few unexplained sounds and disturbing feelings. Instead, much of the drama ensues through interviews and conversations with those being victimized by supernatural activity and confirmations of their experiences by *Paranormal State* mediums such as Chip Coffey and Michele Belanger (Coffey, 2012). The existence of ghosts and demons – like so many ghost hunting reality series – is assumed in *Paranormal State* and the goal of each episode is to assist the living (and sometimes the dead) by allaying fears and often removing negative entities. However, the final frames of nearly every episode, which provide a postscript, often suggest that the spirits remain, but that the human previously tormented by them has less fear about them.

In the season three 2009 episode, "Dead and Back," we meet Vicki, a middle-aged woman who lives in a small, aged white house in Alabama. She is being physically harassed and mentally tormented in her home by a horrific lurking shadow man. She not only hears sounds and sees the figure, but has been struck in the face and back by him. Interviews with Vicki's daughter reveal that this harass-ment is not location-based, but rather an entity that has been following her into each house they rent. The first night's dead time investigation – following the narrative trajectory of most episodes – yields sounds, feelings of dizziness, and a noisy old attic vent. But when reviewing the night's videos the next day, the team sees Vicki by herself in her kitchen. She is speaking on the phone and mentions her deceased father. At that moment, she violently jerks as if she had been struck in the back.

The next day the team brings in psychic Chip Coffey, who channels the tormenting spirit and confirms that it is Vicki's father, who died several years previously from a self-inflicted gunshot that may have been suicide. But more, Coffey reveals that this hateful spirit was a violent and sexually abusive human in life who had targeted Vicki. Vicki listens emotionally to Coffey and confirms that she suspected that the entity might be her father, whom she describes as a violent alcoholic who had sexually abused her when she was very young. She tells the team that she used to beg her mother to kill him.

With this horrific history spoken, the team works with Vicki to remove the entity from her house. PRS leader Ryan Buell tosses holy water into the air and yells "I cast you out in the name of Jesus!" Simultaneously, Vicki and her daughter talk and yell at the spirit, with Vicki shouting at him, "I am your daughter you sick son of a bitch – that should have never happened!" After these dramatic tear-filled scenes, Vicki and her daughter embrace and pray together, feeling that he has left the house.

Following the common structure of most *Paranormal State* episodes, the next scene, announced by Buell's voice-over as "final director's log," sums up the investigation and ends with a suggestion that Vicki may finally find peace. The last scene, featuring the outside of the house, acts as a postscript, explaining through a written summation over the scene that "Though she still experiences a dark presence, Vicki no longer feels like a prisoner in her own home."

This notion that hauntings don't necessarily completely cease can be seen in Third Wave conceptions of demonic oppression as well. For example, the spiritual warfare handbook author Chuck Pierce relates the story of Cathy, a Christian who suffered from periods of deep depression. Visiting Cathy's house, Pierce was led by God to approach a glass bookcase. "I reached up to the top shelf," Pierce recalls, "and pulled out a copy of the handbook for thirty-second-degree Masons" (Pierce and Wagner Systema, 2004: 10). While Cathy did not know she had the book or even where it had come from, Pierce concluded that her depression was caused by a "Masonic curse in her bloodline." The two built a fire and threw the volume into it in an act of ritual destruction. This book burning began the process of freeing Cathy from her generational inheritance. Eventually, "as the curse was broken," Pierce writes, "the gripping, overwhelming depression that had been Cathy's constant companion completely let go of her mind, and she has walked in freedom ever since" (Pierce and Wagner Systema, 2004: 10).

While Cathy's story had a happy ending, Pierce is careful to note that her deliverance from family demons was not immediate. Spiritual warfare manuals and ghost reality television can sometimes resemble secular addiction literature in stressing that getting rid of pasts that haunt is a difficult process that takes time and is not always 100 percent successful (Mate, 2010). While Pierce suggests that "any time we overcome a generational iniquity, it weakens that iniquitous pattern in the blood," he adds the caveat that "sometimes we can do away with it, but sometimes it appears in a weakened form" (Pierce and Wagner Systema, 2004: 74). Third Wave writer Rebecca Greenwood also tells readers that demons, once banished, always try to regain entrance into a person's life (Greenwood, 2006: 177). Demons inherited – or brought on by one's own sinful choices – may be forced out, but they can also return. Spiritual warfare manuals include cautionary tales of failed deliverances. These narratives often have tragic endings that include sickness and death, such as the case in which a former Satanist receives deliverance but later returns to his coven and nearly dies from a diabetic coma, or another in which a woman eventually starves to death from a "demon-imposed diet" (Greenwood, 2006: 178–179; Murphy, 2003: 446–448). Third Wave writer Ed Murphy warns that "the expulsion of one group of evil spirits from a human life will usually lead to the entry of another group if the sin in the life to which the former demonic spirits had attached themselves is not removed" (Murphy, 2003: 109).

While social theorists such as Anthony Giddens and neoliberal economists such as Milton Friedman have proposed a notion of the individual that is increasingly freed from ascribed identities imposed by family, community and history, both ghost reality television and spiritual warfare demonologies reassert the power of the past (Giddens, 1991; Friedman, 1980). And, sometimes, in both ghost reality television and spiritual warfare handbooks, there exists a haunting and traumatic repressed past that is not individual and domestic, but rather corporate and societal. In Third Wave demonology, the ground grieves because of past sins committed upon it, and demons haunt the territory where such horrors occurred. Water, not just land, can grieve and house angry spirits brought on by past tragedy. The Bermuda Triangle is the section of the Atlantic Ocean made famous by media depictions of it as a mysterious, dangerous – even occult – limbo where ships, planes, and people disappear without a trace (Berlitz, 1974). While popular explanations of the Bermuda Triangle have ranged from alien abductions to kidnappers from Atlantis, the body of water appears in one of Peter Wagner's essays as a place demonized by past injustice. The Third Wave founder recounts the story of missionaries Kenneth McAll and his spouse, who, in 1972, became lost in a storm while sailing in the Bermuda Triangle. After they were rescued, McAll decided to research the area in hopes of finding the reason for so many mysterious accidents and disappearances. His investigation uncovered a shocking crime. Specifically, McAll came to believe that "in the Bermuda Triangle area the slave traders of a bygone day, in order to collect insurance, had thrown overboard some two million slaves who were too sick or weak to be sold" (Wagner, 1990: 83). Convinced that the drowning murders of millions of enslaved Africans were the cause of the numerous sea and air tragedies – or, put more precisely, the Triangle's culprits were the demons who had been "invited" to inhabit the region by the combination of the slave traders' sins and the slaves' pagan religion – McAll felt God moving him to act. In July 1977, he organized a "Jubilee Eucharist" celebration in Bermuda. "The stated purpose was to seek 'the specific release of all those who had met their untimely deaths in the Bermuda Triangle'" (Wagner, 1990: 83). While the actual ritual is not described in any detail, it most likely included an intercessory prayer in which the participants prayed for forgiveness in the name of the slave traders and also for the souls of the deceased (and, it is assumed, non-Christian) African slaves. Regardless of its specific form, Wagner writes that the ritual was a success. "As a result the curse was lifted," he asserts, and "McAll reports that 'from the time of the Jubilee Eucharist until now ... no known inexplicable accidents have occurred in the Bermuda Triangle'" (Wagner, 1990: 83).

"If ghosts do not return to reveal crimes that have gone unpunished," writes the scholar Jeffrey Weinstock, "then evil acts may in fact go unredressed" (Weinstock, 2004: 6). In spiritual warfare manuals, the land is not just haunted, but demon-infested, by past injustices, and it cries out for repentance. And even more troubling than the fact of haunting is the fact that the ghosts of the past that are the demons of the present can also cause physical and spiritual harm. Planes and ships disappear; souls are lost at sea *and* from God's grace. The places of past tragedy become places of religious significance, where Satan's demons and God's warriors battle for the land and its inhabitants.

Compare the Third Wave story of the Bermuda Triangle to the 2010 *Paranormal State* episode, "Spirits of the Slave Dungeon." In it, the team investigates the Old City Jail in Charleston, South Carolina. The team begins by taking a ghost tour of the dilapidated stone and metal building where, according to the dramatic telling of the tour guide, "13,000 died in these walls." After the tour, team leader Ryan Buell confronts the building owner to ask him if he feels bad that he is making the dead trapped in the jail perform for his ghost tours. John, the owner, answers "no" and the scene cuts away.

The team conducts their first night of investigations and hear sounds, sense feelings, and walk around in the dark with nightvision. But, as is usually the case for first night "dead time" explorations in this series, no definitive evidence emerges. Despite this, Buell dramatically suggests that "the centuries old stench of death and despair permeates the air within the confines of these cold stone walls, possibly trapping the spirits of the unwilling within it."

In the morning, the team assembles at breakfast to discuss the previous night's experiences and things that they might want to focus on for the second night. Team psychic Michele Belanger points out that history seems to have been "whitewashed" during the ghost tour, with no mention of slaves, just white inmates. Belanger then meets with a College of Charleston history professor who confirms her suspicions – the jail was regularly used to house and torture dis-obedient slaves. The jail was even called "the sugarhouse" because it was known as a place to "sweeten up" recalcitrant slaves through physical abuse. That night, as the team prepares to investigate with this new information in hand, an African American man calling himself "Dr. O" appears at the jail to speak to Buell and his all-white team of investigators. He identifies himself as being both a Yoruba priest and anthropologist. He informs them that he "received a message" that they were disturbing the spirits of the enslaved at the jail site. After a serious discussion with

Dr. O., Buell decides that instead of investigating they would take the anthropologist's suggestion and offer the spirits fruit, water, and white candles as an offering. Standing in a room of the jail, prior to making the offering, Buell leads the team in a prayer and tells the spirits that he is ashamed that he was expecting acts and manifestations from them without thinking about the context of their history of enslavement and abuse. Earlier in the evening, a severe thunderstorm raged and "the shutters sounded like slaves in chains shaking their fists." But, only minutes after making the offering, the storm abruptly ends and the night becomes quiet and calm.

Conclusion

In *The Possession at Loudon*, the French historian and theorist Michel de Certeau writes that "deviltries are at once symptoms and transitional solutions" (De Certeau, 2000: 2). The focus of his statement was 1630s France – which he described as a traditionally religious society that was "becoming less so" – and an incident involving the demonic possession of nuns. For de Certeau, these demonizations were a highly ritualized enactment of "the confrontation ... of a society with the certainties it is losing and those it is attempting to acquire." In some ways, Third Wave spiritual warfare and ghost hunting reality television seem at odds with American "secular" culture, and their ghosts and demons are both symptoms of and solutions to ambivalence toward the current late capitalist, neoliberal moment.

Peppered with notions such as the propensity for both ghosts and demons to return, make themselves known, and even torment the afflicted, Third Wave demonology and ghost reality television suggest a very different conception of self than the notion of an autonomous individual unfettered by her past familial history, social locations, and other historical entanglements. Both Third Wave manuals and ghost reality television such as *Paranormal State* stress that history matters. The past affects the present and sometimes even controls it. One motif of traditional American ghost stories – televised and otherwise–is that the haunting ceases once the tragedies and injustices of the past have been acknowledged and addressed. Similarly, a recurring motif in spiritual warfare deliverance manuals is that, in order to get rid of demons, one must directly confront and repent the sinful past that initially conjured them. Once this "unfinished business" is taken care of, the spirits may depart. But often in *Paranormal State* episodes they don't so much disappear as get acknowledged, accepted, and thus become less frightening. Similarly, in Third Wave spiritual warfare manuals, demons banished may return. Some historical pasts are so tragic, some memories so ingrained, that hauntings continue. The past can never be ignored, and is never fully erased.

Bibliography

Alfano, Sean. "Poll: The Majority Believe in Ghosts." CBS News Online (February 11, 2009). http://www.cbsnews.com/stories/2005/10/29/opinion/polls/main994766.shtml. Accessed 4/16/2017.

Bader, Christopher D., Mencken, F. Carson, and Joseph O. Baker. *Paranormal America: Ghost Encounters, UFO Sightings, Bigfoot Hunts, and Other Curiosities in Religion and Culture.* New York: New York University Press, 2010.

Berlitz, Charles. *The Bermuda Triangle.* New York: Doubleday, 1974.

Buell, Ryan and Stefan Petrucha. *Paranormal State: My Journey into the Unknown.* New York: HarperCollins Publishers, 2010.

Caballeros, Harold. "Defeating the Enemy with the Help of Spiritual Mapping." In *Breaking Strongholds in Your City: How to Use Spiritual Mapping to Make Your Prayers More Strategic, Effective and Targeted.* Edited by C. Peter Wagner, 123–146. Ventura, CA: Regal Books, 1993.

Coffey, Chip. *Growing up Psychic.* New York: Three Rivers Press, 2012.

DeBernardi, Jean. "Spiritual Warfare and Territorial Spirits: The Globalization and Localization of a 'Practical Theology.'" *Religious Studies and Theology* 18, no. 2(1999): 66–96.

de Certeau, Michel. *The Possession at Loudun*, transl. Michael B. Smith. Chicago: The University of Chicago Press, 2000.

Dochuk, Darren. *From Bible Belt to Sun Belt: Plain-Folk Religion, Grassroots Politics, and the Rise of Evangelical Conservatism.* New York: W. W. Norton and Company, 2011.

Friedman, Milton. *Free to Choose.* New York: Harcourt Brace Jovanovich, 1980.

Freud, Sigmund. *The Uncanny.* New York: Penguin Classics, 2003.

Giddens, Anthony. *Modernity and Self-Identity: Self and Society in the Late Modern Age.* Stanford, CA: Stanford University Press, 1991.

Greenwood, Rebecca. *Breaking the Bonds of Evil: How to Set People Free from Demonic Oppression.* Grand Rapids, MI: Chosen, 2006.

Greenwood, Rebecca. *Let Our Children Go: Steps to Free Your Child from Evil Influences and Demonic Harassment.* Lake Mary, FL: Charisma House, 2011.

Heimlich, Russell. "Goblins and Ghosts and Things that go Bump in the Night." Pew Research Center, 2009. http://www.pewresearch.org/fact-tank/2009/10/27/goblins-and-ghosts-and-things-that-go-bump-in-the-night/. Accessed 4/16/2017.

Hill, Annette. *Paranormal Media: Audiences, Spirits and Magic in Popular Culture.* New York: Routledge, 2010.

Holvast, Rene. *Spiritual Mapping in the United States and Argentina, 1989–2005: Geography of Fear.* Boston: Brill, 2009.

Jacobs, Cindy. *Deliver Us from Evil: Putting a Stop to the Occultic Influence Invading Your Home and Community.* Ventura, CA: Regal Books, 2001.

Jagel, Katie. "Poll Results: Exorcism." Yougov: What the World Thinks, September 17, 2013. http://today.yougov.com/news/2013/09/17/poll-results-exorcism/. Accessed 4/17/2017.

Jorgensen, Dan. "Third Wave Evangelism and the Politics of the Global in Papua New Guinea: Spiritual Warfare and the Recreation of Place in Telefolmin." *Oceania* 75(2005): 444–461.

Lyons, Linda. "One-Third of Americans Believe Dearly May Not Have Departed." Gallup, July 12, 2005. http://www.gallup.com/poll/17275/onethird-americans-believe-dearly-may-departed.aspx. Accessed 4/16/2017.

Mate, Gabor. *In the Realm of Hungry Ghosts: Close Encounters with Addiction.* Berkeley, CA: North Atlantic Books, 2010.

Murphy, Ed. *The Handbook for Spiritual Warfare.* Revised and updated. Nashville: Thomas Nelson Publishers, 2003.

O'Neill, Kevin Lewis. *City of God: Christian Citizenship in Postwar Guatemala.* Berkeley: University of California Press, 2010.

Patterson, Alice. *Bridging the Racial and Political Divide: How Godly Politics Can Transform a Nation*. San Jose, CA: Transformational Publications – A Division of Harvest Evangelism, 2010.

Pierce, Chuck D. and Rebecca Wagner Systema. *Protecting Your Home from Spiritual Darkness*. Ventura, CA: Regal Books, 2004.

Richardson, Judith. *Possessions: The History and Uses of Haunting in the Hudson Valley*. Cambridge, MA: Harvard University Press, 2003.

Stephens, Walter. *Demon Lovers: Witchcraft, Sex, and the Crisis of Belief*. Chicago: The University of Chicago Press, 2002.

Wagner, C. Peter. *The Third Wave of the Holy Spirit: Encountering the Power of Signs and Wonders*. Ann Arbor, MI: Vine Books, 1988.

Wagner, C. Peter. "Territorial Spirits." In *Wrestling with Dark Angels: Toward a Deeper Understanding of the Supernatural Forces in Spiritual Warfare*, edited by C. Peter Wagner and F. Douglas Pennoyer, 73–91. Ventura, CA: Regal Books, 1990.

Weinstock, Jeffrey. "Introduction: The Spectral Turn." In *Spectral America: Phantoms and the National Imagination*, edited by Jeffrey Weinstock, 3–17. Madison: University of Wisconsin Press, 2004.

11

AMISH REALITY AND REALITY TV "AMISHNESS"

Agonism in the cultural marketplace

Stewart M. Hoover

The Amish remain an object of fascination in contemporary culture. A distinct and self-referential community, they stand aside from the mainstream cultural landscape. What is most intriguing, perhaps, is precisely how they do this. They are Anabaptists, and share with other Anabaptists a historical memory fraught with persecution and martyrdom. All Anabaptists, then, wish to stand apart. It is in their theological DNA. Amish distinction and uniqueness is expressed by a desire to be apart and hermetic and at the same time to display outward expression of this status through obvious gestures that are flamboyant in their simplicity. The Amish dress plainly in a context where fashion, personal expression, and individualism are valued. Perhaps their most iconic distinction is their mode of travel, with the Amish horse and buggy serving as a direct challenge to the appeal of modernity's speed, efficiency, and individualism in transportation. They are known to live simply, denying themselves the comforts of electricity and home automation.

They thus constitute a direct challenge to the apparatus of modernity, and in ways that are most emotionally fraught in an era of anxiety about the self, identity, and the various crises of the domestic sphere. Rather than participating in modern life's appeals to autonomous subjectivity and domestic success, the Amish deny the most basic cultural markers. As a result, the wider society cannot seem to leave them alone. They have continually been the object of media framing, both journalistic and entertainment (for a review of this history, see Umble and Weaver-Zercher, 2008), and they have been the subjects of (and to some degree willing beneficiaries of) a vibrant tourism industry focused on their "country." And today they find themselves part of the textual repertoire of media genres focused more intently than ever on the private sphere and on domestic life.

There is a vibrant current discourse about the nature and prospects of the domestic sphere as a social and cultural "project." It is, in many ways "the way we never were," (Coontz, 1993) a complex and fragile construction built on the aspirations of post-Second-World-War bourgeois culture. It is also deeply religiously-inflected and can be argued to be particularly marked by Protestantism and the North American Protestant experience (Hoover, 2017). The domestic sphere is also deeply framed and constituted with reference to popular media, particularly television (Silverstone and Hirsch, 1992). In many ways it is not possible to account for or describe contemporary domestic relations without reference to how they are articulated to media production, framing, and especially consumption. For the domestic sphere to "work" – as it were – it must do so with reference to media.

Thus, when we begin to think about how "The Amish" – as a material, lived community, as a cultural form, and as a circulated trope or set of tropes – exist in contemporary discourse, we must take account of their media framing. At the same time, we must understand that framing itself is deeply implicated in how we know and think about the possibilities of contemporary social life. Discourses about social life refer to objects and artifacts, such as "The Amish," in the media repertoire of cultural resources through which we define the domestic sphere. So, to the extent that we begin to unpack the media framing of the Amish, we might expect that both kinds of contemporary media frame – journalism and entertainment media – might actually work together to mediate the Amish within a larger context of cultural exchange focused on the project of "the domestic."

We are all familiar with some of the received images and tropes. We can visualize the Amish horse and buggy. Their manner of dress is also distinctive. Their way of life is easy to conjure, and carries with it salient gestures that in contemporary circulation can easily be coded as "authentic," "pastoral," "meaningful," "family," and "community." Thus, the Amish, in their iconic difference and distinction can be seen to challenge, even contradict, the appeals and anxieties of contemporary culture. As anxieties over the self and of the risks and challenges of modern life seem to accelerate (see Giddens, 1991) the Amish visually and materially stand outside.

They also make an easy and accessible visual reference that can be juxtaposed specifically in relation to media. Amish practice has discouraged, even prohibited, the telephone, at least as a household instrument. Thus the community call-boxes that exist along the roads in "Amish Country" have become nearly as iconic as the buggy. In the same way, Amish experiments with cell technology have drawn attention, and the simple image of someone in Amish dress holding a smartphone serves as a kind of universal trope that binds Amish cultural geography to the geographies of the wider culture as they contend with the challenges and ambiguities of emergent digital media. The Amish thus serve an iconic function in two registers. First, their own quite elaborate cultural challenge through their hermetic practices and spaces stand in direct and pointed contrast to the rest of "modernity," posing a challenge to the taken-for-granted ways of settled, contemporary social life. Second, their representation as such a community of resistance to the temptations, encroachments, and potential pollutants of contemporary mass culture serves as a marker of the ambivalence that typifies contemporary accommodation to digital media. Thus, almost against their will, the Amish have become a singular cultural symbol, with the control of their tropes, symbols, images, and values more or less out of their own hands.

Television

The Amish aspire to stand outside of television and of media more generally. This is not an easy position to maintain. But that trope of the Amish, their rejection of most modern "entertainments," especially those that would be consumed at home, does make them distinct. For most everyone else, though, television remains a more-or-less commonplace and accepted part of life, and one that, as I've said, directly articulates with the projects of contemporary individual and family life. Not that this itself is not without its ambivalences and contradictions, particularly in relation to religious and cultural values and standards of parenting (Hoover, Clark, & Alters, 2003).

While television has remained a central domestic appliance since its inception, its forms of address of the domestic have evolved. Its earliest years yielded to a period often called its "Golden Age," where high-minded drama and culture were made available in living rooms across the nation through its flickering screen. At the same time that television seemingly aspired to a higher order of cultural production, another narrative was also taking shape, that of television as a profitable industrial enterprise, and its content would already in its earliest years be marked by its embedment in emerging cultural markets (Gitlin, 1994). To understand the development of American television, then, it is necessary to look beyond trends in content and format. These are important, but the way that television became an industry and a set of markets is equally important, as it is the market constitution of television that accounts for the success and longevity of many of its "trends." Yes, they make sense because they make cultural sense, but they must necessarily make economic sense first.

And, an important turn in the evolution of American television and of American cultural products more generally came in the 1980s, when US trade policy made an important shift. During the Reagan administration, it became a matter of policy to monetize American culture, and integrate it into the international trade regime (Gagne, 2016). Television, film, art, and other intellectual properties were no longer merely "culture," they became commodities. This was a concrete and material affordance in legal and trade terms of the era of neoliberal globalization, which now defines much of contemporary life. The media are not part of that project simply because they provide images and languages for circulation in contemporary discourse. They do, but at the same time, they conform to and contribute to the political economy of globalization, and more importantly, their content articulates with that project. It is the purpose of this chapter to explore how the mediation of "The Amish" is not only a matter of simple exploitation, as is often said, but is deeply and tellingly integrated into this larger system of exchange, markets, and sense-making. It does important cultural work for the overall project.

The subsequent "eras" of American television make much more sense when seen in the light of economics and markets. American television began as a commercial enterprise, but it was also initially a "loss leader" for the networks. It took years, even decades, for it to come to the place of centrality typical of more recent decades. Part of its evolution was its *market* evolution, with its structure, content, circulation, and practices of audience-making attuned more and more to the market. The contemporary television era, often called the "Peak TV" era, is a product and marker of this evolution. As the television marketplace has become more and more diverse and differentiated, producers have been more and more able to produce for niche markets of taste (Paskin, 2015). This has resulted in exceptional television in traditional cultural terms, but also exceptional television in the most puerile and debased terms. It is all part of the logics of the contemporary media-cultural marketplace.

The "Peak TV" era in American television has coincided with another trend, which is the focus of this volume: "Reality TV." Reality shows first make sense in market terms. They are relatively inexpensive to produce and traffic in tried-and-true themes of the popular media (dare I say "Tabloid"?) marketplace (Murray & Ouellette, 2009). "Reality TV" has been controversial from the beginning. It is widely criticized as "exploitation TV," and among the sacred and set-apart geographies it has exploited, is that of the Amish and Amish life. There has been a good deal of popular and scholarly attention to this fact (for a scholarly take, see Eitzen, 2008). My purpose here is not to simply push analysis and interpretation beyond the simple question of the framing and marketing of "Amish-ness" in reality television, nor to address questions of "authenticity," or "exploitation" directly. Instead, I wish to propose a direction that asks about the ways that Amish reality TV makes particular sense. What purpose does it serve? What work does it do? It is not enough, in my mind, to simply say that the Amish are yet another sacred and protected sector of (supposedly) private life that the rapacious maw of reality TV has engorged itself on (though that is in fact one plausible way to look at it). I want to ask some other questions.

But first, we need to remember that the reality TV "era" is not the first time the Amish have been mediated. In fact, "The Amish" as a cultural trope is a product of mediation, both shallow and deep, across a large span of American media history.

Amish waypoints in media history

The Amish have never been absent from public media. They were of course always present in local news coverage in their home areas, and much of their collective strategy and orientation to public media seems to have been rooted in these experiences. As a result, they have had a traditional approach to media best described as a mixture of apprehension and suspicion (Kraybill, 2008). The Old Order groups also have been modestly active in their own media production, with a variety of regional and national print publications circulating among them (Nolt, 2008). Moreover, they are an object of fascination for general media audiences. In the period of expansion of television content typified by the shift toward the so-called "peak TV era," a notional history of increased Amish presence in media and increased media interest in the Amish would include several important waypoints.

The first among these was certainly the 1985 film, *Witness*, starring Kelly McGillis and Harrison Ford. Set in Lancaster County, the heart of "Amish Country," it was a landmark public presentation of the Old Order Amish culture, and was generally thought to have presented the Amish in a favorable light, framing the dominant public narrative of Amish life as a pure pastoral idyll. Other treatments, including the 1997 *For Richer or Poorer* and several documentary projects in the years following *Witness*, while not as widely-circulated, nonetheless instantiated the "authentic" "pastoral" tropes attached to public framings of Amish life (Umble & Weaver-Zercher, 2008, 20).

A second landmark was of a completely different sort – the tragedy at Nickel Mines, Pennsylvania in October of 2006 when a lone gunman invaded an Amish schoolhouse and took children hostage. Five young girls and the gunman died in the incident. This brought a renewed and very public frame around the Amish community, and projected a new and newly-nuanced set of Amish tropes. The Amish themselves retained their suspicious, even antagonistic, attitude toward journalism and public media, while at the same time, those media found a way to present a new – and in important ways – *authentic* dimension to public under-standing of Amishness, that they seemed uniquely able to express – and to be ennobled by an ethic of forgiveness toward the perpetrator. This dimension of the Amish story led both to increased public focus on the community as it also led many journalists to a round of soul-searching about their exploitation of the story (Umble & Weaver-Zercher, 2008, 248).

The third, and most recent, landmark – and the focus of this account – is the emergence, in the era of "reality television," of a series of Amish-themed programs. Each of these focused on a different aspect of the outside world's fascination with the Amish. The first was *Amish in the City*, a nine-episode series on the UPN network, broadcast in 2004. It keyed off of the Amish practice of "Rumspringa" where young people, before joining the church, are allowed a certain amount of leeway to taste the various enticements of "English" (outside) culture. It followed the standard form of reality for its time, placing Amish teenagers in a living arrangement with non-Amish counterparts in New York City. Eight years later, *Breaking Amish*, on the TLC Network, dealt in a different way with the intriguing (to non-Amish) idea of what would happen to Amish people if they left the protective cocoon of their communities to venture into the wide world, represented again by New York City. This program was re-conceptualized and re-branded as *Return to Amish* after two seasons, and remained in production into 2017. As one academic observer of *Amish in the City* noted about the first series out of the gate, these programs actually bore more resemblance to the rest of reality television than they did to real ground-breaking explorations of the Amish experience (Eitzen, 2008). They were largely domestic in their focus, concerning themselves with relationships, with the temptations of life in the wider culture, and with exploration of meaning and identity. In this way they very much resembled the received vision of the reality genre, focusing on therapeutic discourses about self (see Murray and Ouellette, 2009).

The most tangential of the Amish reality shows was the Discovery Channel's *Amish Mafia*, which also debuted in 2012. The Amish reality genre evolved across the years, with the latter series lacking the actuality and veracity of the earlier ones, as superficial as they also were. The *Amish in the City* teenagers were actual teenagers participating in *a kind of* Rumspringa. The latter series were increasingly subject to questions about their authenticity and veracity. The supposed "Amish" may not have been authentic. The "action" may have been staged. *Amish Mafia* was roundly assessed as nearly fantastical in its premise and execution. It purported to follow an Amish gang in Lancaster County whose purpose was to act as a kind of militia and protection force. The preposterousness of this was matched only by the less-than-effective production itself. The consensus about the program, as declared by Lancaster Online (2017), was that it was simply "fake."

The point here is not to assess whether these representations were true in any absolute sense. It remains clear that they aspire to an account of the Amish that at the same time feeds the appetite among outside culture for insights into the Amish and extends and deepens the sense among the Amish that they remain an object of misdirected fascination. And what is that fascination? What is it that makes the Amish an object that contemporary culture cannot ignore? They do stand outside the culture. They do embody a critique of the pace and direction of contemporary life. They remain available as a pastoral ideal, a reminder of the lost past of *Gemeinschaft*. And the media fascination with the Amish can also be seen to have played a role in the construction of the Amish-modern binary, a role that predates the reality genre and of which that genre is only the most recent iteration. Donald Kraybill, a leading scholar of the Amish, suggested this way of understanding mediation of the Amish:

> it is crucial to recognize that we inhabit a world in which people and institutions are invested, both literally and figuratively, in mediating information to other people. For these mediators – in other words, "the media" – there is money to be made and there are careers to be advanced in the mediation of the Amish ... we must recognize that widespread public interest in the Amish is not an inevitable, let alone accidental, result of differences between the Amish and the English. Rather, this fascination has been created and sustained to a large degree by the media.
>
> *(Kraybill, 1994, 5–6)*

Thus the Amish have always been an available trope in contemporary media. The roles, boundaries, and relationships have been well-established and long set. To this way of thinking, the reality genre is really nothing new. Reality TV as "exploitation television" with regard to the Amish (Eitzen, 2008, 135) does pose some new questions because while it does continue the relations Kraybill points to, it does so in new ways, folding into a broader set of logics unique to the form.

Reality TV as a form

Much has been written about reality television. A wide range of programs fit into the category, everything from home-makeover and tool shows, to talent and other competition programs, to programs dealing with crime and social anomie. None of these formats has been as central to the form as those focused on relations in the domestic sphere. Programs where strangers are put together in a living situation, such as the Dutch "Nummer 28" and the British "Big Brother" franchise stand in as the primogenitors of the form. The central genre, and the one that I think is most telling in relation to my goals here, is one that is a bit broader, and includes not only these "unscripted" domestic dramas, but a wider range of programs where the focus remains on the domestic sphere and evolving subjectivities of self and individual autonomy in private and domestic relations.

In her analysis of one of the important examples of this form, that of the reality "makeover" show, Katherine Sender connects this broader reality genre to the modern liberal project of governmentality. These programs make sense, in this view, to the extent that they portray ways that contemporary life can be and is regulated along norms of acceptability. Reality TV, then, is part of the apparatus described by Nikolas Rose as focused on engaging private and domestic relations "in the name of public citizenship and private welfare…"

> In the name of social and personal wellbeing, a complex apparatus of health and therapeutics has been assembled, concerned with the management of the individual and social body as a vital national resource, and the management of "problems of living," made up of techniques of advice and guidance, medics, clinics, guides and counselors.
>
> *(Rose, 1996, 37)*

In their assessment of the reality genre, Ouellette and Hay (2008), point to ways that these programs essentialize this project, both in content and form. The fact that the programs do not directly present themselves as instructive, but rather do so by example and by violations of the best norms of contemporary self-hood actually strengthens their appeal and their centrality. They are social dramas, intended to illumine by example, especially when the examples are vibrant illustrations of "how *not* to do it." They provide elaborate narratives of what Rose calls "the problems of living," and point to, both directly and indirectly, appropriate therapeutic solutions, most often focused on "the self" and on helping that self.

They are also mediations, deeply involved in the project of constructing the reflexive self (Sender, 2012, 5). They suggest a subjectivity of engagement and individual purpose, offering tools, advice, products, and relationships focused on deepening and developing that self. They address the fundamental crisis of late modernity, as described by Giddens (1991), that the withdrawal of traditional boundaries, structures, and social supports have left contemporary selves deeply anxious, and focused on the risks of modern life. The reality genre addresses this condition in a particularly powerful and salient way. As Katherine Sender concludes in her exploration of a particular reality genre, the project of the self is in a sense "an endless project" (Sender, 2012, 202) always awaiting further attention. As direct circulations into the domestic sphere, where this work is being done, reality shows present themselves as more or less continuous resources to the project.

Thus these shows are deeply embedded and articulated into the project of the self, and more significantly, to that project as a central component and producer of the domestic sphere (Sender, 2012, 17). What seems most significant here is not that the Amish simply provide another convenient set of symbols and tropes for the reality genre but that, as I have argued, there is something unique and particular about "Amishness" as a producer of meaning around contemporary imaginaries of personal and domestic life. It is not just that the Amish are a direct challenge to modernity, though that challenge seems to place them always in the media panopticon, as it seems to enforce an ethic of exhibitionism and exposure and cannot turn its gaze away from those who wish to resist. That could be a plausible explanation for what makes "Amish" a particularly attractive trope for contemporary media. And, in fact, the conventions of media exposure of the Amish in these programs demonstrate the taken-for-granted salience of the idea that somehow the Amish must be culturally "brought to heel," to be leveled into the same media circulations as everyone else.

It is important to keep in mind here that part of what makes the Amish so tantalizing to this exposure is their own self-conscious practices of distinction and resistance. They have been and continue to be quite conscious of "the media" and of their cultural vulnerability to it (Umble & Weaver-Zercher, 2008, 156). This stems in part from their own complex history of negotiation with the broader culture (Kraybill, 1994). They have a theological and existential suspicion of and resistance to the imprecations of state and market power. Their history is one of subjection and even martyrdom to such power. Thus, rather than being naive pastoralists whose approach to culture and media culture is a kind of naivete (which is the way they are typically framed by the media), their reflexive posture in relation to media might be better described as a history of complex negotiation (Kraybill 2008, 175–6).

To the Amish community, then, the reality genre is yet another encroachment on their autonomy from broader "English" culture. And, it is not a trivial or insignificant thing to them. In reviewing scholarly accounts of Amish interactions with the media, a sense of their own project *vis à vis* media and modern mediation begins to form. It is less a matter of them wishing to simply be left alone or ignored (though that is there) than it is a plea that places them in conversation with other cultures, communities, and networks across the globe that wish to claim a right to control their own stories. In recent work, Homi Bhabha (2014) refers to this as a desire to narrate oneself. In an era when social and cultural life is so conditioned and determined by media circulations, those circulations are increasingly determinative of the prospects of individuals, groups, and whole cultures and nations. The Amish thus find themselves subject to a set of conditions that they share with many others across the globe. They must necessarily position themselves, and at the center of that positioning, they see an existential claim to do that without being subject to or framed by the rules imposed by outside forces.

The Amish and logics of contemporary circulation

The outlines of a more nuanced account of the Amish in reality TV begin to form. Yes, the vulnerability of the Amish and of other cultures to exploitation by contemporary media is profound and (regrettably) unexceptional. We are all subject to these forces, and they are increasingly determinative across a wide range of locations and conditions. The Amish are not unique, though they may well be more conscious of these processes than other groups due to their own cultural history. But I wish to argue that, though maybe not unique, they are exceptional in their articulation into contemporary media in general and the reality genre in particular.

An account must be lodged with the relations of the reality genre to a larger project of social regulation and governmentality in the neoliberal cultural marketplace (Rose, 1996). The contemporary logics exercise coercion and control rather more indirectly than in the past, with media circulations playing a prominent role (Ouellette & Hay, 2008). In the center of this, as described earlier by Nikolas Rose, is necessarily a focus on private and domestic life, with a "...complex apparatus of health and therapeutics" proffered to contemporary subjects. A variety of observers of media cultures have charted ways that media circulations come to embody this social and cultural "work." Most intriguing, though, are the ways the reality genre in particular is articulated into all of this. Its direct and indirect address of the domestic, of the project and crisis of the self, and of complex and elaborate remedies to contemporary risks and anxieties, gives reality TV a unique profile.

Summary and conclusion

We can see then that there are several frames through which we should elaborate the relations of the larger dynamics and affordances with the particularities of the reality genre and of the Amish as a distinct field of cultural meaning and resource for symbolic construction in the media sphere. These can serve as a set of tentative conclusions to this inquiry

First there is the frame of "the Amish," their bodies, their materialities, their culture, their social location, their repertoire of symbols and aspirations, and their history of negotiations with mainstream culture, especially the media. Given the situation as I have described it, it is not possible to simply be "the Amish," if by that we mean to exist outside the framework of modern media circulation, and to aggressively police the boundary between an imagined private sphere of action and the public sphere of symbolic exchange. The latter sphere is determinative. Its circulations are deeply embedded in the larger economic and social structures of modernity, and its visual and practical nomenclatures have come to define social and cultural currency in modern life. Anything or anyone that would aspire to stand outside of the media sphere and would do so with some social success would necessarily capture attention. That has certainly been the case with the Amish. I've suggested that part of the reason for this is the way that the Old Order Amish go about being different. Their distinctiveness is a distinctiveness rooted in gestures and practices that quite directly confront modernity. It is not necessary for the Amish to have the "modern conveniences," or to integrate (even in a minor way) to the mainstream culture. Their social distinction is also symbolic distinction and their symbolic distinction presents a set of tropes and images that at one and the same time argue their own authenticity as a coherent, satisfying, pastoral reality *and* present a direct challenge to the presumed architecture of modern meaning-making. In this they function as a valid counter-argument to the presumed superordinate project of modern progress.

This makes them nearly irresistible to modern mainstream mediation. They are simply too distinct, too counter-cultural, and too attractive both in their theological and historical fundamentals and in their gestural critique of modernity. Modern practices of mediation make it impossible for any person or any group to remain invisible. All of modern life is open to scrutiny, and every corner of modern social experience becomes media content. The Amish are attractive to the circulations of the wider culture because of their distinctiveness, but they are sought out because their very existence constitutes a counter-argument to modernity that integrates seamlessly into contemporary anxieties about the nature of being modern. It is not so much that the media panopticon wishes to undermine the will of the Amish to self-narrate, it is more that the Amish constitute a particular way of seeing and arguing about the social anxieties of the present, and in terms that are directly articulated into mediated narratives.

The received and commonplace view – that the Amish need to be thought of as entirely hermetic and separate, standing outside of mainstream culture – is far too simple. The Amish have always been a part of the larger culture, helping mark and define it by means of their distinctiveness. They have for decades been integrated into the larger cultural marketplace owing of course to their visuality, which has become mainstreamed as a set of iconic images and tropes. Their geographies have long been not only invaded by "English" culture, but have been commodified in a vibrant and lucrative tourism industry focused on pilgrimage to the pastoral idyll they are assumed to represent. They have thus been mediated in a number of material and conceptual ways, and have also conducted a complex negotiation with journalistic, entertainment, and now social media. I do not intend to mean by this that the Amish have cynically self-exploited their own culture, but to say that they have necessarily acquiesced to a media-commodity marketplace that has forced a level of complicity on them. That is the contemporary reality of the neoliberal cultural marketplace.

The second frame, then, is the realization that fully self-determinative cultural representation is no longer possible for the Amish. Their distinctiveness and their cultural insistence on a dialogue with a broader context by means of their gestures of living and of display positions them as subject to the gaze, scrutiny, and – in the current moment where all mediations have become commodities – exploitation. Further, their chosen field of cultural practice, identifiable as it is as focused on the contemporary concerns and anxieties over the self and the self in relation to the domestic sphere, makes them doubly accountable to integration into larger media discourses. As we've seen, among the genres and conventions available in the contemporary media marketplace, the reality genre is one that is most centered on the domestic. More significantly, reality formats structure themselves as detailed and supposedly "authentic" explorations of the contemporary crisis on a granular scale. The "pull" that this exerts on the accounts and narratives of Amish life is understandable. The market's need for this intimate gaze is so pressing in fact that (as with many other themes in the genre) true "authenticity" becomes negotiable. Fictive authenticity (re-creations, actor portrayals, dramatizations) become commonplace.

It could not be otherwise. Were the "actual" Amish to "actually" enter into these productions, to cross the proscenium from delectable object of gaze to fully complicit in their own exploitation, the mystery and magic would be lost. The cultural marketplace depends on its ability to circulate images, objects, practices, bodies, and geographies. Those must exist in some absolute form, and to be placed in cultural conversation and circulation requires them to be distinct, yet accessible. They must retain their substance, or at least there needs to be a plausible case for this, or they lose their currency.

But what about those "objects" – the Amish themselves? The case of the Amish gives us an opportunity to reflect on the meaning of all of this for modern subjectivity. For those of us who live in the "broader culture," our own permeability and our own complicity are made more transparent when we think about examples like the Amish. For the Amish, there does remain a central, normative, project. There is such a thing as "authentic" "Amishness" and it wishes to retain its distinct way of life and its distinct critique-by-example of the broader culture. What it lacks, in the contemporary moment, is a means to "self-narrate," as Bhabha puts it. The situation illustrates the layered complexity and completeness of the cultural project of neoliberal circulation. It has become determinative, and alternative voices, wishing to freely engage and articulate, are once again subject to its conditions.

The third frame is one suggested by Sender, Rose, Einstein, and Ouellette and Hay. They describe how the neoliberal cultural market integrates itself well beyond the commercial sphere into the most intimate corners of private and domestic life. It does so by presenting itself as the definitive arbiter of solutions to "the problems of living." Its therapeutic discourses seek to speak to the whole range of modern struggles with self, life and family. Its governmentality thus echoes the Protestant project articulated in the 19th and early 20th centuries through the mediations of the "cult of domesticity." Its resources can serve to compensate for the missing cultural and social tools and supports when we moved beyond the imaged past

Gemeinschaft. This makes the Amish both a tantalizing object (again, as a model of an integrative, pastoral, salubrious ideal) and an object of confusion and curiosity when they wish to separate themselves. Their reticence is even resented. Why shouldn't they – and their stories – be accessible when the overall intention is so innocent and positive? Shouldn't they want to help the "rest of us" understand how to live more simply and happily?

The Amish "project" – if I can use that term – is actually incommensurable with the approaches to therapy and self-help that lie behind the consensual brief of televised reality. They don't think of what they do in those instrumental terms. They do think of it as a way of life, and they resist the encroachments of broader culture on that way of life. And this is where the Amish "religion" enters in, and provides a powerful base for resistance. In a similar way to broader Anabaptist resistance to the encroaching entanglement of the "Protestant Establishment" with the state across the 19th and 20th centuries, the Amish today are true to their Anabaptism in resisting entanglement with implicit but powerful governmentality of the media apparatus. And just as the Protestant establishment – committed as it was to instrumentalizing and projecting its (positive and progressive) values in the public sphere – could never quite grasp the nature of the Anabaptist critique, so the neoliberal media marketplace has little patience for resistance. Especially when that resistance is so directly addressed to, and confounds, the ways and means central to its practice.

Bibliography

Bhabha, Homi. 2014. "The Right to Narrate," *Harvard Design Magazine* 38 (Spring/ Summer) http://www.harvarddesignmagazine.org/issues/38/the-right-to-narrate (accessed December 15, 2017).

Coontz, Stephanie. 1993. *The Way We Never Were: American Families and the Nostalgia Trap.* New York: Basic Books.

Einstein, Mara. 2008. *Compassion, Inc: How Corporate America Blurs the Lines Between What We Buy, What We Are, and Who We Help.* Berkeley, CA: University of California Press.

Eitzen, Dirk. 2008. "Hollywood Rumspringa: Amish in the City," in Diane Zimmerman Umble and David L. Weaver-Zercher, eds. *The Amish and the Media*, 43–66. Baltimore: Johns Hopkins University Press.

Gagne, Gilbert. 2016. *The Trade and Culture Debate: Evidence from US Trade Agreements.* New York: Roman and Littlefield.

Giddens, Anthony. 1991. *Modernity and Self-Identity: Self and Society in the Late Modern Age.* Palo Alto: Stanford University Press.

Gitlin, Todd. 1994. *Inside Prime Time.* London: Routledge.

Hoover, Stewart. 2017. "Residual and Resurgent Protestantism in the American Media (and Political) Imaginary." *International Journal of Communication* 11: 2982–2999.

Hoover, Stewart, Lynn Scofield Clarkand Diane F. Alters. 2003. *Media, Home, and Family.* New York: Routledge.

Kraybill, Donald. 2008. "Amish Informants: Mediating Humility and Publicity," in Diane Zimmerman Umble and David L. Weaver-Zercher, eds. *The Amish and the Media*, 161–180. Baltimore: Johns Hopkins University Press.

Kraybill, Donald. 1994. "The Amish encounter with modernity," in Donald Kraybill and Marc Olshan, eds. *The Amish Struggle with Modernity*, 21–53. Hanover: University of New Hampshire Press.

Lancaster Online. 2017. "Here's Why the Amish Mafia is Fake." http://lancasteronline. com/news/local/amish-mafia-final-season-here-s-why-it-s-fake/article_d45cea48-a3a4-11e3-9cc3-0017a43b2370.html (accessed September 27, 2017).

Murray, Susan, and Laurie Ouellette. 2009. *Reality TV: Remaking Television Culture*. New York: New York University Press.

Nolt, Steven. 2008. "Inscribing Community: The Budget and Di Botshcaft in Amish Life," in Diane Zimmerman Umble and David L. Weaver-Zercher, eds. *The Amish and the Media*, 181–200. Baltimore: Johns Hopkins University Press.

Ouellette, Laurie, and James Hay. 2008. *Better Living through Reality TV: Television and Post-Welfare Citizenship*. London: Wiley-Blackwell.

Paskin, Willa. 2015. "What Does 'Peak TV' Really Mean?" The TV Club. Slate.com. http://www.slate.com/articles/arts/tv_club/features/2015/best_tv_of_2015_slate_s_tv_club_discusses/what_does_peak_tv_really_mean.html (accessed September 21, 2017).

Rose, Nikolas. 1996. "Governing 'Advanced' Liberal Democracies," in Andrew Barry, Thomas Osborne, and Nikolas Rose, eds. *Foucault and Political Reason: Liberalism, New-Liberalism and Rationalities of Government*, 37–64. Chicago and London: University of Chicago Press and UCL Press.

Sender, Katherine. 2012. *The Makeover: Reality Television and Reflexive Audiences*. New York: New York University Press.

Silverstone, Roger, and Eric Hirsch. 1992. *Consuming Technologies: Media and Information in Domestic Spaces*. London: Routledge.

Umble, Diane Zimmerman, and David Weaver-Zercher. 2008. "The Old Order Amish as Media Producers and Consumers," in Diane Zimmerman Umble and David L. Weaver-Zercher, eds. *The Amish and the Media*, 155–158. Baltimore: Johns Hopkins University Press.

PART IV

Commodification of the sacred

12

PRAYING FOR REALITY

The invisible hand in Downey and Burnett's *Answered Prayers*

Sharon Lauricella

Roma Downey, in her gentle voice, communicates to viewers of the reality program *Answered Prayers* that, "the light reaches those who seek it," "we all have the capacity to turn darkness to light," and if we haven't seen light in the darkness, "we haven't travelled far enough." Spiritual development and faith, according to Downey, are our own personal responsibility, achievable only through individual conviction, dedication, and spiritual work. Downey asserts that a primary way to achieve this development and faith is by means of prayer, and the program makes clear to viewers that their prayers are not futile – they will always be answered. The program, created by Downey (an actress made famous by her starring role in the long-running *Touched by an Angel*) and her husband Mark Burnett (known for producing reality series from *Survivor* to *The Apprentice*), depicts individuals and families who "used" prayer to ask for miracles during times of crisis, tragedy, and decision-making. Regardless of the situation, the program suggests that when prayers are offered, and offered with enough conviction, they are *always* answered.

This chapter considers how the spiritual practice of prayer is represented in the reality program *Answered Prayers*. I suggest that the program, in keeping with neo-liberal values expressed by mainstream media, asserts that the individual is responsible for his or her own salvation and agency in being part of a miracle. The "invisible hand" of God is depicted remarkably like the "invisible hand" of the neoliberal economic market, whereby hard work, dedication, and individual agency in both contexts is key to achieving one's desired outcome. I address how Downey and Burnett's objectives of spiritual development and economic success are simultaneously packaged in this program, together with how the contemporary neoliberal agenda is supported. A total of 41 praying individuals were featured in the program across 14 vignettes featured in the series. A closer look at the kinds of prayers and situations featured in the program illustrates how the concept of spirituality and faith coincides with that of the pervasive neoliberal economy.

Why prayer?

There is a wide body of literature around the notion that religion, and particularly a relationship with God, is helpful to people during times of crisis or distress (Kirkpatrick & Shaver, 1990). Prayer, in particular, has been observed as a primary source of haven for people experiencing hardship or adversity. Literature in both health (Kreps, 2012; Baesler & Ladd, 2009) and psychology (Pargament, 2001, 2007) support the practice of prayer as comforting and helpful to the individual. Sociological research has investigated how and why individuals pray, and has linked unique aspects of prayer with race, ethnicity, and life stages (for reviews, see Giordan, 2011 and Lauricella, 2012). For the spiritual-but-not-religious individual, meditation is another meaningful spiritual activity, touted by health practitioners as having significant benefits to one's physical and mental wellness (Kabat-Zinn, 1990). While myriad issues contribute to one's prayer practice, including religion, denomination, and other demographic factors such as age and ethnicity, at its most fundamental, prayer is spiritual communication with God (Baesler, 2003). It is important that studies in communication offer a rich and growing interdisciplinary body of literature on what prayer means, and how, when, and why this practice is pervasive in the religious and spiritual arena (Baesler, 1999, 2002, 2003; Ladd & Spilka, 2002, 2006; Pargament, 2001, 2007). When placed in the broader area of religion and spirituality, prayer is more specifically understood as inherent and important in developing and cultivating a religious and spiritual life.

Neoliberalism, media, and spiritual programming

The framework of neoliberalism considers individualism and competition as the defining characteristic of relationships between and amongst humans. It sees citizens as consumers and customers, whose choices are best practiced by processes that reward merit, hard work, and "deservedness," while at the same time punishing inaction and inefficiency. It purports that the general economy, or "the market" provides benefits, which could not be realized by preparation or even strategic planning on the part of the consumer. This economic structure of production and consumption is applied to all parts of culture and society, including media production and viewership. A cornerstone of neoliberal policy is, in theory, for commercial media and communication markets to be deregulated, though in practice this means that they are "re-regulated" in order to serve corporate interests (McChesney, 2001; Mosco, 2009). The neoliberal media flourishes on profit gained via advertising from corporate organizations which often engage in problematic practices such as environmental degradation, exploitation of developing nations, and the military-industrial relationship (Herman & Chomsky, 1988, p. 17). This relationship thus perpetuates the privatization, corporatization, and globalization of media products (Bagdikian, 1997). Downey's and Burnett's roles in the creation and production of *Answered Prayers* is particularly poignant in the context of neoliberalism.

Media power couple: Downey and Burnett

The concept and construct of *Answered Prayers* is tied closely to the background and objectives of its producers. Roma Downey is an Emmy-nominated actor, having starred in the CBS television series *Touched by an Angel* (1994–2003) and both starred in and produced the mini-series *The Bible* (2013). Downey's role as the kind-hearted protagonist in *Touched by an Angel* is to date her most recognized, having earned her a nomination and win at the TV Guide awards, as well as two Emmy Award and Golden Globe nominations. Downey's husband, Mark Burnett, is a widely recognized television and film producer, well known as director of hit reality show *Survivor* (2002-present), creator and screenwriter for *Are You Smarter Than a Fifth Grader* (2007–11, 2015-present), and also as producer of *Shark Tank* (2009-present), *The Voice* (2011-present) and *The Apprentice* (2004-present). Burnett was named president of MGM Television and Digital Group in 2015, thus adding scripted television programs such as *The Handmaid's Tale* (Hulu) and *Teen Wolf* (MTV) to his growing repertoire. The couple is the catalyst behind two of the most significant Christian television programs to air on national television, *The Bible Experience* and *A.D., The Bible Continues*.

Together Downey and Burnett created the reality program *Answered Prayers*, hosted by Downey and produced by Downey's Lightworkers Media. The 2015 program appeared via a 6-episode series on cable network TLC, a network heavily immersed in producing reality programs and in particular religion-based reality programs. It paints "vivid portraits of ordinary people who faced extraordinary circumstances – and miraculously lived to tell the tale" (Friedlander, 2015). As a media power couple, Downey and Burnett demonstrate their vested interests in both prayer and in the purpose and function of neoliberal media. Both are evangelical Christians, and this background has clearly influenced some of their professional endeavors. In addition to media productions featuring Christian and spiritual issues, the couple are involved in philanthropic outreach including charitable organizations such as Operation Smile and Compassion International. Their intention in *Answered Prayers* is to demonstrate to viewers that, in keeping with Christian values, prayers can be answered, miracles can happen, and it is acceptable to ask for things in prayer, particularly when in crisis.

However, the two are also successful businesspeople, particularly in the case of Burnett, whose role as MGM President clearly demands a focus on profitability. Burnett's background as a self-made capitalist success story is a classic neoliberal script. He began minding the children of affluent families in California, moved on to selling t-shirts on a fence in Venice Beach, and then saw a business opportunity in creating "adventure races" similar to the French *Raid Gauloises*, in which he and his friends participated in 1991. Burnett purchased rights to the format and introduced multi-day expedition race *Eco-Challenge* to the US. The program was broadcast on cable television in the 1990s, and began Burnett's successful career as a television producer. Burnett is best known for producing the markedly successful program *Survivor*, which many argue launched a new brand and style of "reality" television, and is a neoliberal success story. Burnett spent nearly four years pitching the program to different networks, and CBS finally agreed to a summer trial, but only if the program's business model was different: the network asked Burnett to presell advertising sponsorship of the program, and proposed sharing advertising revenue with him. Before shooting began, Burnett secured eight sponsors in exchange for advertising, product placement, and promotion of the sponsor's web address. This program was therefore not only a change in program content, but was also a marked shift in changing sponsorship; as the network did not have to pay to have the show made, the sponsors did (Magder, 2004, p. 140). Burnett went on to create *The Apprentice*, which was hosted for 14 seasons by real estate tycoon, and eventual president, Donald Trump.

Spirituality and neoliberalism: a media match

Each episode of *Answered Prayers* begins with Downey's kind and gentle voice reminding viewers of inspirational, spiritual messages including, "The light reaches those who seek it," or "Hope leads to extraordinary things." The format includes two or three vignettes in each episode, depicting individuals or families in critical situations, such as natural disasters, accidents, robbery, or injury. Of the 41 praying individuals featured in the program, 59% were male (n = 24) and 41% were female (n = 17). Nearly all of the praying people depicted in the program were white; of all 41, only two were visible minorities: Latinx couple Alcides Moreno and his supportive wife Rosario. This section considers how the crisis situations depicted in *Answered Prayers*, together with the characters chosen for the program, support the neoliberal concepts of "hard work," individualism, and personal agency, and perpetuate neoliberal values even in a spiritual context.

Ask and you shall receive

Given the evident crisis in every vignette, it is not a surprise that the program featured petitionary prayer, in which one asked (or even pleaded with) God to do or change something. For example, Trisha Gilles, wife and mother of three, was trapped under debris in the wake of a violent tornado. Separated from her husband and children while yet another storm was approaching, Trisha "was lying there and was praying the whole time, 'God, send someone'" (Episode 1, Vignette 1). During the storm, Trisha clutched a stone given to her by her mother and which bore the inscription, "Protected by angels." Trisha was eventually rescued by a local Good Samaritan who felt called to assist during the disaster. Similarly, intercessory prayer, in which one asks God to do something for someone else is also featured prominently in this program. Roxanne Worsham, whose son's friend collapsed in the cold waters of Lake Tahoe while swimming, "Yelled at the top of my lungs, 'Jesus, help, Jesus save Jake!' with everything I had ... Please, God, Please God" (Episode 5, Vignette 1). In what can only be explained as a miracle within this context, a first-responder happened to be paddling in the area in which Jake had collapsed, rescued him, and brought him to shore. Jake not only survived, but despite his extensive time under the cold waters, made a full recovery. The program therefore infers that if one asks for something in prayer, then the prayer has no purpose but to be answered. Like these examples, each vignette featured in the program has a happy ending, despite even the most challenging of circumstances at its inception.

The notion of eventual success is in keeping with the neoliberal ideal of individual agency or "work." In the neoliberal context, if one works hard enough, and has enough personal agency to change and affect his or her own circumstances, then this dedication and work will be rewarded by the market. The same concept is seen in a spiritual context in *Answered Prayers*: if one prays "the whole time," like Trisha Gilles, or "with everything I had," like Roxane Worsham, then this investment will be returned. The happy endings, resolution, or "miracles" described in each vignette are an unequivocal message that doing the "work" of spirituality will be rewarded with a miracle. There was not one example of an individual being left out, disappointed, or having misfortune after turning toward God and investing time and energy in prayer.

The invisible hand

While petitionary and intercessory prayer were prominently featured in *Answered Prayers*, some of those featured in the program described how they prayed as a means of surrendering to God. This kind of prayer meant relinquishing control by either accepting what was happening or actively and consciously turning the situation over to God. For example, Lindsay Walz was trapped in her sinking car in the Mississippi River after the bridge on which she was driving collapsed. Walz made every human attempt to escape, though after failed attempts, she accepted that she was going to die in her car at the bottom of the river. She reported that, "Surrendering wasn't giving up on life. It was just accepting that whatever would come would come, and I was at peace with it" (Episode 2, Vignette 1). Esther Grachan described a similar notion of surrender, though her act was more about turning her fate over to God. While searching for the "perfect person" with whom to spend the rest of her life, she experienced a series of unsuccessful relationships. Grachan eventually decided to write her first name on a one-dollar bill, and "put it out to God" that the person who found the dollar bill would be the person she would marry. Grachan said, "My faith was, I don't know, on another level ... I knew that God was out there, there's a higher power working in my favour" (Episode 2, Vignette 2).

Walz managed to somehow escape from her car, and reported not being able to remember how she did it. Her survival is framed as only being able to be explained by means of a miracle and giving over to God, as it was only once she let go and had faith that she escaped a disaster. Grachan, about a year after sending her dollar bill out to God, received it back from her boyfriend (and eventual husband), who had put it in a decorative frame and given it to her on their 8-month anniversary. The concept of surrender is also ever-present in neoliberal principles – one must have "faith" in the market, for the market will provide and reward those who trust it. The vignette featuring Grachan is so poignant that it could be a metaphor for neoliberal spirituality – it could not have been better if scripted. Grachan wanted a man, and quite literally released capital (metaphorically represented by the dollar bill) to God. It was then returned in immeasurable multitudes clearly and directly to her. It was only investing her own money and emotional capital in demonstrating her faith that she received the capital back, with a return on her investment in the form of her eventual husband. The use of money in this vignette is eerily demonstrative of the neoliberal idea of investment, work, and surrender to the market. The "invisible hand" of both God and the market are clearly evident in both of these vignettes. Faith in God can be correlated to faith in the market. God can work in one's favor, and so too can the "Invisible Hand" of the free market.

The program even features situations that are either caused or illustrated by neoliberalism. For example, Verhaeghe (2014) suggests that after some 30 years of adherence to neoliberal values, privatization, and the "free market," people in our culture are experiencing increased loneliness, depression, and feeling like a "one-person enterprise." The sense of loneliness was described by Mary Owen, a 25-year-old mountaineer and explorer, who prayed for God's support while she was lost on Mt. Hood in Oregon. She said, "My first thing was to pray and to search for God … I actually did not feel His presence for the first time in my entire life. I wasn't sure how close I was to hypothermia … feeling so entirely alone" (Episode 4, Vignette 2). Mary's loneliness is symbolic of the need to participate in the neoliberal game of the one-person show whereby we are each responsible for our own personal success or failure. Mary's pleas and surrender to God are what saw her through her solitary days on the mountain and her eventual salvation by rescuers. The same parallel can be drawn with neoliberalism – we must have our own agency, own work, and our own personal brand to succeed. When one has enough conviction and dedication, neoliberal principles dictate that the market will reward us with financial salvation.

Alcides and Rosario Moreno, the only non-white characters in the program, described how Rosario prayed for Alcides's survival after suffering an employment-related accident. Alcides reported that his own survival was a miracle and reason to believe in God. Rosario described praying for her husband even though the doctors told her that she ought not to have much hope. Their story is one of believing in the possibility of miracles, and having, as Downey touts, "unwavering faith" in Alcides's unlikely survival. However, as the only visible minorities featured in the program, Alcides and Rosario exemplify how neoliberal economics marginalize minorities in the US. White people in the program are shown vacationing at Lake Tahoe, visiting beaches at the Great Lakes, going skiing, or driving cars to and from their professional jobs. Mr. Moreno, a non-English-speaking Latino, was a window washer in New York City when he suffered his near-fatal accident. Son Hing (2014) argues that neoliberalism is a particularly harsh system for minorities. Neoliberal prescriptions reward active participation, risk taking, and innovation, all of which are difficult for minority groups. Further, neoliberal market principles can function in ways which justify antipathy toward minorities, and thus the structural restraints that marginalize minority communities can be largely ignored. The vignette featuring Mr. and Mrs. Moreno shows them having none of the privilege that other families in the program possessed, such as taking vacations, living in affluent neighborhoods, or participating in organized sports or higher education. Even the placement of the vignette within the series is positioned as if it were an afterthought; the Morenos are the final characters in the final vignette in the final episode of *Answered Prayers*. Thus this vignette exemplifies the unfortunate marginalization of minorities, which is a byproduct of the neoliberal socioeconomic framework.

Miracles don't just happen

The central message in *Answered Prayers* is that miracles *can* and *do* happen. However, in order for miracles to occur, there must be two inherent elements: the miracle must be requested in prayer, and faith must be demonstrated. Each of the stories featured in the program demonstrates these requirements in "achieving" or "acquiring" a miracle.

The stories feature crises of various forms, including serious illness, accident, natural disaster, or loneliness. While the real-life subject of the story narrates, actors are shown in prayer. These prayers are characterized by either people petitioning God for a miracle in their own lives, or asking for intercession in the lives of others. Often, they depict desperation and panic. The most obvious response to these kinds of prayer is that a miracle – an otherwise inexplicable event that can only be attributable to the work of divine agency – occurred.[1] In the program, a miracle is depicted as an "against-the-odds" event, and one in which the praying individual gives credit to God for performing something which would be impossible for a human to accomplish. Often, this took the form of survival after a physical accident or problem. For example, the survival of Jake Blackmon (who collapsed while swimming in Lake Tahoe, Episode 5, Vignette 1) was described as a miracle – rationally, and under "ordinary" circumstances, the teenager should have died. Family friend Roxane Worsham, who frantically prayed on the beach at Lake Tahoe and even mobilized others to pray at the scene of the accident, described Jake's survival: "I think the Lord breathed new life into Jake again ... This was everybody's miracle ..." Her husband Rob Worsham similarly stated, "There is no question in my mind that Jake's rescue and recovery and survival was a miracle." At the conclusion of the program, Downey tells viewers to hold on "until the story is over, and we are together once again." These miracles of survival conclude with togetherness and unity as a result of the miracle.

The miracle of transformation is a theme that Downey and Burnett also chose to demonstrate and perpetuate in *Answered Prayers*. Transformation is demonstrated by means of people in crisis changing after a problem was resolved, and recognizing that they had been given a second chance to either find purpose or to create a positive impact for others. This was clearly shown in the example of Pastor Kevin

Ramsby who believed that he was dying after being robbed and assaulted at home (Episode 3, Vignette 1). Ramsby shared that, "I think God gave me a second chance [by letting me survive] because He saw what I could become. To become a guide and to serve and be a little bit of a light for others to how to [sic] go through darkness in their lives. It amazes me how God can take darkness and turn it into light, a new beginning." Similarly, Chase Kear, who suffered a serious head injury while pole vaulting (Episode 3, Vignette 2) shared, "I thank God every day for that second chance. For that opportunity to do something better." These instances of being given "another chance" demonstrate the theme of the opportunity to contribute positively and to make a difference.

The active "ask" and receipt of miracles is central to the message in *Answered Prayers*. This proactive pursuit of one's desired outcome adheres to the neoliberal economic principle of "hard work." The program infers that if one prays hard enough, and with enough conviction, then the miracle is sure to happen. The same parallel can be drawn with neoliberal economics, which focuses upon the individual's personal agency and commitment to economic success; enough hard work and participation in the market will result in profit and security. The notion of personal contribution to success is integral to the neoliberal framework, and thus active involvement in "creating" a miracle is essential to the message in this program.

The neoliberal value of family is also pervasive in this program. For example, images of couples' wedding rings are shown throughout the duration of crises. During the aftermath of the tornado that separated Trisha and Darrel Gilles, the program showed Trisha's trapped hand bearing her wedding band. In the same episode, Jodi and Brett Bainter reported the stress placed upon their marriage when Brett accidentally backed the lawnmower onto their toddler son's leg, causing permanent damage and eventually requiring amputation. Jodi reported that while Brett emotionally withdrew from the family, their marriage was not going to be lost because "that would be an even bigger tragedy. It wasn't going to happen. Not on my watch" (Episode 1, Vignette 2). Brecher (2012) argues that the family is integral to the success of neoliberal capitalism, and Cooper (2017) argues that even though personal responsibility is integral to the neoliberal ethos, neoliberalism promotes familial bonds, for family and kinship are a counterpart to freedom of the markets. Thus the messages chosen in *Answered Prayers* fit with perpetuating the intact family unit, commitment, and a complete, whole family as foundational to the socioeconomic order. Downey's message at the end of the vignette featuring Jodi, Brett, and their injured son Jake is that, "As a family, they healed together." This theme of togetherness and the intact family unit adheres to the neoliberal expectation of family function and unity.

Conclusion

The 2015 reality program *Answered Prayers* implies that when a prayer is offered, a prayer is answered. The program suggests that, as host Roma Downey asserts in the introduction to each episode, an answered prayer is difficult to explain – "you just know it." This reality program suggests to viewers that if one prays "hard enough," or with enough conviction, prayers will be answered. These answers are recognized as miracles, and are orchestrated by God's invisible hand working on behalf of the individual. The principles of hard work and the function of a system larger than the individual are in close keeping with neoliberal values: the program promotes the notion that engaging in committed spiritual prayer will result in success. Neoliberal principles such as an intact and fully functional family are also promoted in this program. The role of Downey and Burnett as creators of the program and self-made success stories is integral to the messages in and construction of this program. Their financial values and objectives align with those of Donald Trump. Mr. Trump's background as real estate magnate, host and star of Burnett's *The Apprentice*, and eventual United States president, is nothing short of a neoliberal fairy tale.

It is helpful to note that *Answered Prayers* is limited in its portrayal of prayer life. Most spiritual traditions teach and encourage prayers of gratitude, thanksgiving, and confession. No such prayers were featured in this series. The program is further limited to representing only crisis situations; it does not feature ritualized prayer, including prayers before meals, or contemplative/meditative prayer (Keating 2002, 2009) which facilitates direct contact with the Divine. Omission of these kinds of prayers may be because such prayers don't make compelling viewing – watching one contemplate/meditate or engage in rote prayer is neither dynamic nor exciting for audiences. Further, these kinds of prayers are not directly relatable to neoliberal values. Thus, their omission is largely tied to the program's specific purpose to promote commitment and dedication, while also bolstering viewership and profit on the part of the producers.

In the early twentieth century, the "nouveau riche" were discredited by those with "old" or inherited money. Those who created their own economic success by means of entrepreneurship or "hard work" sought acceptance by passing themselves off as landlords or having passive income. Neoliberalism has changed this social construct: those who inherited their money seek to present themselves as self-made success stories. Claiming to have "earned" one's income is the more desirable story of economic wellbeing. The same pride in "earning" a miracle is evident in the reality program *Answered Prayers*. It is clear that the producers assert that miracles do not just happen as random blessings – they must be asked for with conviction and earned. Pride in one's agency associated with the miracle means that one *achieved* it, rather than *received* it. This neoliberal principle of personal agency is a straightforward parallel in this program. Downey and Burnett therefore promote a constructed neoliberal spirituality, which they both manufacture and endorse in this program.

Note

1 For the purposes of this paper, a miracle is defined as a welcome or surprising event that is not explicable by natural or scientific laws, and is the work of Divine agency. Other sources, for example Foundation for Inner Peace (1976), *A Course in Miracles*, defines a miracle as a correction or shift in perception, and that miracles occur naturally as expressions of love.

Bibliography

Baesler, E. J. 1999. "A Model of Interpersonal Christian Prayer." *The Journal of Communication and Religion* 22: 40–64.

Baesler, E. J. 2002. "Prayer and Relationship with God II: Replication and Extension of the Relational Prayer Model." *Review of Religious Research* 44: 58–67.

Baesler, E. J. 2003. *Theoretical Explorations and Empirical Investigations of Communication and Prayer.* Lewiston, New York: Edwin Mellen Press.

Baesler, E. J. and Ladd, K. 2009. "Exploring Prayer Contexts and Health Outcomes: From the Chair to the Pew." *Journal of Communication and Religion* 32(2): 347–374.

Bagdikian, B. 1997. *The Media Monopoly.* Boston: Beacon Press.

Brecher, B. 2012. "The Family and Neoliberalism: Time to Revive a Critique." *Ethics and Social Welfare* 6(2): doi: doi:10.1080/17496535.2012.682503.

Cooper, M. 2017. *Family Values: Between Neoliberalism and the new Social Conservatism.* Cambridge: MIT Press.

Foundation for Inner Peace. 1976. *A Course in Miracles.* Schuchman, H., Thetford, B., Wapnick, K., Eds. New York: Viking.

Friedlander, W. 2015. "Roma Downey's 'Answered Prayers' Premieres in July on TLC". *Variety.* July 11. http://variety.com/2015/tv/news/roma-downey-answered-prayers-tlc-1201517281/

Giordan, G. 2011. "Toward a Sociology of Prayer." In G. Giordan and W.H. Swatos, Jr., Eds. *Religion, Spirituality and Everyday Practice.* Dordrecht: Springer.

Herman, S. & Chomsky, N. 1988. *Manufacturing Consent: The Political Economy of Mass Media.* New York: Pantheon Books.

Kabat-Zinn, J. 1990. *Full Catastrophe Living: Using the Wisdom of Your Body and Mind to Face Stress, Pain, and Illness.* New York: Delecorte Press.

Keating, Thomas. 2002. *Open Mind, Open Heart: The Contemplative Dimension of the Gospel.* New York: Continuum.

Keating, Thomas. 2009. *Intimacy With God: An Introduction to Centering Prayer.* New York: Crossroad Publishing Company.

Kirkpatrick, L. A. and Shaver, P. R. 1990. "Attachment theory and religion: Childhood attachments, religious beliefs, and conversion." *Journal for the Scientific Study of Religion* 29: 315–334.

Kreps, G. L. 2012. "The Role of Prayer in Promoting Health and Well Being." *Journal of Communication and Religion* 35(3): 237–254.

Ladd, K. L. and Spilka, B. 2002. "Inward, Outward, and Upward: Cognitive Aspects of Prayer." *Journal for the Scientific Study of Religion* 41: 475–484.

Ladd, K. L. and Spilka, B. 2006. "Inward, Outward, Upward Prayer: Scale Reliability and Validation." *Journal for the Scientific Study of Religion* 45: 233–251.

Lauricella, S. 2012. "The Lifetime of Prayer: A Review of Literature on Prayer Throughout the Life Course." *Journal of Communication and Religion* 35(3): 209–236.

McChesney, R. (2001). "Global Media, Neoliberalism, and Imperialism." *Monthly Review* 52(10). https://monthlyreview.org/2001/03/01/global-media-neoliberalism-and-imperialism/

Magder, T. 2004. "The End of TV 101: Reality Programs, Formats, and the New Business of Television." In S. Murray and L. Ouellette, Eds. *Reality TV: Remaking Television Culture.* New York: New York University Press.

Mosco, V. 2009. *The Political Economy of Communication.* Los Angeles: Sage.

Pargament, K. 2001. *The Psychology of Religion and Coping: Theory, Research, and Practice.* New York, NY: Guilford Press.

Pargament, K. 2007. *Spiritually Integrated Psychotherapy: Understanding and Addressing the Sacred*. New York, NY: Guilford Press.

Son Hing, L. S. 2014. "Stigmatization, Neoliberalism, and Resilience." In Peter A. Hall and Michèle Lamont, Eds. *Social Resilience in the Neo-Liberal Era*. Cambridge: Cambridge University Press.

Verhaeghe, P. (2014). *What About Me? The Struggle for Identity in Market-Based Society*. Trans. Jane Hedley-Prole. Melbourne: Scribe Publications.

13

"THE SEARCH FOR A YOUNG IMAM BEGINS NOW"

Imam Muda and civilizational Islam in Malaysia

Andrea Stanton

In May 2010, Malay-speaking viewers in Southeast Asia began tuning in to a new kind of reality television – a contest-based talent show, like many on air in the region, but with a twist. The first episode opened with an evening shot of a graceful mosque, then panned down to the courtyard, where a man in a grey suit, turquoise dress shirt, black tie and black *songkok* (a Malaysian man's hat that appears similar to a *tarboosh*) emerged. "*Salaam `aleikum*," he greeted viewers, saying that "for the first time in our broadcasting history," viewers would see the first show "in the world" aimed at finding a man of authority, integrity, and credibility who could serve as "*imam muda*," a young imam. Stressing that the man selected would be "versatile and relevant to the community," he emphasized that viewers would be witnesses to this process, and concluded: "The search for a young imam begins now."[1]

The scene then shifted to an internal shot of a stage, with traditional Islamic tile patterns, composed of green, purple, and blue lights, illuminating the walls. (Although much of the show took place with contestants on this stage, and some media reports mentioned a studio audience, the camera did not show audience members.) As the ten contestants[2] came into focus, an ornamented call to prayer provided the musical backdrop. When it ended, the candidates and the host began to sing an Arabic-language *nasheed*, or hymn, about Muhammad.[3] The host, Ustaz Haji Dzulkarnain Hamzah, a religious scholar and former Malaysian military chaplain, had served previously as host of a Qur'an instruction and sharia interpretation talk show called *Kalam Suci*, which had broadcast on Astro Oasis, the station now broadcasting *Imam Muda*.[4] He introduced the ten candidates, and said that they had been selected after the channel conducted a month of auditions. The candidates ranged in age from 18 to 28, and described themselves as a college student, a farmer, an imam, a bank official, a motivational speaker, and Qur'an memorization teacher, among other professions. The variety suggests both the contestants' middle-class, educated status and the close intertwining of piety and ordinary life that characterizes Islam in contemporary Malaysia. Their qualifications came from personal study – of *fiqh* and *tawhid*, among other areas, as the host noted – not necessarily from a formal degree program.

After praising the contestants, the host turned to introducing their first task: death. "Every living creature will face death," he said somberly, adding: "Death is very close to everyone." He recited from the Qur'an – a beautiful, ornamented recitation, whose impact was enhanced by the reverberation added to the microphone. Serious music played as the host continued: "Every person has a time limit. When their time has come, they cannot turn back time for even one second." His speech seemed almost a *khutba* in itself, and an invocation to viewers to contemplate their own mortality, within a pious framework.[5] He then turned to the issue of *janaza*: "It is compulsory to bathe a corpse, shroud it, pray for it, and bury it." The *Imam Muda* candidates would be asked to do this for an "unclaimed," "risky" corpse – understood as the body of a person who had been infected with the AIDS virus. They would be guided in this process by three men introduced as a *mudir* and two *murshids* – a director and two guides – who would also serve as their judges.[6] The contestants would be assessed half on their answers to a written exam, and half on their performance in the actual event. When interviewed, several contestants mentioned their experience bathing and shrouding family members – or their regret at missing the opportunity to do so because they were out of the country when a loved one died. Abe Syara, one candidate, explained that he was excited to learn how to manage a corpse, to contribute to his society and his hometown. Another mentioned that his mother will be happy that he has learned *janaza* practices, because she hopes that he will manage her corpse one day. The candidate interviews include almost no background music.

Before showing the bathing, shrouding, burial, and prayer scenes (done in groups of five candidates, working as a team, with the face of the corpse blurred), the show cut away from the narrative. A text-screen appeared, with five questions that the candidates had answered in their exam: What are the seven rules of funeral prayer? Who are the five people who can bathe the corpse? Can a Muslim son manage the corpse of his non-Muslim father? What is the law of autopsy? What is the law of laying flowers and planting trees on a grave? The question screen allowed viewers to test their own knowledge; a set of answer screens appeared later in the program. The commercial break ended with Ustadh Hamzah delivering another *khutba*-style reflection on death. "It is the way of life: everyone will face death," he noted. "What is our preparation to face the moment of death?" His comments, and this question, reinforce the idea that *Imam Muda* was intended to cultivate viewers' piety not solely by improving their perception of imams, but also by pushing them toward self-reflection. Rather than locate the show's narrative drama in the question of which candidates would succeed and which would fail, the host's comments focused the drama on the weighty nature of their task, and its relevance to all viewers. In the end, the judges praised all contestants, saying that they had each done well. No contestant was eliminated, and the first episode ended with the contestants thanking their judges by bowing to them individually and kissing their hands, while singing another Arabic-language *nasheed* in praise of Muhammad.

With this opening episode, *Imam Muda* demonstrated both its allegiance to and a move away from typical reality television contests. This chapter looks at the context, response, impact, and criticism that surrounded *Imam Muda*, and argues that the show was not a one-time deviation from the standard reality television model. Instead, it marks an important diversification of that model, which harmonizes both with the idea of "Islamic lifestyle" television (and the conceptual expansion of "halal" from butchered meat to incorporate all aspects of modern daily life) and with the specific national-religious-consumerist nexus of Islamic piety in Malaysia. That a reality television show whose first episode focused on corpse management and ended with all contestants continuing to the next round could attract Muslim viewers in Malaysia and across Southeast Asia suggests the need to take it seriously. That it could be both popular and retired after three years due to push-back from religious figures and more conservative Muslims suggests that the contours of the nexus mentioned above are continually evolving as various members of Malay society weigh in on what constitute appropriate modern expressions of Malay Muslimness.

Context

Malaysia was formed in 1963, when the independent Federation of Malaya joined with several other former colonies to form a federal constitutional monarchy. Since 2009, the government has been led by Prime Minister Mohamed Najib bin Abdul Razak. Its territories are roughly divided between the western and eastern sides of the South China Sea, totaling roughly 127,000 square miles of land. Its population of 31 million is roughly 50% ethnic Malay, 23% ethnic Chinese, 12% indigenous, 7% Indian, and 8% non-citizen. Bahasa Malay is the official spoken language, although English is widely spoken, as are Chinese and other languages. Islam is the official state religion, and all ethnic Malays are considered legally Muslim. Muslims make up 61% of the population, Buddhists 20%, Christians 9%, and Hindus 6%. The median age is 28, and 86% of the population is 55 or younger, making Malaysia's population relatively youthful. Nearly 95% of the population age 15 and over is literate, with fourteen years of primary and secondary schooling expected for all citizens, regardless of sex. 53% of the labor force works in the service sector, with 36% in industry and only 11% in agriculture, reflecting Malaysia's position as a middle-income country moving toward high-income standing with a multi-sector, services-focused economy.

Malaysia is among the more advanced countries of the world in terms of its communications, with 145 mobile phone subscriptions per 100 inhabitants and 71% of the population using the Internet. There is a state-owned television station, Radio Television Malaysia, which operates two nationally-available TV networks, five national radio stations, and thirteen regional ones. It historically has broadcast primarily Malay-language locally produced programs and English-language foreign programs, drawing criticism from Chinese speakers. In 1984 the government supported the creation of a third, private TV station that broadcast partly in Chinese. In the mid-1990s, the government authorized the creation of additional private stations. Satellite television is also popular: Malaysia launched two East Asia Satellites in 1996, covering southeast Asia as well as India, Vietnam, Taiwan, and parts of Australia. Astro, the All Asia Radio and Television Company, operates the satellite broadcasting networks, with exclusive broadcasting rights through 2017.[7] Described as the largest pay television operator in Southeast Asia in terms of the number of its subscribers, Astro had an estimated 3.3 million subscribers by 2013. Since 2012, Astro has also worked with the Malaysian government to provide a free, direct-to-home satellite television option, called NJOI, which offers 22 television and 20 radio channels; the program is seen as increasing viewership across a broader income spectrum.[8]

Imam Muda fit smoothly into the Malaysian television landscape. It aired on Astro Oasis, Astro's Islamically oriented channel, and was available through both its pay and free-to-air (NJOI) satellite packages. The show was jointly developed by the satellite network and the governmental Federal Territory Islamic Affairs Department (JAWI), which governs religious affairs for Muslims in Malaysia's three federal territories. (An official from the Department appeared on the final episode, along with an executive from Astro's entertainment division.)

But *Imam Muda* also fit smoothly into the broader Malaysian landscape. Barendregt notes that, around Southeast Asia, "a fancy Islamic lifestyle increasingly serves as an identity tool kit for the well-to-do" – that education, professionalization, and middle-class wealth are mutually reinforcing of religious identity. "All sorts of Islamic chic, [including] modern Muslim entertainment such as Malaysia's *Imam Muda* reality soap have arisen to address the needs of the new Islamic well-to-do of Southeast Asia's metropoles," he argues.[9] This fits with what Fischer describes as the "halalization" that constituted the Malay middle class as a suburban, national community for whom Muslim and Malay are mutually reinforcing, mutually productive identities.[10] This iteration of national, Muslim identity places increasing emphasis on constituting and reinforcing oneself as a pious, national subject through consumption and lifestyle choices. It dovetails (but does not fully map onto) the notion of "*Islam hadhari*" or civilizational Islam, which was endorsed and espoused by Abdullah Badawi, who promoted it as a progressive, authentically Malaysian form of Islam during the 2004 general elections. "*Islam hadhari*" has a longer history, growing out of several decades in which Malay politicians and activists sought to amplify the role of religion in Malay identity.[11] Hence shows like *Imam Muda* might be reflective both of the consumerist turn in Malay identity, and also of the Malaysian state's success in promoting a more confident, religio-ethnic identity for Malays.

Response

Imam Muda attracted almost instant international attention, with stories in European and North American news media: France, Germany, Switzerland, Canada, and the

United States (Bernama, 2010). They delighted in noting that it was a reality television show – but about religion. Yet beyond the media appeal of this wholesome, religion-focused show, some reports described *Imam Muda* as signaling a new era for Islamic television programming, helping shed its reputation "as a dull and conservative programming block." One analyst described *Imam Muda*'s broadcaster Oasis as learning from "the growth of 'lifestyle' Islamic TV in both the Middle East and countries in Europe with significant Muslim populations," like the United Kingdom.[12] These claims were supported by *Imam Muda*'s popularity: "The show had a huge viewership, the highest one on Astro Oasis," Nestorovic stated, "and more than 1000 candidates auditioned to enter the show."[13] An advertising trade publication described Astro's 2010 Malay household penetration at 55%, and said that the first season of *Imam Muda* drew an average viewership of 416,000, with the finale drawing 800,000 viewers.[14] Further, its theme song, "HambaMu" or "Your Servant," referring to God, became a popular song in its own right.[15]

Yet one key element was absent from *Imam Muda*: women. While several contestants mentioned missing their wives, and almost all mentioned their mothers, the presence of actual women on the show was minimal. The host was male, the judges were male, the contestants were male – the stage was almost always entirely male, and even most of the tasks involved the contestants engaging with men or boys. Given the success of *Imam Muda*'s first season, it was unsurprising that the show was extended. It was also perhaps unsurprising that *Imam Muda 2* would be joined by a companion show: *Ustazah Pilihan* (Ideal Female Teacher, also translated as Chosen Female Teacher, and similar to *Imam Muda* in having a title that included one Arabic-origin word and one Malay-origin word). It launched the same year as *Solehah* (*Saliha*, in Arabic, meaning pious or upright woman), which also sought to find an ideal young woman leader, in this case in a preacher-educator role.

The producers of *Ustazah Pilihan* and *Solehah* created shows that were more conservative than *Imam Muda*, particularly in their presentation and treatment of contestants. *Ustazah Pilihan* borrowed the same font from *Imam Muda*, but with the word "*Ustazah*" in pink. This was a cosmetic difference, however. Where the candidates of *Imam Muda* appeared in sharp suits with bright shirts, the women appeared in their first episode dressed in brown. Further, rather than being seated on a bench, they were all seated behind a long, black table, obscuring their bodies from the upper torso down. The episode began with one of the candidates reciting from the Qur'an, followed by another candidate translating the verse (30:20) into Malay. While this issue has aroused less concern in southeast Asia than in other Muslim-majority societies, the idea of women Qur'an reciters engaging in public recitation has been controversial, because women's voices are sometimes considered part of their `*awra*, the nakedness or intimate parts of the body that must be covered in public.[16] But here, the candidates spoke as authorities: reciting the Qur'an in Arabic, translating it into Malay, and narrating and translating *hadith* – the latter primarily about women's roles, but the Qur'anic passages were broader statements about God and humanity. Similarly, the candidates' guides and judges were also women, which created a mono-gender show that complemented *Imam Muda*, but also thereby presented women as authorities on Islam – figures from whom viewers could learn, regardless of their own gender.

Impact

With this point in mind, might it be more appropriate to speak of *Imam Muda*, and the shows that have followed it, as a show about authority of its imam candidates, or as about helping viewers to cultivate a pious self? Wok et al. suggest that Malay viewers perceive religious television shows to be informational, and hence "are motivated to watch due to [their] educational content."[17] Hasan Mahmud al Hafiz, one of the show's judges, described *Imam Muda* as different from "other programs that have no religious values." He added: "We provide spiritual nourishment. We are not looking for a singer or a model."[18] Viewers described themselves as watching the show to improve their knowledge of Islam, fitting the model of spiritual self-cultivation through media engagement noted by Hirschkind and others.[19] Channel manager Izelan Basar stated that the show's aim was "to get both the contestants and the audience to know, understand, and practice their religion," through entertaining them positively (Henderson, 2010). In this sense, *Imam Muda* and the shows that followed it could be seen as promoting a kind of socio-religious activism. As John and Michael Voll note, "The changing models of Muslim tele-vangelistic presentation [here, from televised *khutbas* to reality TV programs] are central to the evolution of important types of Muslim social and religious activism" today – types that are often decentralized, non-hierarchical, and transnational.[20] The idea of television-led activism is supported by instances like that in the seventh episode, which had asked the candidates to spent time teaching the Qur'an to two teenage boys at Dar al-Fuqaha (House of the Jurists, in Arabic), a home for children of impoverished families. During the episode, the host described helping people in need as a source of Muslim pride, and asked viewers to donate to Dar al-Fuqaha, giving its address and a Bank Islam account number. Historically, *sadaqa* or personal charitable giving was individual and private. By encouraging viewers to donate to Dar al Fuqaha via a "halal" or no-interest Islamic bank, *Imam* Muda encouraged them to see themselves as part of a community of pious viewers supporting fellow Malay Muslims, and in doing so, giving a good name to Islam and to Malayness.[21]

The show was also described as intended to help improve the popular image of imams, and Islam in general, to make it more relevant to young Malaysians. "When we talk about imams, the first impression is always someone who is old-fashioned or just does his work in the mosque," one viewer explained, adding that he found it easier to relate to the young imam candidates.[22] The youthful element appears important here: Wok et al. suggest that *Imam Muda* and similar shows are attempting "to utilize elements of popular culture to tackle the religious concerns of Muslims in a fresh and relevant manner, especially to the younger generation."[23] This is a pious and a national goal, since the Malaysian government promoted Muslim identity and Malay identity as both pious and patriotic. And along with youth come expectations of modernity and professionalism: observers noted that while the judges sometimes appeared on the show's main stage in clerical robes, the contestants always appeared in matching, sharply tailored suits, with *kopiahs* (also known as *songkoks*) on their heads, signaling their Muslimness, Malayness, and modernity. As host Ustaz Haji Dzulkarnain Hamzah explained in the opening episode, the candidates had to be good role models, because imams are followed "not only in prayer but by society."

Yet the impact of *Imam Muda* and its spin-offs might also be understood as the further knitting together of a Malaysian or Southeast Asian notion of consuming, Muslim modernity. This is evident in the promotions run by one of *Imam Muda* and *Ustazah Pilihan*'s sponsors, Bank Islam. Established in 1983 after the passage of the Islamic Banking Act, Bank Islam describes itself as "the first Shariah based banking institution in Malaysia and Southeast Asia," and a leader in developing Malaysia's Islamic banking sector.[24] In addition to financial and in-kind support for *Ustazah Pilihan* and its contestants, for example, Bank Islam also ran several contests for viewers.[25] One small-scale competition required contestants to like the bank's Facebook page and post answers to a set of questions, in hopes of winning a new smartphone or *Ustazah Pilihan* merchandise. But Bank Islam also offered three RM 10,000 ($2270) awards to winners of its "Program Prihatin" (Caring Program), who proposed initiatives to support women's economic development or business opportunities. One winner proposed adding a kneading machine, yam cutting machine, and packaging machine to his filled pastry business, to employ more "local women." Another asked for funding to support a course teaching women hand embroidery and entrepreneurship, including basic accounting and marketing skills. And one proposed to share skills around cabbage growing.[26] The initiative did not directly connect to the religious leadership focus of *Ustazah Pilihan*. But by connecting women's empowerment, economic development, and Islamic finance, under the umbrella of Bank Islam's sponsorship of the show, this contest helped reinforce the sense of connection between being Malay, Muslim, middle class, and modern – a connection seen as foundational to Malay national discourse and to the state, as Fischer argues.[27]

Criticism

One challenge for *Imam Muda*'s larger goals of improving the popular image of imams and promoting modern piety, is that reality show contestants do not disappear after the show ends. In 2016, Ammar Wan Harun, one of the contestants in Season 2, was criticized for commenting on the death of several unvaccinated children. "I didn't know that the Angel of Death does not take the lives of vaccinated children," he said on his Facebook page. When questioned, he said "I just want those who denied vaccines be respected for their choice. Don't make it as if vaccines are more powerful than fate." Reportedly, he was pressured to delete his Facebook page by government officials. Liberal columnist Zurairi AR criticized Ammar for "playing the religious card" in trying to persuade Malaysians to follow him.

"Satellite TV provider Astro and its religious channel Oasis are partly to blame for lending these hacks made-up titles such as 'Imam Muda'," Zurairi said. He argued that their TV fame gave contestants credibility with their fans – credibility they did not deserve. A secularist, Zurairi criticized "religious folks [pulling] wool over the public's eyes," and blamed Islamic television stations for enabling them.[28]

The criticism above came from a secular writer, but *Imam Muda* received criticism from religious Malays and Southeast Asians as well. According to Nestorovic, religious criticism led to its cancellation after three seasons: "Astro discontinued the show due to complaints from members of religious circles in Malaysia about the com-mercialization and commoditization of the institution of imamate."[29] One concern appears to have been the tendency of at least some show contestants to turn their performance into a career boost, as with Najdy, who parlayed his appearance in the 2011 season into moderate fame as a religious pop singer.[30] (Its cancellation does seem to have been something of a surprise: articles written in 2012 describe it as popular and seem to assume that it will be renewed.) But neither Astro Oasis nor competing Islamic lifestyle channel Al-Hijrah, operated by a government-owned corporation, have abandoned the reality show contest model. Astro Oasis has focused on Islamic reality television contests that are less likely to spark resistance, like *Pencetus Ummah*, which focuses on the search for the next influential preacher. (Preachers call people to return to the faith and to become more pious, but are not considered authoritative or scholarly figures in Sunni Islam.) The channel's head of reality programming, Namanzee Harris, in 2014, described that show in contrast to *Imam Muda*: funny, relaxed, and non-traditional in its approach to finding, training, and evaluating contestants. "*Pencetus Ummah* is everything a traditional religious program is not," he said in an interview with a local newspaper. "There are *nasyid* [*nasheed*] artistes performing and fun-filled moments for fans to get to know their favorite new preacher."[31] Other shows avoid controversy by integrating existing forms of pious competition into the reality television format. In spring 2016, it launched *Tahfiz Muda*, which showcased ten children, age 6 to 12, who compete in their memorization of the Qur'an. Qur'an recitation competitions are nothing new, nor is televising them; the only change that Astro has made is to turn a one-day or weekend-long competition into a serial.

Conclusion

The burst of international news coverage that accompanied the launch of *Imam Muda* in 2010 has not been matched by similar interest in Malaysia's subsequent Islamically-focused reality television contests. Yet within Malaysia, and secondarily around the region, these programs are no longer newsworthy departures from a normative reality television contest model. They have become part of the model. Further, they have become a normalized part of the landscape of daily Malay television watching. Even in 2012, a survey of 535 Malay respondents found that only 5.2% reported watching less than one hour of Islamic reality television per television watching session. 25.2% said that they watched at least one hour per session, 32.0% that they watched at least two hours, and 17.7% that they watched at least three hours per session. While only 9.4% reported paying "very much attention" to these shows, 59% reported paying "moderate" or "much" attention – and the fact that they were tuning in for such extended time, and with such a high percentage of viewers, suggests the degree to which Islamic reality television has become a normal, standard genre for Malay television viewers.[32]

In this process of normalizing Islamic reality television, the shows and their parent channel, Astro Oasis (and, to a lesser extent, Al-Hijrah) also serve the state. Even the post-*Imam Muda* shows, which appear intentionally designed to arouse less pushback from more conservative religious figures in Malaysia, still promote what Fischer describes as a state-driven project "that envisions the amalgamation of Malay ethnicity, consumption practices, and Islam" and which is "intimately linked to challenging Islamic discourses or *dakwah*."[33] Astro Oasis' reality television shows challenge *dakwah*'s revivalist, salvation-oriented claims as well – sometimes quite explicitly. An Astro Media Sales promotion for the 2016 season of *Pencetus Ummah*, aimed at marketing managers, promised: "No *dakwah* misconceptions, no false numbers. That's us." It suggested both that *dakwah* proponents and the media teams of other TV programs lied – the first about Islam, and the second about how many viewers their shows enjoyed. "Catch our mentors and contestants as they challenge misconceptions and false portrayals of *dakwah* in Malaysia," the ad continued, adding: "Now armed with an award [Best Religious TV Program 2016], season 4 looks set to reach even more *real* consumers." Again linking the authenticity of the program in terms of content and viewership, the ad concluded: "Check out the performance, they're no lie."[34]

Yet these shows, as noted above, may be fostering a new kind of activism, in line with what the Arab Muslim world has seen with Egyptian preacher Amr Khaled's "Life Makers" and "Renewers" initiatives.[35] Like Khaled's followers, Malay Muslim activism may also take explicitly non-political, social movement forms. However, as Wasli and Hussin note, *Imam Muda, Ustazah Pilihan, Solehah, Pencetus Ummah* and similar programs "share the objective to find a good leader in the Muslim world" – with leadership roles for men and for women. "The participants in these programs are trained to be leaders, equipped with good communication skills and pious personality," they add, noting that the weekly challenges "encourage proactive and creative solutions" to difficult and societally awkward situations: marriages between Malaysians and non-Malaysians, for *Ustazah Pilihan*, or dealing with children born out of wedlock, for *Imam Muda*. [36] While *Ustazah Pilihan* couched its rationale for focusing on women leaders in traditional terms, using the expression that "to educate a woman is to educate a generation," this should not obscure its impact. If these shows have indeed become part of the standard television landscape for Malay viewers, then the models of leadership – and the positive emphasis on leadership – that they put forth may become models as well. These may support the Malaysian state's vision of modern, Muslim, consumerist Malays, or they may oppose it – or they may move Malaysian Muslims in a different direction entirely.

Notes

1 Various episodes from *Imam Muda*'s first and subsequent season can be found online, often with English subtitles. The opening episode of the first season, with English subtitles can be found at: https://vimeo.com/62833222.

2 The show's contestants were described in Malay as "*peserta*" and "*calon.*" This chapter uses "contestants" as the English translation. However, "participant" and "candidate" suggest the more collaborative nature of the contest, as well as the show's respectful treatment of all contestants.

3 Musician Rhoma Irama and other scholars have discussed the phenomenon of "*dakwah* music" in Malaysia: pious popular music that addresses religious or moral themes and may incorporate stories from the hadith or even passages from the Qur'an. See Rhoma Irama, "Music as a medium for communication, unity, education, and dakwah", in Islam and Popular Culture in Indonesia and Malaysia, edited by Andrew N. Weintraub (Oxford; New York: Routledge, 2011), 185–192. The songs on *Imam Muda* follow the more typical contemporary *nasheed* format: male voices in restrained harmony, with no instruments, singing in Arabic and primarily about Muhammad.

4 Information about Ustaz Hamzah like many personalities, tends to come from celebrity sites. In this case, the relevant article is from 2008, two years before *Imam Muda* aired. See https://rockon2012.wordpress.com/2008/04/24/personaliti-ustaz-dzul-dakwah-guna-multimedia/. His Facebook fan page (https://www.facebook.com/DzulkarnainHamzah/) and the many videos of his Qur'anic recitation (Sura Yasin, e.g.: https://www.youtube.com/watch?v=bAQM9-OMUEY) appear to have been created and uploaded after *Imam Muda* began airing, suggesting that his visibility increased after the show began.

5 This resonates with what Charles Hirschkind describes for cassette sermon listening in Egypt – an older media genre. See "The Acoustics of Death" in his *The Ethical Soundscape: Cassette Sermons and Islamic Counterpublics* (New York: Columbia University Press, 2006).

6 Like many of the religious terms used in *Imam Muda, murshid* and *mudir* are Arabic-language imports.

7 Samsudin Rahim, "Development, Media, and Youth Issues in Malaysia," in Husken, Frans and Dick van der Meij, editors, *Reading Asia: New Research in Asian Studies* (London: Routledge Curzon, 2004), 29–48.

8 See IBP, Inc., *Malaysia: Doing Business and Investing in Malaysia Guide* (Washington, DC: International Business Publications, 2016), 99–100.

9 Bart Barendregt, "Sonic Discourses on Muslim Malay Modernity: The Arqam Sound," *Contemporary Islam*, Vol. 6 (2012), 315–40.

10 Johan Fischer, Proper Islamic Consumption: Shopping Among the Malays in Modern Malaysia (Copenhagen: Nordic Institute of Asian Studies Press, 2008), 188.

11 See for example Terence Chong, "The Emerging Politics of *Islam Hadhari*", in *Malaysia: Recent Trends and Challenges*, edited by Saw Swee-Hock and K. Kesavapany (Singapore: Institute of Southeast Asian Studies, 2006), 26–46. For a broader history, see Sylvia Frisk, "Islamization in Malaysia", *Submitting to God: Women and Islam in Urban Malaysia* (Copenhagen: Nordic Institute of Asian Studies, 2009), 27–62.

12 Michael O'Neill, "Meet the New Muslim Consumer", *Campaign Asia-Pacific*, October 2010, 60–66.

13 Cedomir Nestorovic, *Islamic Marketing: Understanding the Socio-Economic, Cultural, and Politico-Legal Environment* (Switzerland: Springer, 2016).

14 Astro Entertainment Adverts & Commercials Archive, Advertolog, http://www.advertolog.com/astro-entertainment/promo/imam-muda-16533905/.

15 The official music video for "Hambamu," produced by Astro Entertainment, can be viewed at: https://www.youtube.com/watch?v=ETTGMY5i-SQ. Mawi had been a 2005 contestant on *Akademi Fantasia*, and although he had been eliminated early in the competition, the judges were persuaded by an outpouring of popular support to reinstate him. He went on to win the contest. See Bart Barendregt's "Islam's Got Talent: Television and the Islamic Public Sphere in Malaysia," in Lifestyle Media: Consumption,

Aspiration, and Identity, edited by Fran Martin, Tania Lewis, Bart Barendregt, and Chris Hudson (London: Routledge, 2016), 176–190 for more on Mawi, and Nestorovic, *Islamic Marketing*, for more on *Imam Muda*'s popularity.

16 See for example Elizabeth Thompson, "Public and Private in Middle Eastern Women's History," *Journal of Women's History* 15 (1), Spring 2003, 52–69. Anne Rasmussen notes that some Indonesian religious scholars actively distance themselves from that view, arguing that it is a Middle Eastern, rather than Islamic, interpretation. See Anne K. Rasmussen, *Women, the Recited Qur'an, and Islamic Music in Indonesia* (Berkeley and Los Angeles: University of California Press, 2010).

17 Saodah Wok et al., "Extended Hierarchy-of-Effect Model and its Application on Islamic Reality Shows Towards Malay Community in Malaysia", paper presented at the i-COME (International Conference on Communication and Media), Penang, November 2012, 5.

18 Sean Young, "La television malaisienne part 'la recherché du nouvel imam' avec un concours," La Presse Canadienne 6.28.10.

19 See Charles Hirschkind, "Experiments in Devotion Online: The YouTube Khutba," *International Journal of Middle East Studies* 44 (1), 2012, 5–21, and *The Ethical Soundscape*.

20 See John O. Voll and Michael O. Voll, "Muslim Activism and Social Movement Theory for the 21st Century," paper presented at the APSA (American Political Science Association) Annual Meeting, August 2010, 23.

21 On the contemporary use of charitable activities to build community and develop networks among pious, middle class Muslims in the Middle East, see Janine A. Clark, *Islam, Charity, and Activism: Middle-Class Networks and Social Welfare in Egypt, Jordan, and Yemen* (Bloomington: Indiana University Press, 2004).

22 See Al Jazeera, "Malaysia Hit Show Picks 'Imam Muda',", 7.31.10, http://www.alja zeera.com/news/asia-pacific/2010/07/2010731503766963.html.

23 Wok et al. 3.

24 See http://www.bankislam.com.my/home/corporate-info/about-us/corporate-profile/. The bank was established in part as a means of supporting the economic development of Muslim Malaysians, and to address government concerns that Malays were lagging behind Chinese Malaysians, economically. Hence its activities are also located at the religious-national nexus that characterizes Muslim Malayness.

25 See http://www.bankislam.com.my/home/corporate-info/news-room/media-release/bank-islam-taja-peserta-ustazah-pilihan-musim-pertama/.

26 See: http://www.bankislam.com.my/home/corporate-info/news-room/corporate-events/ustazah-pilihan/.

27 Fischer, 9.

28 Zurairi AR, "Do not trust an 'imam muda' with your lives," *Malay Mail Online* 6.26.16, http://www.themalaymailonline.com/opinion/zurairi-ar/article/do-not-trust-an-imam-muda-with-your-lives.

29 Nestorovic, 237.

30 See for example his Facebook page, https://www.facebook.com/imammudanajdy/. He sings as part of UNIC, a *nasyid* group founded in 2003, with a changing roster of singers and musicians.

31 See Dennis Chua, "Interesting Stories to Draw Audience", *New Straits Times*, December 15, 2014, http://www.nst.com.my/news/2015/09/interesting-stories-draw-audience

32 See Saodah Wok, Rizalawati Ismail, Zakirah Azman, and Siti Sakinah Latif, "Extended Hierarchy-of-Effect Model and its Application on Islamic Reality Shows Towards Malay Community in Malaysia", paper presented at the i-COME International Conference on Communication and Media, Penang, November 2012, 11.

33 Fischer, 9. *Dakwah* is the Malay indigenization of the Arabic term *da'wa*, calling or evangelizing Muslims to a closer relationship with Islam.

34 See "No *dakwah* misconceptions, no false numbers. That's us." *Marketing Magazine*, http://www.marketingmagazine.com.my/newsletter/pencetus-ummah.html. Emphasis in original.

35 See http://www.amrkhaled.net/ for Khaled's official website.
36 See Mohamad Muhidin Patahol Wasli and Zaharah Hussin, "Directed Content Analysis of *Akhlak* in Islamic Reality Television Programme 'Imam Muda'," *Online Journal of Islamic Education*, Special Issue 2014, 3.

Bibliography

Al Jazeera, "Malaysia Hit Show Picks 'Imam Muda'," July 31, 2010, http://www.aljazeera.com/news/asia-pacific/2010/07/2010731503766963.html

Barendregt, Bart, "Sonic Discourses on Muslim Malay Modernity: The Arqam Sound," *Contemporary Islam* Vol. 6 (2012), 315–340

Barendregt, Bart, "Islam's Got Talent: Television and the Islamic Public Sphere in Malaysia," in *Lifestyle Media: Consumption, Aspiration, and Identity*, edited by Fran Martin, Tania Lewis, Bart Barendregt, and Chris Hudson (London: Routledge, 2016), 176–190

Bernama, "German and Swiss Media in Frenzy over 'Imam Muda' show," *The Star Online*, July 15, 2010, \t "_blank" https://www.thestar.com.my/news/nation/2010/07/15/german-swiss-media-in-frenzy-over-imam-muda-show/

Chong, Terence, "The Emerging Politics of Islam Hadhari," in *Malaysia: Recent Trends and Challenges*, edited by Saw Swee-Hock and K. Kesavapany (Singapore: Institute of Southeast Asian Studies, 2006), 26–46

Chua, Dennis, "Interesting Stories to Draw Audience," *New Straits Times*, December 15, 2014, http://www.nst.com.my/news/2015/09/interesting-stories-draw-audience

Clark, Janine A., *Islam, Charity, and Activism: Middle-Class Networks and Social Welfare in Egypt, Jordan, and Yemen* (Bloomington: Indiana University Press, 2004)

Fischer, Johan, *Proper Islamic Consumption: Shopping Among the Malays in Modern Malaysia* (Copenhagen: Nordic Institute of Asian Studies Press, 2008)

Frisk, Sylvia, "Islamization in Malaysia," in *Submitting to God: Women and Islam in Urban Malaysia* (Copenhagen: Nordic Institute of Asian Studies, 2009), 27–62

Henderson, Barney, "X Factor for Muslim Preachers in Malaysia Wows Television Audience," *The Telegraph*, June 25, 2010, http://www.telegraph.co.uk/news/worldnews/asia/malaysia/7855062/X-factor-for-Muslim-preachers-in-Malaysia-wows-television-audience.html

Hirschkind, Charles, "Experiments in Devotion Online: The YouTube Khutba," *International Journal of Middle East Studies* 44(1), 2012, 5–21

Hirschkind, Charles, *The Ethical Soundscape: Cassette Sermons and Islamic Counterpublics* (New York: Columbia University Press, 2006)

IBP Inc. *Malaysia: Doing Business and Investing in Malaysia Guide* (Washington, DC: International Business Publications, 2016)

Irama, Rhoma, "Music as a medium for communication, unity, education, and dakwah," in *Islam and Popular Culture in Indonesia and Malaysia*, edited by Andrew N. Weintraub (Oxford; New York: Routledge, 2011), 185–192

Marketing Magazine, "No dakwah misconceptions, no false numbers. That's us." *Marketing Magazine*, http://www.marketingmagazine.com.my/newsletter/pencetus-ummah.html (n.d.)

Nestorovic, Cedomir, *Islamic Marketing: Understanding the Socio-Economic, Cultural, and Politico-Legal Environment* (Geneva: Springer, 2016)

O'Neill, Michael, "Meet the New Muslim Consumer," *Campaign Asia-Pacific*, October2010, 60–66

Rahim, Samsudin, "Development, Media, and Youth Issues in Malaysia," in *Reading Asia: New Research in Asian Studies*, edited by Frans Husken and Dick van der Meij, (London: Routledge Curzon, 2004), 29–48

Rasmussen, Anne K., *Women, the Recited Qur'an, and Islamic Music in Indonesia* (Berkeley and Los Angeles: University of California Press, 2010)

Thompson, Elizabeth, "Public and Private in Middle Eastern Women's History," *Journal of Women's History* 15(1), Spring2003, 52–69

Voll, John O. and Michael O. Voll, "Muslim Activism and Social Movement Theory for the 21st Century," paper presented at the APSA (American Political Science Association) Annual Meeting, August 2010

Wasli, Mohamad Muhidin Patahol and Zaharah Hussin, "Directed Content Analysis of Akhlak in Islamic Reality Television Programme 'Imam Muda'," *Online Journal of Islamic Education*, Special Issue 2014, 1–10

Wok, Saodah, Rizalawati Ismail, Zakirah Azman, and Siti Sakinah Latif, "Extended Hierarchy-of-Effect Model and its Application on Islamic Reality Shows Towards Malay Community in Malaysia," paper presented at the i-COME (International Conference on Communication and Media), Penang, November 2012

Young, Sean, "La television malaisienne part 'la recherché du nouvel imam' avec un concours", *La Presse Canadienne*June 28, 2010, http://search.proquest.com.du.idm.oclc.org/docview/522940496?accountid=14608&rfr_id=info%3Axri%2Fsid%3Aprimo

Zurairi, AR, "Do not trust an 'imam muda' with your lives," *Malay Mail Online*June 26, 2016, http://www.themalaymailonline.com/opinion/zurairi-ar/article/do-not-trust-an-imam-muda-with-your-lives

14

PREACHERS OF OXYGEN

Franchising faith on reality TV

Mara Einstein

In October of 2013, the Oxygen network launched what was supposed to be a limited-run reality series entitled *Preachers of LA*. The show is described by the producers as a "docu-series" – in an attempt to distinguish it from the negative connotations of "reality TV" – and it focused on the personal lives of six of Los Angeles' flamboyant male mega-pastors – five out of six of whom are African American. The show turned out to be "the most watched freshman series in Oxygen history… averaging over 1 million total viewers" according to Nielsen research.[1] More important for the network, it increased viewership among young women, its key target audience.[2] It was also the most social cable reality program, meaning that it was the most active as it relates to social media. This success led not only to a second season of the show, but to two program spinoffs – *Preachers of Detroit* and *Preachers of Atlanta* – with the franchise coming to be dubbed the "Preachers of Oxygen." Any correlation to Bravo's *Real Housewives* franchise is, of course, intentional, as Oxygen and Bravo are both owned by media giant NBCUniversal/Comcast.

Economically, it is easy to see why religion and reality TV have become such a powerful combination, and therefore, why programming like the *Preachers* would be produced. First, reality television has grown exponentially over the last 20 years fueled by its inexpensive production costs, the ability to export successful program franchises around the world, and the flexibility of the format to incorporate product placement.[3] As it has grown, there have arisen a number of subgenres[4] – for example, makeover shows, celebrity-based shows, shows about extreme life situations such as *Hoarders* or *My Fabulous Fat Life*, and now shows with religious themes. The *Preachers of Oxygen* combine the newer emotion-provoking religious subgenre with the long-successful exposition of celebrity lifestyles. What is new in this latter format, however, is that the current generation of celebrity commodities invite cameras into their homes to promote themselves as ordinary. These preachers being "just like everybody else" was integral to the promotion of this programming and ties in with accessibility to their audience. Second, the choice of religion as a topic for this genre fits well with its dependence on social media. While reality TV grew in the 1990s because of its positive economic structure, in the last five years it has been buoyed by the advent of social media – a medium reliant on heightened emotion and strong opinions. The *Preachers* use social media to enhance and supplement the on-air content and to directly engage with their audience. Continuous content is facilitated by the shows' large size casts consisting of multiple celebrity preachers and their wives, most of whom are active socially. In addition, these religious leaders come with a built-in audience – their megachurch-sized congregations. Third, as the media landscape becomes increasingly fragmented and social media dependent, network executives seek audiences that not only spend significant time with media, but who are also willing to share content and engage in conversation with others. African Americans are the heaviest consumers of media – television as well as social media,[5] and so content is being tailored for this demographic. Moreover, according to the Pew Research Center, African Americans "are markedly more religious on a variety of measures than the U.S. population as a whole."[6] Thus, programming with religious elements and social media attached could be expected to appeal to the young, female, African American audience Oxygen was targeting in an effort to define their image.[7] In sum, African Americans were an underserved audience, and religion was an underrepresented topic. The combination of this media-attentive demographic with emotionally-charged content that can be shared on social media led to a win–win–win for producers.[8]

While the economics of this are evident, the implications of marrying religion to reality are less clear. In this chapter, I will discuss the *Preachers of Oxygen* through the lens of political economy with attention to changing media industry structures, the rise of social media and its impact on television genres, as well as the imperative of church marketing, particularly as it relates to the African American church. In analyzing *Preachers*, we can begin to theorize the rise of religion as a topic within the reality TV format during late capitalism and its propensity toward promoting personal improvement and the therapeutic self, a source for erecting "altars to individualism and consumerism in the pursuance of 'self'."[9] Social media contributes to this reflection as these online platforms work synergistically with the reality TV genre, and through them provide a space wherein discussions about the self, spirituality, and faith occur. So while *Preachers of LA* is, according to CNN, "a chaotic mix of prayer, 'house porn,' and neatly orchestrated dust-ups between senior pastors and their 'first ladies,'" it is also a conduit for raising questions about religion – both personal and societal – such as why does God help one person and not another, how are the roles of women changing (or not) within the church, and how do traditional and liberal church members negotiate their conflicting beliefs.

Reality TV and social media

Social media has perpetuated the success of reality television because it has changed the way we think about privacy.[10] Not so long ago audiences might have thought it untoward to watch the foibles of their ministers. Not so today when less and less of our lives remains private. Resumes are now personal branding on Twitter, and photo albums are amassed on Facebook. Exposing the personal within media formats did not start with blogging and reality television. Rather, prying into people's personal lives became not only accepted, but expected within the context of talk shows like *Oprah* and *Donahue* and *Maury*. [11]

So, too, have technology and social media fundamentally changed the way viewers interact with television. Moe and Schweidel write, "Increasingly, viewers are moving away from the passive absorption of television entertainment and seeking a more interactive relationship with programming and with other audience members while they watch their favorite shows."[12] This need for engagement is what has driven the appeal of live programming, such as the *Academy Awards*, contest shows like *The Voice*, and sports. In an attempt to replicate this with filmed content, networks create online content that requires viewers to interact with it while the show is in progress. In this, *Preachers* was no exception. The producers provided viewers with real time content that was linked with the show, had cast members available after the show for personal interaction, worked with the preachers and their wives to be active on social media, and even produced content specifically for social media, notably a Twitter sermon presented by multiple preachers. Additional content like this is necessary because 87% of Americans watch television with a second device in hand. While some may use the second screen to purchase products they see – either between programs or within programming itself – much of it is used to interact with other viewers or with program cast members.[13]

Social media, however, are not simply about conversation with cast members; they are about promotion, which means sharing content with others. The network marketing department produces some of the content, but the tweets and Instagram posts that get the most response are those generated by the cast members themselves. Needing to engage with the audience helps explain why the show is about six preachers (rather than one preacher and his family). Remember, too, that these preachers come with an existing fan base, be they members of their congregation or listeners to their music. More important is the quality of the content itself. Researchers have found that audiences are more likely to share content when it generates strong emotions,[14] and religion is a topic that does this well – both positively and negatively.

In the case of *Preachers of LA*, Twitter was widely used as space to both praise and disparage the show. Comments included:

- #PreachersofLA: Coming this fall, I don't know the difference between them and pimps ... seriously
- Watching #PreachersofLA, boy I tell ya! I see less bibles and more Bentleys and Ferraris!
- Pastors arguing like Atlanta Housewives ... Jesus take the wheel

Alternatively, Instagram generated praise as viewers interacted with the cast members, even while the pastors blatantly promoted the show. In one example, a pastor posted a picture of himself on one knee with his head down amid a drab, rocky, mountainous backdrop. The pastor's comment with the picture was "You can't appreciate the mountain without 1st going through the valley! #Preach-ersofLA coming to @oxygen weds oct 9th." People commented: "this pic is tough!" and "a testimony will come out of all of it." Some people posted comments that disparaged the show, but even so, those said they would tune in. Thus, audiences are turned into marketing evangelists for the show, which is the ultimate goal of word-of-mouth marketing via social media.[15]

The amalgamation of the ability to ignite strong feelings and society's implied consent to almost unlimited exposure (making what was private public) has birthed a staggering array of reality programming with a religious theme. On multiple levels, there is a feeling of the forbidden in watching these programs. Religion has most recently been one of the most private of practices. These reality shows provide an "insider's view" on what has formerly been hidden. Moreover, preachers, rabbis, and imams are held up as pinnacles of the community. Their foibles and humanness were not meant for public consumption. No more. Now these forbidden fruits are fair game for the market because they have innate controversy. In addition to others covered in this text, there are *Snake Salvation* (National Geographic), *Breaking Amish* (TLC), *Breaking the Faith* and *Escaping the Prophet* (TLC), *Divas for Jesus* and *Mary Mary* (WE), *Preach* (Lifetime), and *Match Made in Heaven* (WE), among many, many others. Within this media environment, it makes perfect sense that shows like *Preachers of LA* and *Detroit* and *Atlanta* have been successful.

Preachers of LA

The *Preachers* franchise aired on the Oxygen TV Network, which launched in 2000. It was created by Gerry Laybourne (former president of Nickelodeon), Marcy Carsey (who famously produced *The Cosby Show* and *Roseanne*), and Oprah Winfrey. It was initially envisioned as a competitor to female-targeted Lifetime. However, even after a decade, Oxygen could not establish a coherent identity and remained a third-tier cable network.

At the time of *Preachers*, the network had begun a repositioning fueled by its acquisition by Comcast in early 2013. Rather than compete with Lifetime, which targeted older women, Oxygen set out to attract younger women and particularly "urban" women, industry speak for African American. Social media was fundamental to this strategy of attracting younger viewers who spend significant time online. Moreover, like its Bravo counterpart, the network was pursuing a strategy that relied heavily on reality programming and broadcast this to viewers with a new tagline, "very real." *Preachers of LA* (POLA) was created as integral to this strategy.

Preachers of LA was produced by Lemuel (Lemmie) Plummer and Holly Carter. Plummer – only 26 at the time – previously produced a number of other reality series, including *Mary Mary*, a reality series about a sister gospel duo, and BET's *The Sheards*. This latter show is about a family headed by a megachurch pastor and a gospel singer which was co-created with Carter, his co-producer on the *Preachers* franchise. Carter is the founder and CEO of Relevé Entertainment, a management and production company that creates "family and faith inspired content." Her clients include Usher, Mary Mary, and Deitrick Haddon. Both producers are children of pastors. In addition, Carter holds a Doctorate of Ministry from the Southern California School of Ministry.

The preachers are a hodgepodge group. A few are older, four are married and two are not; the ones that are not married have girlfriends, and one of those girlfriends had a baby with a pastor outside of marriage. Relationships, more than religion, are the cause for drama in the show. Note, too, that these preachers front large congregations, which allows them to promote the show through their built-in networks. Here is a list of the preachers:

- **Bishop Noel Jones** is the brother of singer Grace Jones and the leader of a neo-Pentecostal congregation at the City of Refuge Church, which serves 20,000 congregants including several celebrities. An early press release suggested that the program would focus on issues related to the church and stated, "Bishop Jones is headed towards retirement and looking for a successor who he can entrust his life's work. But finding the right man is harder than it sounds." In the series, however, the attention has mostly been paid to his long-term (16-year) ill-defined relationship with Loretta. When attention is given to his preaching, the camera focuses on the number of body guards that surround him, and the yoga and other meditative practices he needs to do in preparation for appearing before a large audience. Attention is also given to his dog, JJ, who is identified with an on-screen title as much as the preachers.
- **Deitrick Haddon** is a Gospel recording artist and the son of an evangelical bishop. He began preaching by age eleven and leading the church choir by thirteen. The series focuses in large part on the salacious aspects of his messy divorce and the fact that he had a child out of wedlock with Dominique, the woman who will be his new wife by the end of the series. Haddon is a client of Relevé Entertainment, run by Holly Carter, one of the company's executive producers. He is not currently associated with the church as he was kicked out because of the scandal. The show is about his comeback.
- **Bishop Clarence McClendon** is an international televangelist and the leader of the Full Harvest Church and McClendon Ministries, his televangelistic enterprise. While as flashy in house and car as the other pastors, he appears little in the show itself. A clash in an early episode with Deitrick Haddon suggests that the pastor did not sign on for the reality aspects of the show, but truly expected a docu-series. His wife does not participate, and, in a *POLA* special, McClendon did not show up.
- **Pastor Wayne Chaney** is the pastor of Antioch church (3,500 members), which was started by his grandfather. He is married to Myeshia Chaney, a gospel artist. They have two children and their lives are fairly drama-free. That is until Myeshia loses a lot of weight and begins a women's ministry.

- **Bishop Ron Gibson** is the other high-drama "character" in the series. He was born in Compton and spent his early life as a gang leader (Crips), a pimp, and a drug addict. He is the leader of the Life Church of God in Christ, a 4,500-member congregation. The series focuses on his forays back to Compton to help other gang members, a story arc about getting his addicted sister out of the "hood" and clean, and his incredible opulence as evidenced by his many cars and multiple mansions. The first press release for the show states, "there's one thing he and his wife would give it all away for – a child." This storyline never emerges.
- **Pastor Jay Haizlip** is the only white member of this predominantly African-American cast. Haizlip was a pioneering competitive skateboarder who became a drug addict. Now he is the Senior Pastor of The Sanctuary Church, which has two outlets serving 3,500 members. He is married to Christy, the most integrated first lady of all the couples. They are both much tattooed, and they primarily minister to troubled youth.

As these descriptions suggest, the women in the lives of the pastors are central to the show, and they are a source of conflict, for sure. However, they also inspire moral and religious discussions on topics such as "shacking," who qualifies as a "first lady," and even whether tattoos are sinful or an art form. Perhaps more important, the ladies provide representation for the target audience Oxygen is trying to attract.

Marketing the *Preachers of LA*

Product placement is integral to the reality formats. In the case of *Preachers of LA*, however, the interplay between product and content becomes a bit more complex. Yes, there is product placement in the show, but I would suggest it is the preachers themselves – and perhaps religion – that is being sold here, rather than the venue for Deitrick Haddon's wedding or the airline that takes the pastors to the Essence festival in New Orleans.

We see this in a number of ways. First, the show is formatted so that the names of the pastors and their congregations are constantly provided. In the first episode, the number of congregants is also listed as if to solidify these preachers' credentials. This formatting makes sense in early episodes when viewers are not familiar with the cast. Its persistence throughout the season seems to be for no other reason than to provide promotion for the preachers. Second, all of the preachers come from megachurch congregations. The smallest is 3,500 (Chaney) and the largest 20,000 (Bishop Jones). This creates a built-in audience for the show and provides a continuous loop of promotion – reminding me of the brilliant promotion surrounding *The Secret*, a book made up of content derived from numerous New Age ministers who already had sizable followings. For sure, the congregations alone would not provide the audience needed to sustain the show. However, these pastors have broad networks of churches where they have led worship services that also promote the show, particularly through social media.

The lengths to which faith can be presented on TV are being tested within this series, and in the genre overall. Rarely on the *Preachers of LA* are there long scenes of the pastors preaching. There is a 30–50 second montage of preaching at the beginning of the first episode. God and Jesus are mentioned, but not within the context of a religious service. Faith is presented as a seamless aspect of everyday life, as lived religion. In one example, Ron Gibson prays with his sister, Shaun, who is addicted to drugs; in another Jay Haizlip prays with an anorexic woman whom he meets in a park. I liken this to what I saw with Joel Osteen, which I discuss in *Brands of Faith*. In order to appeal to the largest audience possible, mentions of God, Jesus and outright prayer are kept to a minimum for Osteen. A short prayer about the Bible at the beginning of the show and the virtual altar call at the end of the show are the only blatant religious acts.[16]

More flagrant forms of promoting the faith occur outside of the television program itself. For example, the after-show program online readily mentions Jesus, blessings, Easter, and so on. When the pastors appear on talk shows on TV, religion is *the* topic of conversation. On *The Wendy Williams Show*, for example, Jay Haizlip talks about a woman coming to his church for a healing, and on *Arsenio Hall*, the pastors had a "preach off." Oprah Winfrey used a similar format when promoting the work of spiritual writer, Eckhart Tolle; when on TV, Tolle and Oprah had a discussion of his book in broad terms, but online the two had long, in-depth conversations about God and spirituality. Online participants self-selected to spend additional time with more intense religious content, whereas television viewers might look for a makeover show and Oprah's Favorite Things and be disappointed by overly religious fare. As the *Preachers* franchise has progressed, more and more religious practice has been presented. On the second season of *Preachers of LA*, we see people speaking in tongues. In the *Detroit* and *Atlanta* shows, there is more content shot within the church. We also see issues related to the black community and the importance of the church in providing support.[17]

Finally, the preachers are packaged like other celebrities within this Third Generation of the reality genre. As suggested above, each has a brand – the preacher from the hood, or the skateboarder preacher, and so on – that allows viewers to make emotional connections with them the same way consumers connect to branded products. The most flamboyant brand is that of Deitrick Haddon. Haddon is a Grammy-winning singer, he was a "baby preacher," he is the bad-boy who divorced his wife and had a baby out of wedlock. The first season revolved around much of the upheaval in his private life, and was about reviving his gospel career, including launching a new gospel album (the timing of which worked in conjunction with the show schedule). It is also not surprising, then, that Oxygen created a spinoff reality show to give him – and his music – additional exposure.

African Americans, television, and the Black Church

The surfeit of religious reality television shows with African American casts is not surprising given the current media industry landscape. African Americans watch more television than other demographic groups – 200 hours per month versus 140 for the general population – and their media usage overall exceeds other demographics.[18] If we look at social media, and Twitter specifically, African Americans who use the Internet use Twitter more than white Americans (28 percent versus 20 percent), and they use the service more often – tweeting multiple times throughout the day.[19] This cohort has long been underserved by the television producers. New networks have been able to establish a niche by creating content for them. The Fox Network did this when they launched in the 1980s, and it has been a recipe for success ever since.[20]

Religious programming targeting African Americans, as for other demographics, has traditionally been televangelism. As Walton (2009) describes in *Watch This! The Ethics and Aesthetics of Black Televangelism*, the world of the televised Black Church is a mix of patriotism, capitalism, and patriarchy. "And in this media-constructed Christian realm, American flags drape the cross of Christianity, material wealth is divinely ordained, and hypermasculinity models God's power just as female docility signifies purity and virtue."[21] The Oxygen pastors follow in this tradition, preaching the prosperity gospel and presenting an idealized world where wealth and racial equality are seemingly readily achievable. While the wives and girlfriends are integral to driving the narrative of the show, they remain showpieces and fodder to drama, and are not the primary actors in events.

Today's black preachers know they are speaking to a consumerism-drenched audience. In her book *Brand New Theology* about mega-pastor T.D. Jakes, McGee explains that these pastors "have interpreted and translated the mythology of black religion for a new generation of African Americans – a generation steeped in neoliberalism and a culture of advanced capitalism."[22] This is different from traditional Black Churches which looked to liberate the self and the community, rather than the "individual over community." Rather, these pastors, like their counterparts of other races, preach a prosperity gospel suggesting that viewers can achieve wealth, health and individual happiness by following them. Women are most affected by this come-on as they are the primary participants in religious practice,[23] and are the primary followers of charismatic preachers like Jakes. As McGee puts it, "The churches of the New Black Church and their pastors promote a theology that is much more about brand loyalty than the gospel and spiritual healing" (p. 31). As noted above, these preachers have been fostered as brands that become perpetuated by reality programming.

Preachers of Oxygen, then, is part of a larger trend of commodifying the Black Church. Preachers like T.D. Jakes are the epitome of this trend, but the *Preachers* of reality TV are not far behind. Whether it is through books, music, conferences or television programs, the expectation is that preachers will become a brand or, better yet, a celebrity brand.[24] As more preachers move to create these money-making enterprises, the pressure to achieve this level of success and maintain it increases both for up-and-coming preachers as well as the more established ones.[25] Moreover, the prosperity gospel they teach is fundamentally rooted in neoliberal ideas of individualism. Rather than creating choice and community and spiritual fulfillment, branded preachers strive for attention and engagement which benefits them and the corporations and congregations they serve. This is true even if those who watch the shows or buy the books or attend an event never set foot in their church.

Religion, reality, or just revenues?

The producers of the *Preachers* are Lemmie Plummer and Holly Carter – both African American, both children of pastors, and both producers of previous religious reality content. Given this, it seems they would be sincere in their mission to promote faith. In fact, they claim to have selected the LA pastors because of their "global footprint," with Carter noting she wanted to "give a platform to the voice of pastors, and create an opportunity to see them not only as religious leaders, but as fathers and husbands and friends."[26] The truth is more complex. Given the economics, the media environment and the push to market the Black Church, it is likely more true that the pastors were selected based on the formulas of reality TV, and the business relationships among the players. As Jervette Ward (2015) notes, "The choice of these preachers and the first ladies ... seamlessly continues the Black church's reputation for sexism from society to the reality television world. Though sexism is prevalent in the Black church, there are several churches in the Los Angeles area with amazing Black female preachers who could have theoretically been cast for such a groundbreaking show."[27] By casting men with sexist attitudes on a network that targets "young, multicultural women," the stage was set for strong emotions, considerable debate, and significant program sampling as evidenced by the ratings. Ultimately, in catering to a female audience, as the show progressed more attention was directed toward the first ladies and girlfriends. However, the preachers remained the stars of the show and even in subsequent spinoffs, the number of male preachers continued to outweigh the number of women.

Beyond casting, the series is manipulated for maximum drama, as all reality shows are. Some of this centers around the women in the preachers' lives. Who is a real "first lady" in the church, who is married and who isn't, and so on. Mostly, though, the series focuses on the salacious aspects of gospel singer Deitrick Haddon's life. The first season of the show is about his comeback, both to the church and the music industry – which included an additional spinoff show with former Destiny's Child member, Michelle Williams, called *Fix My Choir*.

The *Preachers* format gets refined a bit with the two spinoff shows. Perhaps in deference to the female audience, two female preachers are part of the *Detroit* cast of seven. However, even that does not eliminate the stereotypes so fundamental to the format. One of the women is Bishop Corletta Vaughn; the other is Evangelist and Grammy winner Dorinda Clark-Cole. While the latter has no quarrel with women preaching, she believes the church belongs to men and women should not serve as bishops. This, of course, becomes a main source of conflict in the show. Other stereotypes from the first show continue – one pastor is a former gang member, one a young upstart, and so on. As for *Atlanta*, the five preachers are purposefully cast for the drama. The group is made up of three African Americans (one female and two males) and, for the first time, two white cast members – one male, one female. As the show's website states, they are preachers with "drastically different approaches to their ministry, [and] the show explores many of the most hot-button and polarizing issues in America today." This show has the youngest cast, with an eye to appealing to the young female audience. Moreover, three of the five preachers are also recording artists, furthering the ability to promote the show through multiple outlets including social media. Similar to Deitrick Haddon in the first show, this spinoff gets the most drama from a young, argumentative (read: cursing) preacher and Grammy winner – Le'Andria Johnson – who learns that her husband had a baby with another woman.

What is surprising, perhaps, is that social media – Twitter but more extensively YouTube – have provided a space where viewers can talk not only about the show but also larger societal issues related to faith. So while these shows are entertainment, they are also a conduit for raising serious questions about religion – both personal and societal – such as why does God help one person and not another, how are the roles of women changing (or not) within the church, how do traditional and liberal church members negotiate their conflicting beliefs, and finally, what is the role of the church in today's mediated culture.[28] These conversations arise because of events on the show, such as Pastor Haizlip talking with an anorexic woman and conversations among the First Ladies. Even so, narrativizing the intimacy of everyday life of pastors provides little insight into their humanity, nor does it elucidate their conception of faith. It merely sensationalizes their failings through the staging of mundanity. As for viewers, these shows do little to move them beyond an individualistic form of spirituality and affirm egotism, rather than introducing forms of practice such as discipline, commitment and sacrifice[29] – ideas in opposition to late capitalist ideology. Moreover, even while produced by African Americans, the shows do little to move away from racialized stereotypes. Rather than providing insights, this celebrated media culture of participation allows little ability to challenge prevailing norms of race, gender, and faith.

Notes

1 Delivering growth in the network's targeted demo of young women, Oxygen's "Preachers of L.A." earned a season high among F18–34 (221,000), F18–49 (462,000) and F25–54 (514,000), according to Nielsen. The series continues to increase among all key demos including up 11 percent among F18–34 and F18–49, up 9 percent among P18–49 and up 7 percent among F25–54, compared to the previous week. Every episode of the hit series has delivered over one million total viewers. In the 10pm hour, Oxygen was the #4 cable network among F18–49. See TV by the Numbers, "Oxygen Media's 'Preachers of LA' Delivers Season Highs Among Key Demos."

2 Beginning in 2017, Oxygen reformatted its programming brand again, this time to focus on true crime shows targeted to women.

3 For more on reality formats/formulas of reality, see: Kavka, *Reality TV*; Kraidy and Sender, *The Politics of Reality Television*; Murray and Ouellette, *Reality TV*. For commercialization of the genre, see Deery, *Consuming Reality*; Jenkins, "Buying into American Idol.".

4 Orbe, "Representations of Race in Reality TV."

5 Nielsen, "Multifaceted Connections."
6 Pew Research Center.
7 Raphael, "The political-economic origins of Reali-TV."
8 For more on reality TV and racism, see: Andrejevic & Colby, "Racism and reality TV"; Boylorn, "As seen on TV." For gender and reality TV, see Pozner, *Reality Bites Back* and Weber, *Reality Gendervision.*
9 Carrette and King, *Selling Spirituality*, p. 15.
10 Andrejevic, *Reality TV*; Poniewozik, "Reality TV at 10."
11 Abt and Seesholtz. "The shameless world of Phil, Sally and Oprah"; Shattuc, *The Talking Cure.*
12 Moe and Schweidel, *Social Media Intelligence*, 20.
13 Flomenbaum, "Accenture report."
14 Berger, *Contagious*; Guadagno, Rempala, Murphy and Okdie, "What makes a video go viral?"
15 Jenkins, Ford and Green, *Spreadable Media.*
16 Einstein, *Brands of Faith.*
17 These shows never lived up to the success of the first show, and subsequent spinoffs were cancelled, as was the first one.
18 Nielsen, "Multifaceted Connections."
19 Duggan, "Mobile Messaging and Social Media 2015."
20 Zook, *Color by Fox.*
21 Walton, *Watch This!*, p. xxi.
22 McGee, *Brand New Theology*, p. 14.
23 Gilkes, "Plenty Good Room."
24 McGee, *Brand New Theology*, p. 47.
25 Frederick, *Colored Television.*
26 Oxygen Blogger, "Q&A with 'Preachers of L.A.'"
27 Ward, *Real Sister.*
28 For information on religious conversation, see Besecke, "Seeing invisible religion"; Wuthnow, "Taking talk seriously."
29 Buxton, "Not Exactly a Selling Point?"

Bibliography

Abt, Vicki, and Mel Seesholtz. 1994. The shameless world of Phil, Sally and Oprah: Television talk shows and the deconstructing of society. *The Journal of Popular Culture*, 28(1), 171–191.

Andrejevic, Mark. *Reality TV: The work of being watched.* Boulder, CO: Rowman & Littlefield, 2004.

Andrejevic, Mark, and Dean Colby. Racism and reality TV: The case of MTV's Road Rules. In *How real is reality TV? Essays on representation and truth*, ed. David Escoffery, 195–211. Jefferson, NC: McFarland, 2006.

Berger, Jonah. *Contagious: Why Things Catch On.* New York: Simon & Schuster, 2013.

Besecke, Kelly. 2005. Seeing invisible religion: Religion as a societal conversation about transcendent meaning. *Sociological Theory* 23(2), 179–196.

Boylorn, Robin M. 2008. As seen on TV: An autoethnographic reflection on race and reality television. *Critical Studies in Media Communication* 25,(4), 413–433.

Buxton, Nicholas. Not Exactly a Selling Point? Religion and Reality TV. In Thomas, L. (Ed.) *Religion, Consumerism and Sustainability: Paradise Lost?* New York: Palgrave Macmillan, 2011.

Carrette, Jeremy R., and Richard King. *Selling Spirituality: The Silent Takeover of Religion.* London: Routledge, 2005.

Deery, June. *Consuming Reality: The Commercialization of Factual Entertainment*. New York: Palgrave Macmillan, 2012.

Duggan, Maeve. Mobile Messaging and Social Media 2015: The Demographics of Social Media Users. Accessed July 2, 2016. http://www.pewinternet.org/2015/08/19/the-dem ographics-of-social-media-users/.

Einstein, Mara. *Brands of Faith: Marketing Religion in a Commercial Age*. London: Routledge, 2008.

Flomenbaum, Adam. Accenture Report: 87% of Consumers Use Second Screen Device While Watching TV. Accessed September 5, 2017. http://www.adweek.com/lostremote/ accenture-report-87-of-consumers-use-second-screen-device-while-watching-tv/51698

Frederick, Marla. *Colored Television: American Religion Gone Global*. Stanford: Stanford University Press, 2016.

Gilkes, Cheryl Townsend. 1998. Plenty Good Room: Adaptation in a Changing Black Church. *The Annals of the American Academy of Political and Social Science* 558, 101–121.

Guadagnoa, Rosanna E., Daniel M. Rempala, Shannon Murphy and Bradley M. Okdie. 2013. What makes a video go viral? An analysis of emotional contagion and internet memes. *Computers in Human Behavior*, 29(6), 2312–2319. Doi: doi:10.1016/j. chb.2013.04.016

Jenkins, Henry. Buying into American Idol: How We Are Being Sold on Reality TV, in *Convergence Culture*, 59–93. New York: New York University Press, 2006.

Jenkins, Henry, Sam Ford and Joshua Green. *Spreadable Media: Creating Value and Meaning in a Networked Culture*. New York: New York University Press, 2013.

Kavka, Misha. *Reality TV*. Edinburgh: Edinburgh University Press, 2012.

Kraidy, Marwan M. and Katherine Sender (eds). *The Politics of Reality Television: Global Per-spectives*. London: Routledge, 2011.

McGee, Paula. *Brand® New Theology: The Wal-Martization of T.D. Jakes and the New Black Church*. Ossining, NY: Orbis Books, 2017.

Moe, Wendy W. and David A. Schweidel. *Social Media Intelligence*. New York: Cambridge University Press, 2014.

Murray, Susan and Laurie Ouellette. *Reality TV: Remaking Television Culture*. New York: New York University Press, 2008.

Nielsen. Multifaceted Connections: African-American Media Usage Outpaces Across Plat-forms. Accessed July 2, 2016. http://www.nielsen.com/us/en/insights/news/2015/ multifaceted-connections-african-american-media-usage-outpaces-across-platforms.html

Orbe, Mark P. 2008. Representations of Race in Reality TV: Watch and Discuss. *Critical Studies in Media Communication* 25(4), 345–352.

Oxygen Blogger. Q&A with 'Preachers of L.A.' Producers Holly Carter & Lemuel Plum-mer, Accessed September 5, 2017. http://www.oxygen.com/preachers-of-la/season-2/ blogs/qa-with-preachers-of-la-producers-holly-carter-lemuel-plummer.

Pew Research Center. A Religious Portrait of African Americans. Accessed August 4, 2017. http://www.pewforum.org/2009/01/30/a-religious-portrait-of-african-americans/

Poniewozik, James. Reality TV at 10: How its changed television and us. *Time magazine*. February 22, 2010. Accessed June 5, 2011. http://www.time.com/time/magazine/a rticle/0,9171,1963739,00.html

Pozner, Jennifer. *Reality Bites Back: The Troubling Truth About Guilty Pleasure TV*. Berkeley, CA: Seal Press, 2010.

Raphael, Chad. The political-economic origins of Reali-TV. Accessed April 21, 2017. http://scholarcommons.scu.edu/cgi/viewcontent.cgi?article=1020&context=comm

Shattuc, Jane M. *The Talking Cure: TV Talk Shows and Women*. New York: Routledge, 2014.

TV by the Numbers. Oxygen Media's "Preachers of LA" Delivers Season Highs Among Key Demos. November 21, 2013. http://tvbythenumbers.zap2it.com/network-press-re leases/oxygen-medias-preachers-of-la-delivers-season-highs-among-key-demos/, accessed December 13, 2017.

Walton, Jonathan L. *Watch This! The Ethics and Aesthetics of Black Televangelism*. New York: New York University Press, 2009.

Ward, Jervette R. *Real Sister: Stereotypes, Respectability, and Black Women in Reality TV*. New Brunswick: Rutgers University Press, 2015.

Weber, Brenda R. *Reality Gendervision: Sexuality & Gender on Transatlantic Reality Television*. Durham: Duke University Press, 2014.

Wuthnow, Robert. 2011. Taking talk seriously: Religious discourse as social practice. *Journal for the Scientific Study of Religion* 50(1), 1–21.

Zook, Kristal B. (1999). *Color by Fox: The Fox Network and the Revolution in Black Television*. New York: Oxford University Press.

INDEX